Sir John Froissart's chronicles of England, France, Spain, and the adjoining countries, from the latter part of the reign of Edward II. to the coronation of Henry IV

Jean Froissart, Thomas Johnes

SIR JOHN FROISSART'S

CHRONICLES

OF

ENGLAND, FRANCE, SPAIN,

AND THE

ADJOINING COUNTRIES,

FROM THE LATTER PART OF THE REIGN OF EDWARD II.
TO THE CORONATION OF HENRY IV.

NEWLY TRANSLATED FROM THE FRENCH EDITIONS,
WITH VARIATIONS AND ADDITIONS FROM MANY CELEBRATED MSS.

BY THOMAS JOHNES.

Who so shall telle a tale after a man,
He moste reherse, as neighe as ever he can,
Everich worde, if it be in his charge,
All speke he never so rudely and so large;
Or elles he moste tellen his tale untrewe,
Or feinen thinges, or finden wordes newe.

CHAUCER'S PROLOGUE

THE SECOND EDITION.

TO WHICH IS PREFIXED,
A LIFE OF THE AUTHOR, AN ESSAY ON HIS WORKS,
A CRITICISM ON HIS HISTORY,
AND A DISSERTATION ON HIS POETRY

VOL. IV.

LONDON:
PRINTED FOR LONGMAN, HURST, REES, AND ORME, PATERNOSTER-ROW;
AND J. WHITE, FLEET-STREET.
1806.

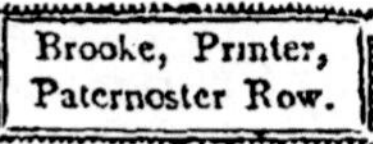
Brooke, Printer,
Paternoster Row.

THE

CONTENTS

OF

THE FOURTH VOLUME.

CHAP.

CHAP.

THE

CHRONICLES

OF

ENGLAND, FRANCE, SPAIN, &c.

CHAP I.

THE DUKE OF BURGUNDY MARCHES FROM THE CITY OF ROUEN, WITH THE INTENTION OF COMBATING THE DUKE OF LANCASTER AND THE ENGLISH.—THE TWO ARMIES ARE ENCAMPED OPPOSITE TO EACH OTHER AT TOURNEHEM *.

WHEN the duke of Lancaſter was arrived at Calais, as has been before mentioned, and had refreſhed his army a little, he was not willing to remain there without performing ſome warlike deeds upon the French: he therefore marched out with his two marſhals and full three hundred lances, with as many archers. They paſſed through Guines†, and continued their march until they had croſſed the river Doſtre, and overran that whole country. They turned towards the abbey

* Tournehem,—a ſmall town of Artois, bailiwick of St. Omer.

† Guines,—a town in Picardy, two leagues and a half from Calais.

of Liques*, where they collected a large booty, which they brought safe with them to Calais.

On another day, he made an excursion towards Boulogne, where he did much damage to the flat countries.

The count Guy de St. Pol and sir Galeran his son were at the time in the city of Terouenne, with many men at arms; but they made no sally against the English, when they were on these expeditions, for they did not think themselves sufficiently strong to oppose them in the field.

News was brought to the king of France, who at that time was holding his court at Rouen in the greatest pomp and magnificence, that the duke of Lancaster was come to Calais, and that from thence he was daily making inroads into France. When the king and his council heard this, their minds were occupied on a different subject; for this same week the duke of Burgundy was to embark with his whole army, consisting of upwards of three thousand fighting men, to invade England.

The king demanded from his prelates and council what was best to be done, supposing the English had crossed the sea, whether to advance to them and offer battle, or to continue their plan of operation for the invasion of England. This last proposition was given up, and orders sent to the French army to break up their quarters in and near Rouen as soon as possible, and to prepare every thing for marching towards Calais with the duke

* Abbey of Liques,—diocese of Boulogne sur mer.

of

of Burgundy. Such were the commands of the king of France, for he was desirous of combating the English on that side of the water.

The men at arms heard these orders with great joy, and were soon ready. The duke of Burgundy, with his whole army, took the field, and formed his march so as to cross the river Somme at Abbeville. He continued until he came to Montrieul * sur mer, and from thence to Hesdin † and St. Paul ‡, where they halted for the rear of the army to join them.

News was brought to the duke of Lancaster, that the French were on their march to offer him battle; upon which the duke, with his whole army, left Calais, and took up their quarters in the valley of Tournehem. He had not been long there before that gallant knight sir Robert de Namur came in grand array to serve under him, with a hundred lances of good men at arms, accompanied with knights and squires.

The duke of Lancaster was much rejoiced on his arrival, and said: 'My good uncle, you are heartily welcome; for they say that the duke of Burgundy is on his march, and wishes to fight with us.' Sir Robert replied, 'My lord, by God's help, we will willingly meet him.'

---

* Montrieul,—a town in Picardy, seventeen leagues and a half from Calais.

† Hesdin,—a strong town in Artois, eighteen leagues and a half from Calais.

‡ St. Paul,—a small town in Picardy, diocese of Beauvais.

The English found good quarters in the valley Tournehem, where they fortified themselves with strong hedges, and there came daily to them provision in abundance from Calais. Their light horse scoured the country of Guines, but they gained little, for all the low countries had been spoiled, and their most valuable things carried for safety to the adjoining fortresses.

The duke of Burgundy arrived with all his chivalry, and fixed his quarters at the hill of Tournehem, where his marshals immediately encamped the men at arms opposite to where the English lay.

The French lodged themselves orderly, and without delay: they took up much ground, and with good reason; for I have had it mentioned to me as a certain fact, that the duke of Burgundy had under his command four thousand good knights. You may judge therefore of the great difference between the two armies.

Each army remained in these positions a considerable time without doing any thing; for the duke of Burgundy, notwithstanding he was so much superior in force, and had with him, of good men at arms, seven to one, would not engage without the positive orders of the king of France, his brother, who was not desirous of it. In truth, had the French come forward to battle, the English would not have refused it; for they were daily drawn out, and in readiness to receive them. They had made every preparation, and each person knew what he was to do, should the enemy shew any

any inclination to fight: but because they were so small a body, and so well fortified, they would not foolishly lose an advantage by quitting their camp.

Some knights advanced from each army to skirmish; and, as usual in such cases, sometimes one side gained, and sometimes the other.

The earl of Flanders, at this time, was very anxious for the honour and reputation of the duke of Burgundy, his son-in-law: he resided in a handsome house which he had lately built near to Ghent: he frequently heard from or sent to the duke, by messengers who were constantly employed on this service. The earl strongly advised his son-in-law, for his own honour, not to exceed, on any account, the orders which he had received from his brother the king of France, or from his council.

We will now return to the affairs of the distant provinces, where the knights had frequently more employment, and met with adventures in greater abundance than any where else, on account of the war being carried on more vigorously.

CHAP II.

SIR JOHN CHANDOS DOES GREAT MISCHIEF TO THE PROVINCE OF ANJOU.—HE DESPOILS THE ESTATES OF THE VISCOUNT DE ROCHE-CHOUART, EXCEPT THE FORTRESSES AND STRONG HOLDS.

DURING the time of this expedition to Tournehem, and in that neighhourhood, ſome feats of arms were performed in Poitou, which ought not to be forgotten. Sir John Chandos, being ſénéſchal of Poitou, and a hardy and valiant knight, had a great deſire to meet the French: he therefore did not remain long idle, but collected, during the time he paſſed at Poitiers a body of men at arms, Engliſh and Poitevins, and ſaid he would make an incurſion with them towards Anjou, and return by Touraine, to look at the French who were aſſembled in thoſe parts. He ſent information of the expedition he meditated to the earl of Pembroke, who was in garriſon at Montagne * ſur mer, with two hundred lances.

The earl was much pleaſed with this intelligence, and would willingly have been of the party; but his attendants and ſome knights of his council prevented him, by ſaying; 'My lord, you are a young and noble knight, formed to excel: if you

* Montagne,—a town in Saintonge, [illegible] C[illegible]e.

at

at this moment unite yourself with sir John Chandos and his army, he will obtain all the glory of the expedition, and you will be only named as his companion. It is therefore more proper for you, who are of such high rank and birth, to act for yourself, and let sir John Chandos do so on his part, who is but a knight-bachelor when compared with you.'

These and such like words cooled the ardour of the earl of Pembroke, who, having no longer any wish to go, sent an excuse to sir John Chandos.

Sir John would not, however, give up his enterprise, but ordered his rendezvous at Poitiers; from whence he marched, with three hundred lances, knights and squires, and two hundred archers. In this number were, lord Thomas Percy, sir Stephen Cossington, sir Richard de Pontchardon, sir Eustace d'Ambreticourt, sir Richard Taunton, lord Thomas Spencer, sir Nêle Loring, the earl of Angus*, sir Thomas Banastre, sir John Trivet, sir William de Montendre, sir Maubrins de Linieres, sir Geoffry d'Argenton, and several other knights and squires.

These men at arms and archers marched boldly forth and in good array, as if going upon some

* David king of Scotland created sir John Stuart of Bonkill earl of Angus. He and his heirs held the estates, but the Umphravilles of England (the earl mentioned in the text) grasped at the title for many generations.—*Pinkerton's Hist. of Scotland*, vol. i p 7.

grand enterprise, and, having passed through the province of Poitou, entered that of Anjou. When they were arrived in that country, they fixed their quarters in the flat parts of it, and sent out their light divisions to burn and destroy every thing. They did infinite mischief to this rich and fine country, without any one attempting to prevent them; and they remained there upwards of fifteen days, especially in that part of it called the Loudunois.

They retreated from Anjou down the river Creuse, which separates Touraine from Poitou; and sir John Chandos, with his army, entered the lands of the viscount de la Rochechouart, where every thing, excepting the fortresses, was ruined. They advanced to the town of Rochechouart, and vigorously assaulted it, but without effect; for there were excellent men at arms within it, commanded by Thibault du Pont and Helyons de Talay, who prevented it from being taken or injured.

The English continued their march to Chauvigny *, where sir John Chandos received information that the lord Louis de Sancerre, marshal of France, with a great body of men at arms, were at la Haye † in Touraine. He was very desirous to march that way, and sent in great haste to the earl of Pembroke to signify his intentions, and to beg of him to accompany him to la Haye in Touraine,

* Chauvigny,—a town in Poitou, on the Vienne, six leagues from Poitiers.

† La Haye,—a town in Touraine, on the Creuse.

raine, and that he would meet him at Châtelherault *. Chandos the herald was the bearer of this meſſage. He found the earl of Pembroke at Mortagne buſily employed in muſtering his men, and preparing, as it appeared, to make an excurſion. He excuſed himſelf a ſecond time, by the advice of his council, ſaying he could not accompany him.

The herald, on his return, found his maſter and the army at Châtelheraut, to whom he delivered his anſwer. When ſir John Chandos heard it, he was very melancholy, knowing that pride and preſumption had made the earl refuſe to be a party in this expedition, and only replied, ‘ God's will be done.’ He diſmiſſed the greater part of his army, who ſeparated, and he, with his attendants, returned to Poitiers.

CHAP. III.

THE LORD LOUIS DE SANCERRE SURPRISES THE EARL OF PEMBROKE.—SEVERAL OF HIS MEN ARE SLAIN, AND THE EARL IS BESIEGED IN A HOUSE AT PUIRENON.

WE will now relate how the earl of Pembroke proſpered. As ſoon as he knew that ſir John Chandos had diſbanded his army, and was

* Châtelheraut,—a town in Poitou, on the Vienne.

returned

returned to Poitiers, he aſſembled his own forces, which conſiſted of three hundred Engliſh and Poitevins, and marched from Mortagne. He was joined by ſome knights and ſquires of Poitou and Saintonge, as well as by ſome Engliſh knights that had been in ſir John Chandos' army.

Theſe men at arms, therefore, advanced under the command of the earl of Pembroke, and took the direct road to where ſir John Chandos had been, burning and deſpoiling all thoſe parts of Anjou which the firſt had left, or which had been ranſomed. They halted to refreſh themſelves in the Loudunois, and then took the road for the lands of the viſcount de Rochechouart, to which they did great damage.

The French who were in garriſon on the frontiers of Touraine, Anjou and Poitou, conſiſting of a large body of men at arms, heard the whole truth of theſe two excurſions, and how the earl of Pembroke, who was a young man, would not, through pride, ſerve under ſir John Chandos. They therefore reſolved to conquer him, if they could; for they thought they ſhould more eaſily defeat him than ſir John Chandos.

They made, in conſequence, a ſecret levy of their forces from all the garriſons; and ſir Louis de Sancerre, marſhal of France, took the command of them. They marched all night to la Roche-poſay * in Poitou, which was in the French intereſt. There were in this expedition, ſir

* La Roche-poſay,—a town in Touraine, on the Creuſe.

Robert

Robert de Sancerre, cousin to the marshal, sir John de Vienne, sir John de Bueil, sir William des Bourdes, sir Louis de St. Julien and Carnet le Breton; in the whole, seven hundred fighting men.

The earl of Pembroke had finished his excursion, and re-entered Poitou, having completed the total destruction of the viscount de Rochechouart's estate. In his company were, sir Baldwin de Franville, sénéschal of Saintonge, lord Thomas Percy, lord Thomas Spencer, the earl of Angus, sir John Orwich *, sir John Harpedon, sir James de Surgeres, sir John Cousins, sir Thomas de St. Alban, sir Robert Twiford, sir Simon Ausagre, sir John de Mortain, sir John Touchet, and several others.

The English and Poitevins marched on without any thought or precaution, having heard nothing of these men at arms: they had entered Poitou with all their pillage, and came, one day about noon, to a village called Puirenon, where they halted, after the manner of persons in perfect security. But when the servants were about to put the horses in the stable, and to prepare the supper, the French, who well knew what they were about, entered the village of Puirenon, with their lances in their rests, bawling out their cry, 'Our Lady, for Sancerre the marshal!' and then overthrew all they met in the streets. The noise became so

* Sir John Orwich. Q. Barnes calls him sir Nêle Loring. Why not Norwich?

violent

violent, that the English ran to the head-quarters with great alarm, to inform the earl of Pembroke, lord Thomas Percy, sir Baldwin de Franville and the others, that the French had suddenly attacked and surprised them. These lords were soon armed, and, sallying out from their hotels, collected their men together, but they could not all assemble, for the numbers of the French were so considerable that the English and Poitevins were overpowered; and, in this first attack, more than one hundred and twenty were killed or made prisoners. The earl of Pembroke and some knights had no other remedy but to retire, as quickly as they could, into an unembattled house, which belonged to the knights-templars, without a moat, and only enclosed with a stone-wall. All who could get there time enough shut themselves in: the greater part of the others were slain or made prisoners, and their arms and horses taken. The earl of Pembroke lost all his plate.

The French, who closely pursued them, finding those who could get together had shut themselves up in this house, where much rejoiced, saying among themselves; 'They must be our prisoners, for they cannot escape; and we will make them dearly repay the damages they have done in Anjou and Touraine.' On which, they advanced to this house in regular order, and with a good will to assault it: when they were come thither, it was evening: after they had examined it narrowly on all sides, to see if it might be easily taken, they began the attack, in which were performed many

gallant

gallant deeds of arms, for the French were in great numbers, and were all well tried men.

They made different attempts on this houſe, which was very ſtrong, and gave the earl Pembroke and his men enough to do; for the Engliſh, being ſo few, laboured hard to defend themſelves, as it was to them of the greateſt conſequence. Scaling ladders were brought, and fixed againſt the walls, which ſome bold adventurers mounted, with their ſhields over their heads to ſhelter themſelves from ſtones and arrows; but when they were got to the top they had done nothing, for they found there, ready to receive them, knights, ſquires, men at arms, with lances and ſwords, with which they handſomely fought hand to hand, and made them deſcend much quicker than they had mounted. Add to this, that there were Engliſh archers intermixed with theſe men at arms, at two feet diſtance on the walls, who ſhot ſo well that the French beneath ſuffered much.

The Engliſh continued under conſtant alarm, repelling theſe attacks until night, when the French tired with fighting and fatigue, ſounded their trumpets for the retreat, ſaying they had done enough for one day, but that they would return to the attack on the morrow; adding, that, as they could not eſcape from them, they would ſtarve them to ſurrender. They returned to their quarters in high ſpirits, and made merry, having placed a ſtrong guard in front of the houſe to be more ſecure of their enemies.

It

It will readily be believed that the earl of Pembroke and thofe who were thus blockaded were not much at their eafe: they were aware that this houfe was not of fufficient ftrength to hold out long againft fo many men at arms. It was as badly provided with artillery, to their great forrow, as with provifion; but this laft was not of much confequence, for they could well faft a day and night, if neceffary, in defending themfelves.

When it was dark, they entreated a fquire, an expert foldier, and in whom they placed great confidence, to fet out directly by a poftern, and ride as faft as he could to Poitiers, to inform fir John Chandos and his friends how awkwardly they were fituated, and to beg they would come to their affiftance; in the hopes of which they would hold out until noon; and, if he made hafte, he might eafily make this journey by early morning.

The fquire, who perceived the extreme danger in which all the lords were, very cheerfully undertook it, but boafted a little too much of his knowledge of the roads. He fet out about midnight by a poftern-gate, and took the ftraight road, as he thought for Poitiers; but it fo fell out, that during the whole night he wandered about, until it was broad day, before he hit upon the right road.

At day-break, the French, who were befieging the Englifh at Puirenon as you have before heard, founded their trumpets to arm, faying it would be better to make their attacks in the cool of the morning than in the heat of the day.

The

The earl of Pembroke and the knights ſhut up with him, inſtead of ſleeping, had fortified themſelves with whatever they could find, making uſe even of benches and ſtones, which they had carried to the top of the walls. They found the French were preparing to renew the attack, and comforted each other upon it.

Some time before ſun-riſe, the French were ready, when they marched by companies, and with great vigour, to the aſſault of the hôtel. They acquitted themſelves too well, and having brought ſcaling ladders, placed them againſt the walls, mounting them with the utmoſt eagerneſs, covered by their ſhields, otherwiſe they would not have ventured: it was held highly honourable to thoſe who mounted the firſt, as in truth it was a very brave act.

The Engliſh were not idle nor faint-hearted in their own defence, but fought marvellouſly well, and flung down upon the ſhields of the aſſailants ſtones and great beams of wood, with which they beat them ſo ſeverely, that they killed or wounded ſeveral. They did their duty excellently well, and ſo ſmall a fort was never ſeen to hold out ſo long againſt ſuch a force. This aſſault continued from early dawn until ſix o'clock.

CHAP

CHAP. IV.

SIR JOHN CHANDOS COMES TO THE ASSISTANCE OF THE EARL OF PEMBROKE, BESIEGED IN PUIRENON.

BETWEEN six and nine o'clock, after the heat of the attack, the French, indignant that the English had made so long a defence, sent orders to all the villagers thereabouts to bring pick-axes and mattocks to undermine the walls, which was what the English were most afraid of. The earl of Pembroke called one of his own squires, and said to him, 'My friend, mount a horse, and sally out from the back gate, where they will make way for you, and ride as fast as possible to Poitiers to sir John Chandos, to tell him our situation and the imminent danger we are in: recommend me to him by this token.' He then took off his finger a rich ring of gold, adding, 'Give him this from me: he will know it well again.' The squire, who thought himself much honoured by this commission, took the ring, mounted the best courser he could fine, and set off by the back gate during the attack, for they opened it for him. He took the road to Poitiers; and, whilst he was making all the haste he could, the assault was carried on warmly by the French, and as vigorously opposed by the English: indeed, it behoved them so to do.

We

We will now ſay ſomething of the firſt ſquire, who had left Puirenon at midnight, and who, having loſt his road, had wandered about all the night. When it was broad day, he knew his road, and made ſtraight for Poitiers; but, his horſe being tired, he did not arrive there until about nine o'clock, when he diſmounted in the ſquare before the hôtel of ſir John Chandos, and immediately entered it, having learnt that he was at maſs: he approached him, and, falling on his knees, delivered his meſſage.

Sir John Chandos, who had not yet recovered his vexation at the earl of Pembroke's refuſal to join him in his expeditions, was not very eager to give him aſſiſtance: he coldly ſaid, 'It will be almoſt impoſſible for us to get there in time and hear the whole maſs.' Soon after maſs, the tables were ſpread, and dinner ſet out. His ſervants aſked ſir John, if he would dine: 'Yes,' ſaid he, 'ſince it is ready,' and then entered the hall, where his knights and ſquires had preceded him with water to waſh his hands. As he was thus employed, and before he ſat down to table, the ſecond ſquire from the earl of Pembroke entered the hall, and, having knelt down, drew the ring from his purſe, ſaying; 'Dear ſir, my lord the earl of Pembroke recommends himſelf to you by this token, and entreats you moſt earneſtly to come to his aſſiſtance, and reſcue him from the imminent danger he is now in at Puirenon.'

Sir John Chandos took the ring, and, having examined it, knew it well. He then replied, 'It will not be poſſible for us to arrive there in time, if they be in the ſituation you deſcribe.' He added, 'Come, let us dine.' Sir John ſeated himſelf with his knights at table, and eat of the firſt courſe: as the ſecond was ſerved, and indeed begun on, ſir John Chandos, who had much thought on this buſineſs, raiſed his head, and, looking at his companions, ſpoke as follows, which gave much pleaſure to thoſe around him.

'The earl of Pembroke (a lord of ſuch high birth and rank that he has even married a daughter of my natural lord the king of England, and is brother in arms as in every thing elſe with my lord of Cambridge,) entreats me ſo courteouſly that it behoves me to comply with his requeſt to ſuccour and reſcue him, if it be poſſible to arrive in time.' He then puſhed the table from him, and, riſing, ſaid to his knights and ſquires, 'Gentlemen, I am determined to go to Puirenon.' This was heard with joy, and they were ſoon ready to attend him. The trumpets ſounded, and every man at arms in Poitiers was mounted in the beſt way he could; for it had been ſpeedily told abroad, that ſir John Chandos was marching to Puirenon, to the aſſiſtance of the earl of Pembroke and his army, who were there beſieged by the French

When theſe knights and ſquires took the field, they amounted to upwards of two hundred lances, and increaſed every moment. They marched with all haſte: news of this was brought to the French, who had conſtantly been engaged at this aſſault from day-break until noon, by their ſpies, who ſaid; 'Dear lords,

lords, look well to yourſelves, for ſir John Chandos has marched from Poitiers with upwards of two hundred lances, and is advancing with great haſte and a greater deſire to meet with you.'

When ſir Louis de Sancerre, ſir John de Vienne, ſir John de Beuil and the others who were preſent, heard this, the beſt informed among them ſaid; ' Our men are tired and worn down by their aſſaults upon the Engliſh, yeſterday and to-day: it will be much wiſer for us to make a handſome retreat with all we have gained, and our priſoners, than to wait the arrival of ſir John Chandos and his company, who are quite freſh; fot we may loſe more than we can gain.'

This plan was immediately followed, for there was not a moment to loſe: the trumpets were ordered to ſound a retreat: their men aſſembled in a body, and, having ſent off their baggage, they themſelves took the road to la Roche-poſay.

The earl of Pembroke and thoſe with him, imagining the French muſt have had ſome intelligence, ſaid among themſelves; ' Chandos muſt certainly be on his march, for the French are retreating, not daring to wait his coming: come, come, let us immediately quit this place and take the road towards Poitiers and we ſhall meet him.' Thoſe who had horſes mounted them: and others went on foot, and ſeveral rode double. They thus left Puirenon, following the road to Poitiers: they had ſcarcely advanced a league before they met ſir John Chandos and his army in the condition I have before told; ſome on horſeback, ſome on foot, and ſome riding double. Much joy was ſhewn on both ſides at this meeting; but ſir John ſaid, he was ſorely vexed that he had not been in time to have met the French. They rode together converſing for about three leagues, when they took leave of each other and ſeparated. Sir John Chandos returned to Poitiers; the earl of Pembroke to Mortagne, the place he had marched from; and the marſhal of France and his army to la Roche-poſay, where they refreſhed themſelves and divided their booty: they then retired to their garriſons, carrying with them their priſoners, whom they courteouſly admitted to ranſom, as the French and Engliſh have always been accuſtomed to act towards each other.

We will now return to the armies in Tournehem; and ſpeak of the death of the moſt courteous, noble and liberal queen that ever reigned in her time, the lady Philippa of Hainault, queen of England and of Ireland.

CHAP. V.

THE DEATH OF QUEEN PHILIPPA OF ENGLAND: SHE MAKES THREE REQUESTS TO THE KING ON HER DEATH-BED.—SOME FRENCHMEN, HAVING ATTACKED THE ENGLISH CAMP AT TOURNEHEM, ARE REPULSED BY SIR ROBERT DE NAMUR.

DURING the time that ſuch numbers of noblemen of the kingdom of France were aſſembled at Tournehem under the command of the duke

duke of Burgundy, and the duke of Lancaſter was encamped with his army in the valley oppoſite to them, a circumſtance happened in England, which, though ſo very common, was not the leſs unfortunate for the king, his children, and the whole kingdom. That excellent lady the queen of England (who had done ſo much good, and during her whole life had aſſiſted all knights, ladies and damſels who had applied to her, who had had ſuch boundleſs charity for all mankind, and who had naturally ſuch an affection for the Hainault nation, being the country from which ſhe ſprung,) lay at this time dangerouſly ill at Windſor-caſtle, and her diſorder daily increaſed.

When the good lady perceived her end approaching, ſhe called to the king, and, extending her right hand from under the bed-clothes, put it into the right hand of the king, who was very ſorrowful at heart, and thus ſpoke; 'We have enjoyed our union in happineſs, peace, and proſperity: I entreat, therefore of you, that on our ſeparation, you will grant me three requeſts.' The king, with ſighs and tears, replied; 'Lady, aſk: whatever you requeſt ſhall be granted.' 'My lord, I beg you will acquit me of whatever engagements I may have entered into formerly with merchants for their wares, as well on this as on the other ſide of the ſea. I beſeech you alſo to fulfil whatever gifts or legacies I may have made, or left to churches, here or on the continent, wherein I have paid my devotions, as well as what I may have left to thoſe of both ſexes who have

 been

been in my ſervice. Thirdly, I entreat that, when it ſhall pleaſe God to call you hence, you will not chooſe any other ſepulchre than mine, and that you will lie by my ſide in the cloiſters of Weſtminſter.' The king, in tears, replied, 'Lady, I grant them.'

Soon after, the good lady made the ſign of the croſs on her breaſt, and, having recommended to God the king and her youngeſt ſon, Thomas, who was preſent, gave up her ſpirit, which, I firmly believe, was caught by the holy angels and carried to the glory of Heaven, for ſhe had never done any thing, by thought or deed, that could endanger her loſing it. Thus died this queen of England, in the year of grace 1369, the vigil of the aſſumption of the Virgin, the 15th of Auguſt *.

Information of this loſs was carried to the Engliſh army at Tournehem, which greatly afflicted every one, but particularly her ſon the duke of Lancaſter. However, as there is no death but what muſt be paſſed over and forgotten, the Engliſh did not neglect to keep up very ſtrict diſcipline in their camp, where they remained a long time facing the French.

It happened that ſome of the French knights and ſquires, ſeeing the enemy every day before their eyes, held a converſation, and, after diſcuſſing the matter, agreed to meet on the morrow, at day-break, to ſkirmiſh with them, and beat up the guard.

* See her monument in Gough's Sepulchral Monuments, vol. i.

There were upwards of three hundred knights and ſquires, the greater part of them from the Vermandois, Artois, and Corbiois, who had entered into this agreement, and, without mentioning it to their marſhals, had each informed the other of their intentions. When the morning came for this expedition, they were all ready armed, mounted, and aſſembled. They rode forth in this array, nothing doubting of ſucceſs, and began to make a circuit round the hill of Tournehem, in order to gain an advantageous poſition, and to fall upon one of the wings of the Engliſh army.

This wing was allotted to ſir Robert de Namur and his people. Sir Robert had been on guard that night, but towards day-break had entered his tent, and was then ſitting at ſupper, quite armed, except his helmet, and the lord Deſpontin* with him. The French at this moment arrived at the quarters of ſir Robert, which were alſo thoſe of ſome other German and Engliſh lords; but the guard very fortunately had not diſarmed themſelves: they immediately oppoſed the Frenchmen who came up ſpurring and galloping, and checked their career. News ſoon reached ſir Robert that his men were fighting, having been attacked by the French. In an inſtant, he puſhed the table from him where he had been ſeated, and ſaid to the lord Deſpontin, 'Come, come to the aſſiſtance of our men.' Inſtantly he fixed his helmet

* Lord Deſpontin. Q. Barnes calls him lord of Ponthieu.

on his head, and ordered his banner, which was placed before his tent, to be difplayed. Some one faid, 'My lord, fend to the duke of Lancafter, and do not engage without him.' He bluntly replied: 'Not I: I fhall go the fhorteft way I can to help my men. Thofe may fend to my lord of Lancafter who will, but let all who love me follow me.'

He then advanced, fword in hand, to meet the enemy: the lord Defpontin and fir Henry de Sancelle were with him, as well as his other knights, who directly engaged in the battle, having found their men fighting with the French, in great numbers, and who, to fpeak truth, ought to have done much this day: but no fooner did they perceive fir Robert de Namur marching with his banner than they wheeled about and gave up their plan, for they thought the whole army was ready to fall on them: indeed, it was fo in different parts of the camp, for the fun was now rifen.

A Vermandois knight was flain under the banner of fir Robert de Namur, called fir Robert de Coulogne, who was much regretted; for he was rich, amiable, and courteous, and an honourable knight in every ftation.

Thus ended the affair. The French retreated without doing any thing more, for they were afraid of greater lofs than gain. Sir Robert did not purfue them farther than was wife, but brought back his men when he found the enemy was quite gone, and returned to his quarters.

CHAP.

CHAP. VI.

THE DUKE OF BURGUNDY AND HIS ARMY DECAMP WITHOUT A BATTLE.—THE DUKE OF LANCASTER RETURNS TO CALAIS.

SINCE this laſt affair, nothing happened worth relating. It was very diſpleaſing to many on both ſides that they thus remained ſo long without a battle: every day it was ſaid, 'We ſhall engage to-morrow;' but that morrow never came; for, as I have ſaid before, the duke of Burgundy would not act contrary to the orders of the king: The orders he received were very ſtrict; for there were continually meſſengers going from the king to the duke, and from the duke to the king on this ſubject.

At laſt the duke of Burgundy, as I was then informed, having conſidered that he was encamped at a very heavy expenſe, and could not remain ſo much longer with any honour; for he had upwards of four thouſand knights, while the enemy was but a handful in compariſon, with whom, however, he had not fought, nor had had any intentions of ſo doing: the duke, I ſay, ſent ſome of his knights to lay his ſituation before the king, and to explain to him his wiſhes. The king thought the duke judged rightly, and ordered him, on the receipt of his letters, to break up his camp,

to

to diſmiſs his army, and come to Paris, where he himſelf was going.

When the duke received theſe orders, he ſent for the principal lords of his army, and told them ſecretly their contents; ſaying, 'We muſt break up our camp, for the king ſends for us back.' When it was midnight, thoſe to whom he had given this information, having packed up every thing, were mounted, and had ſet fire to their quarters. At this hour, ſir Henry de Sancelle was returning to his tent, having been on guard with ſir Robert de Namur's men, to whom he was attached; and ſeeing firſt one, then two, and then three fires in the enemy's camp, he ſaid to himſelf, 'Theſe French think, perhaps, to ſurpriſe us: they have the appearance of intending it: Let us go,' ſaid he to thoſe near him, 'to ſir Robert's tent, and awaken him, that, ſhould it be ſo, he may be prepared in time.' Sir Henry went thither, and, calling his chamberlains, told them, they muſt inſtantly awaken ſir Robert. They went to his bed-ſide and ſir Henry de Sancelle with them, who awakened him, and told him all that he had ſeen. Sir Robert made anſwer, 'We ſhall ſoon hear other news: let our men be inſtantly armed and made ready.' He himſelf was ſoon armed. When his men were drawn up, he had his banner diſplayed, and marched to the tent of the duke of Lancaſter, who was arming alſo, for he had received ſimilar information. It was not long before the different lords came thither, one after another: as they arrived,

rived, they were drawn up, and remained quiet, without any light.

The duke of Lancaſter ordered his marſhals to march the archers to where he hoped the French would make their attack, if they came; for he certainly expected a battle. When they had remained at their poſts for two hours, and ſaw no one advancing to them, they were more ſurpriſed than before. The duke called to him his lords, and aſked them what he had beſt now to do. Some replied one thing, and ſome another, and each defended his own opinion. The duke, perceiving that valiant knight ſir Walter Manny, ſaid; 'And you, ſir Walter, what do you adviſe?' 'I do not know,' replied ſir Walter; 'but, if you will follow my advice, I would draw up my men at arms and archers in order of battle, and would advance ſlowly; for, as it will ſoon be day, we ſhall then ſee clearly before us.'

The duke aſſented to this propoſal: but others were of a contrary opinion, and adviſed him not to march from where he was.

This diſcuſſion continued until orders were given for ſome of the troops of ſir Robert de Namur and ſir Waleran de Bourne* to mount their horſes, becauſe they were lightly accoutred and rode well. Thirty horſemen were choſen from the beſt mounted, and ſent off towards the French camp.

---

* Sir Waleran de Bourne. Q. Barnes calls him Van Bornico.

Whilſt

Whilſt they were gone on this expedition, ſir Walter Manny, addreſſing the duke, ſaid; ' My lord, never believe me again, if theſe French be not fled: mount your horſe, and order the others to do the ſame, that you may purſue them, and I will engage you will have a fine day of it.'

The duke replied; ' Sir Walter, I have hitherto always followed the advice of my council, and intend now doing ſo'; for I can never believe that ſo many brave men at arms and noble knights would thus run away. Perhaps the fires we ſee may have been lighted to entrap us. Our ſcouts will ſoon return, and then we ſhall know the truth.'

As they were thus converſing, the ſcouts returned, and confirmed all that ſir Walter Manny had thought: they ſaid they had found none but ſome poor victuallers, who followed the army. Sir Walter Manny gained great credit. The duke went to his tent to diſarm: he would that day have dined in the French camp, but the fire was too great: he and his men at arms, however, ſupped there, and took up their quarters on the mountain for the night, and made themſelves comfortable with what they found there. On the morrow they decamped, and returned to Calais.

The duke of Burgundy, when he marched off, made his quarters at St. Omer, where he and all his army remained until they were diſbanded, and every man returned to his home. There was afterwards much trouble to re-aſſemble them again.

CHAP.

CHAP. VII.

THE EARL OF PEMBROKE, DESIROUS OF AVENGING HIMSELF FOR THE DEFEAT HE RECEIVED AT PUIRENON, MAKES AN INCURSION TO ANJOU.—THE ABBEY OF ST. SALVIN IN POITOU IS BETRAYED TO THE FRENCH, AND FORTIFIED.

THE ſame week that the armies quitted Tournehem, the earl of Pembroke (who was in Poitou, and had been much mortified at the defeat he had ſuffered from ſir Louis de Sancerre, ſir John de Vienne, ſir John de Bueil and the others at Puirenon, as has been related) reſolved to have his revenge, if poſſible; and for this end he marched from Mortagne with his army, which conſiſted of about two hundred lances, and came to Angoulême, where the prince received him moſt courteouſly. The earl entreated of him permiſſion to lead another expedition, and to lend him ſome of his men, as he was very anxious to avenge himſelf of the affronts he had ſuffered from the French. The prince, who had much affection for him, immediately granted his requeſt. Sir Hugh Calverly was juſt returned from his excurſion into the county of Armagnac, with five hundred fighting men; and the prince gave him leave to accompany the earl of Pembroke in his intended expedition.

He

He alſo requeſted the company of ſir Louis de Harcourt, ſir Guiſcard d'Angle, ſir Percival de Coulongne, the lords de Pons, de Partenay and de Pinane, lord Thomas Percy; ſir Richard de Pontchardon, and ſeveral knights of the prince's houſehold, who willingly accepted the invitation, for they were ready for any excurſion: ſo that, when they were aſſembled, they amounted to five hundred lances, three hundred archers, and fifteen hundred foot ſoldiers, armed with pikes and ſhields, who followed the army on foot. This army marched, under the command of the earl of Pembroke as their leader, and took the road towards Anjou: where they no ſooner arrived than they began to deſtroy, and to do every damage to the country they paſſed through, by razing caſtles and ſorts, burning ſuch towns as could not hold out againſt them, and levying contributions on all the flat country as far as Saumur * on the Loire. They gained poſſeſſion of the ſuburbs, and began an aſſault on the town; but they could not take it, for ſir Robert de Sancerre was in it with a large body of men at arms, who defended it from ſuffering any damage: all the country round about it, however, was pillaged, burnt, and ruined.

Sir Hugh Calverly and his diviſion advanced to a bridge on the Loire, called le Pont de Cé †; when he defeated thoſe who guarded it, took the bridge, and placed ſuch a garriſon of his own men

* Samur,—on the Loire, dioceſe of Angers.

† Pont de Cé,—Pont de Sé,—two leagues from Angers.

there,

there, after he had fortified it well, that they kept possession of it for a long time.

The English, in this expedition, took a large abbey called St. Maur *, on the Loire, which they repaired and fortified, and placed therein a considerable garrison, which, during the ensuing winter and summer, did great mischief to the adjacent country.

At this time, there was in Poitou an abbey which still exists, called St. Salvin †, situated seven leagues from Poitiers; and in this abbey there was a monk who hated the abbot, as he afterwards shewed. It was on account of this hatred which he bore him that he betrayed the abbot and the whole convent, and delivered up the abbey and the town to sir Louis de St. Julien and to Carnet le Breton, who took possession of it, repaired it, and made it a strong garrison.

Sir John Chandos was much vexed at St. Salvin being thus surprised, and not being able to retake it; for, as he was sénéschal of Poitou, he was angry that such a house should have been taken in his government, and declared, that if he should live long enough, he would have it again by some means or other, and make them pay dearly for the insult they had put upon him.

We will now quit Poitou, and return to the duke of Lancaster.

---

* St. Maur,—on the Loire, election of Saumur.

† St. Salvin.—St. Savin,—a village in Poitou, election of Poitiers.

CHAP.

CHAP. VIII.

THE COUNTY OF ST. POL IN PICARDY IS PILLAGED AND RUINED BY THE ENGLISH.—SIR HUGH DE CHASTILLON IS TAKEN PRISONER.

WHEN the duke of Lancaſter had retreated to Calais after the decampment of Tournehem, as has been before related, and had refreſhed himſelf and men for three days, he reſolved, by advice of his council, to draw out his troops, and make an excurſion into France. His marſhals, the earl of Warwick and ſir Roger Beauchamp, were ordered to muſter the army, which orders they very readily obeyed, for they were deſirous of making an inroad on France.

The men at arms and archers marched from Calais in excellent array: every man was appriſed what he was to do, and where he was going. The firſt day's march was only five leagues from Calais. On the morrow, they came before St. Omer, where there were many ſkirmiſhes at the gates; but the Engliſh did not make any long halt: they continued their march, and that night encamped on the heights of Herſault *. On the third day,

* Herſault Q. if not Heriſſart; but that ſeems to be too great a diſtance.

they

they arrived at the city of Terouenne *, where was the count de St. Pol with a large company of men at arms. The Engliſh did not halt, but continued their march, taking the road to Heſdin †, and fixed their quarters at night on a ſmall river.

When the count de St. Pol found that the Engliſh were taking the road to his country, he knew they were not going thither for his good, for they hated him too much: he ſet out, therefore, in the night, and gave the government of the city to the lord de St. Py and ſir John de Roye ‡; and, riding hard, he arrived at his town of St. Pol ‖.

The Engliſh came before the place very early on the morrow morning, and ſeveral ſevere ſkirmiſhes happened; but the arrival of the count was fortunate for himſelf and for the town, as he, with the aſſiſtance of thoſe who had accompanied him, prevented the place from being taken. The duke of Lancaſter, therefore, and his army refreſhed themſelves at their eaſe in the county of St. Pol, which they overran, and did great damage to all the flat

* Terouenne—is now in ruins. It was taken by Henry VIII. by a ſtratagem of pointing wooden guns painted, which were thought to be real ones, and threatening to batter down the town, if not ſurrendered.

† Heſdin,—a ſtrong town in Artois, on the Canche.

‡ Two of my MSS. have different names—the lord de Sampy, ſir Guy de Roye. One has ſir John de Roye.

‖ St. Pol,—a town in Artois, five leagues from Heſdin.

 country,

country. They advanced to the caſtle of Pernes *, where the counteſs dowager reſided. They examined well the fort, and the duke ſounded the depth of the ditches with a lance: notwithſtanding this, they made no attack, though they ſhowed every appearance of it. They made no long ſtay, but continued their march, and went towards Lucheux †, a handſome town, which belonged to the count. They burnt the town, and, without touching the caſtle, continued their road for St. Riquier ‡.

The Engliſh did not march more than three or four leagues a-day, ſo that they burnt and deſtroyed all the countries they paſſed through. They croſſed the river Somme at Blanchetaque below Abbeville, and then entered the country of Vimeu ||, with the intention of puſhing forward to Harfleur on the Seine, in order to burn the navy of the king of France.

The count de St. Pol, and ſir Moreau de Fiennes, conſtable of France, with a large body of men at arms, purſued and hovered about the Engliſh army, ſo that they could not diſperſe nor quit the ſtraight road, but were obliged to keep in a compact body, to be ready to combat the French ſhould they be ſo inclined.

---

* Caſtle of Pernes,—a town in Artois, three leagues from St. Pol.

† Lucheux,—a town of Picardy, near Doulens.

‡ St. Riquier,—an ancient town in Picardy, two leagues and a half from Abbeville.

|| Vimeu,—in Picardy. St. Valery is its capital.

In this manner they marched through Vimeu and the county of Eu: entering the archbishoprick of Rouén, they passed Dieppe, and then continued their march until they came before Harfleur, where they fixed their quarters.

The count de St. Pol had out-marched them, and had entered the town with two hundred lances at the utmost. The English remained three days before Harfleur, but did nothing: on the fourth, they decamped, and returned through the lands of the lord d'Estouteville, whom they did not love much, and burnt and destroyed the whole or greater part. They then passed through Vexin Normand in their way to Oisemont*, to recross the Somme at Blanchetaque.

Sir Hugh de Chastillon, master of the crossbows in France, was at this time captain and governor of Abbeville. When he heard that the duke of Lancaster was returning that way, he armed himself, and ordered twelve of his people to do the same. On mounting their horses, he said he was going to view the guard of the gate of Rouvray, that it might not be wanting in defence, and that the English should not find it too weakly guarded. It was early in the morning, and there was a thick fog.

Sir Nicholas Louvaine, who had been sénéschal of Ponthieu, and whom, this very year, sir Hugh de Chastillon had taken and ransomed for ten thou-

* Oisemont,—a market-town in Picardy, five leagues from Abbeville.

 sand

ſand francs, remembered this ſo ſorely that, having a great deſire to recover his loſſes, he ſet out on the point of day from the duke's army, accompanied by only twenty men. As he was well acquainted with all the roads and paſſes of that country, having reſided there for upwards of three years, he intended lying in ambuſcade between Abbeville and the caſtle of Rouvray, in the hope of taking ſome prize: he had croſſed a ſmall rivulet which ran through a marſh, and hid himſelf and men in ſome old uninhabited houſes.

Sir Hugh never dreamed that the Engliſh would form an ambuſcade ſo near the town. Sir Nicolas and his men kept themſelves very quiet: they perceived ſir Hugh de Chaſtillon riding down the road which leads to Rouvray, with only twelve others, armed at all points, except his helmet, which one of his pages bore on a courſer behind him. He croſſed the little rivulet, and made for the gate of Rouvray, to ſee what the guard of croſs-bowmen were about, and to enquire if they had heard or ſeen the Engliſh.

When ſir Nicholas Louvaine, who was on the watch, ſaw him, he recogniſed him directly, and was more rejoiced than if any one had given him twenty thouſand francs. He ſallied out from his ambuſh, ſaying, 'Follow me: here is what I wiſhed for: it is the maſter of the croſs-bows, and I aſk for nothing better.' Then ſticking ſpurs into his horſe, and pointing his lance, he came upon ſir Hugh, crying, 'Surrender, Chaſtillon, or thou art a dead man.' Sir Hugh, who was much

much puzzled to conjecture whence these men could come, had neither time to put on his helmet nor to mount his courser: finding himself in such a strait, he asked, 'To whom am I to surrender?' Sir Nicholas replied, 'To Louvaine, to Louvaine.' In order, therefore, to avoid the danger he could not escape from, he said, 'I surrender.' He was then taken, and told, 'Ride on quickly, for the army of the duke of Lancaster marches on before us.' On this occasion was slain, a very valiant citizen of Abbeville, called Lawrence Dancons*, who was much regretted.

Thus was taken and entrapped sir Hugh de Chastillon, at that time master of the cross-bows in France and governor of Abbeville, through the good fortune of sir Nicholas Louvaine: with which capture the duke of Lancaster and the English were much rejoiced. On the other hand, the inhabitants of Abbeville were exceedingly vexed at it; but for the present they could not better themselves.

The English marched on, crossed the Somme at Blanchetaque, and then passed through the towns of Rue sur mer and Montrieul sur mer, until they at last arrived at Calais. The duke of Lancaster there dismissed all the foreigners, when sir Waleran de Bourne and the Germans departed. The duke returned to England, and the Germans to their own country, as there was not any intention of continuing the war until the ensuing summer, for now

* Dancons. My two MSS. have Dentels.

Martinmas was paſſed: but the duke informed them, that in the approaching ſpring, he ſhould croſs the ſea with a greater force than he had hitherto done, and ſhould entreat his couſins the dukes of Gueldres and Juliers to accompany him into France.

We ſhall now be ſilent as to the affairs of Picardy, for indeed nothing of great moment happened ſince this time, and return to Poitou, where warlike deeds were oftener performed.

CHAP. IX.

SIR JOHN CHANDOS IS SLAIN IN A SKIRMISH.—THE FRENCH, AT FIRST VICTORIOUS, ARE IN THE END DEFEATED.

SIR John Chandos, being ſénéſchal of Poitou, was ſeriouſly afflicted with the loſs of St. Salvin: he was continually deviſing means to retake it, whether by aſſault or by ſcalado was perfectly indifferent to him, ſo that he could gain it. He made many nightly ambuſcades, but none ſucceeded; for ſir Louis, who commanded in it, was very watchful, as he knew the capture of it had highly angered ſir John Chandos.

It happened that, on the night preceding the eve of the new year (1370), ſir John Chandos, who reſided refided in the city of Poitiers, had fent out his fummons to the barons and knights of Poitou to come to him as fecretly as they could, for he was going on an expedition. The Poitevins would not refufe him any thing, being much beloved by them: they obeyed his fummons, and came to Poitiers. Sir Guifcard d'Angle, fir Louis de Harcourt, the lords de Pons, de Partenay, de Pinane, de Tannaybouton, fir Geoffry d'Argenton, fir Maubrun de Linieres, lord Thomas Percy, fir Baldwin de Franville, fir Richard de Pontchardon, came thither, with many others.

When they were all affembled, they were full three hundred lances.

They left Poitiers in the night, and no one, except the principal lords, knew whither they were going. The Englifh, however, had fcaling ladders, and every thing they might have occafion for with them. They marched to St. Salvin; and, when there arrived, were told what was intended; upon which they all difmounted, and, giving the horfes to their valets, the Englifh defcended into the ditch. It was then about midnight.

They were in this fituation, and would very fhortly have fucceeded in their expedition, when they heard the guard of the fort wind his horn. The reafon was this. That very night Carnet le Breton had come from la Roche-pofay, with forty lances, to St. Salvin, to requeft fir Louis de St. Julien to accompany him in an expedition to Poitou: he therefore awakened the guard and thofe within the fort.

The Engliſh, who were on the oppoſite ſide, ignorant of the intentions of this body of Frenchmen wanting to enter the fort, thought they had been ſeen by the guard, or that ſpies had given information of their arrival to the garriſon. They immediately left the ditch, and ſaid; 'Let us away; for this night we have been diſappointed in our ſcheme.' They mounted their horſes, and advanced in a body to Chauvigny on the river Creuſe, two ſhort leagues diſtant.

When all were arrived there, the Poitevins aſked ſir John Chandos if he wiſhed them to remain with him: he anſwered, 'No: you may return in God's name: I will to-day ſtay in this town.' The Poitevins departed, and with them ſome Engliſh knights: in all, about two hundred lances.

Sir John Chandos entered a hôtel, and ordered a fire to be lighted. Lord Thomas Percy, ſénéſchal of la Rochelle, and his men remained with him. Lord Thomas aſked ſir John Chandos if he intended ſtaying there that day: 'Yes,' replied ſir John: 'why do you aſk?' 'Becauſe, ſir, if you be determined not to go further, I ſhall beg of you to give me leave to make an excurſion, to ſee if I ſhall meet with any adventure.' 'In the name of God, go then,' replied ſir John. At theſe words, lord Thomas Percy ſet out, attended by about thirty lances. Sir John Chandos remained with his own people. Lord Thomas croſſed the bridge of Chauvigny, taking the longeſt road to Poitiers, having left ſir John

Chandos

Chandos quite low ſpirited for having failed in his intended attack on St. Salvin. He continued in the kitchen of the hôtel, warming himſelf at a ſtraw fire which his herald was making for him, converſing at the ſame time with his people, who very readily paſſed their jokes in hopes of curing him of his melancholy.

After he had remained ſome time, and was preparing to take a little reſt, and while he was aſking if it were yet day, a man entered the hôtel, and came before him, ſaying, ‘ My lord, I bring you news.’ ‘ What is it?’ aſked ſir John. ‘ My lord, the French have taken the field.’ ‘ How doſt thou know this?’ ‘ My lord, I ſet out from St. Salvin with them.’ ‘ And what road have they taken?’ ‘ My lord, that I cannot ſay for a certainty; but it ſeemed to me they followed the road to Poitiers.’ ‘ And who are theſe French?’ ‘ My lord, they are ſir Louis de St. Julien and Carnet le Breton, with their companies.’ ‘ Well, it is indifferent to me,’ replied ſir John: ‘ I have not any inclination to exert myſelf this day: they may be met with without my interference.’

He remained a conſiderable time very thoughtful: after having well conſidered, he added; ‘ Notwithſtanding what I have juſt ſaid, I think I ſhall do right to mount my horſe; for at all events I muſt return to Poitiers, and it will be ſoon day.’ ‘ It is well judged,’ replied the knights who were with him. Sir John ordered every thing to be got ready, and his knights having done the ſame, they mounted and ſet off,

taking

taking the road to Poitiers, following the courſe of the river. The French might be about a good league before them on this ſame road, intending to croſs the river at the bridge of Luſſac*. The Engliſh ſuſpected this from perceiving the tracks of the horſes, and ſaid among themſelves, 'Either the French or lord Thomas Percy are juſt before us.' Shortly after this converſation, day appeared; for in the early part of January the mornings begin to be ſoon light. The French might be about a league from the bridge of Luſſac, when they perceived lord Thomas Percy and his men on the other ſide of the river. Lord Thomas had before ſeen them, and had ſet off full gallop to gain the bridge. They ſaid, 'There are the French: they are more in number than we are; let us haſten to take advantage of the bridge.'

When ſir Lewis and Carnet ſaw the Engliſh on the oppoſite ſide of the river, they alſo made haſte to gain the bridge: however, the Engliſh arrived firſt, and were maſters of it. They all diſmounted, and drew themſelves up to defend and guard it.

The French likewiſe diſmounted on their arrival, and, giving their horſes for the ſervants to lead them to the rear, took their lances, and advanced in good order, to attack the Engliſh and win the bridge. The Engliſh ſtood firm, although they were ſo few in compariſon with the enemy.

* Luſſac,—a town in Poitou, dioceſe of Poitiers.

Whilſt

Whilst the French and Bretons were considering the most advantageous manner to begin the onset, sir John Chandos arrives with his company, his banner displayed and flying in the wind. This was borne by a valiant man at arms, called James Allen, and was a pile gules on a field argent. They might be about forty lances, who eagerly hastened to meet the French. As the English arrived at a small hillock, about three furlongs from the bridge, the French servants, who were between this hillock and the bridge, saw them, and, being much frightened, said, 'Come away: let us save ourselves and our horses.' They therefore ran off, leaving their masters to shift as well as they could.

When sir John Chandos, with displayed banner, was come up to the French, whom he thought very lightly of, he began from horseback to rail at them, saying; 'Do you hear, Frenchmen: you are mischievous men at arms: you make incursions night and day at your pleasure: you take towns and castles in Poitou, of which I am sénéschal. You ransom poor people without my leave, as if the country were your own, but, by God, it is not. Sir Louis, sir Louis, you and Carnet are too much the masters. It is upwards of a year and a half that I have been endeavouring to meet you. Now, thanks to God, I do so, and will tell you my mind. We will now try which of us is the strongest in this country. It has been often told me, that you were very desirous of seeing me: you have now that pleasure. I am John

John Chandos: look at me well; and, if God please, we will now put to the proof your great deeds of arms which are ſo renowned.'

With ſuch words as theſe did ſir John Chandos greet them: he would not have wiſhed to have been any where elſe, ſo eager was he to fight with them.

Sir Louis and Carnet kept themſelves in a cloſe body, as if they were willing to engage. Lord Thomas Percy and the Engliſh on the other ſide of the bridge knew nothing of what had paſſed, for the bridge was very high in the middle, which prevented them from ſeeing over it.

During this ſcoffing of ſir John Chandos, a Breton drew his ſword, and could not reſiſt from beginning the battle: he ſtruck an Engliſh ſquire, named Simkin Dodenhale, and beat him ſo much about the breaſt with his ſword that he knocked him off his horſe on the ground. Sir John Chandos, who heard the noiſe behind him, turned round, and ſaw his ſquire on the ground and perſons beating him. This enraged him more than before: he ſaid to his men, 'Sirs, what are you about? how ſuffer you this man to be ſlain? Diſmount, diſmount:' and at the inſtant he was on foot, as were all his company. Simkin was reſcued, and the battle began.

Sir John Chandos, who was a ſtrong and bold knight, and cool in all his undertakings, had his banner advanced before him, ſurrounded by his men, with the ſcutcheon above his arms, he himſelf was dreſſed in a large robe which fell to the ground,

ground, blazoned with his arms on white sarcenet, argent a pile gules; one on his breast, and the other on his back; so that he appeared resolved on some adventurous undertaking; and in this state, with sword in hand, he advanced on foot towards the enemy.

This morning there had been a hoar frost, which had made the ground slippery; so that as he marched he entangled his legs with his robe, which was of the longest, and made a stumble: during which time a squire, called James de St. Martin (a strong expert man), made a thrust at him with his lance, which hit him in the face, below the eye, between the nose and forehead. Sir John Chandos did not see the aim of the stroke, for he had lost the eye on that side five years ago, on the heaths of Bourdeaux, at the chace of a stag: what added to this misfortune, sir John had not put down his vizor, so that in stumbling he bore upon the lance, and helped it to enter into him. The lance, which had been struck from a strong arm, hit him so severely that it entered as far as the brain, and then the squire drew it back to him again.

The great pain was too much for sir John, so he fell to the ground, and turned twice over in great agony, like one who had received his death wound. Indeed, since the blow, he never uttered a word. His people, on seeing this mishap, were like madmen. His uncle, sir Edward Clifford, hastily advanced, and, striding over the body, (for the French were endeavouring to get posses-

sion

ſion of it), defended it moſt valiantly, and gave ſuch well-directed blows with his ſword that none dared to approach him. Two other knights, namely ſir John Chambo and ſir Bertrand de Caſſilies*, were like men diſtracted at ſeeing their maſter lie thus on the ground.

The Bretons, who were more numerous than the Engliſh, were much rejoiced when they ſaw their chief thus proſtrate, and greatly hoped he was mortally wounded. They therefore advanced, crying out, 'By God, my lords of England, you will all ſtay with us, for you cannot now eſcape.'

The Engliſh performed wonderful feats of arms, as well to extricate themſelves from the danger they were in as to revenge their commander, ſir John Chandos, whom they ſaw in ſo piteous a ſtate. A ſquire attached to ſir John marked out this James de St. Martin, who had given the blow: he fell upon him in ſuch a rage, and ſtruck him with his lance as he was flying, that he ran him through both his thighs, and then withdrew his lance: however, in ſpite of this, James de St. Martin continued the fight.

Now if lord Thomas Percy, who had firſt arrived at the bridge, had imagined any thing of what was going forwards, ſir John Chandos' men would have been conſiderably reinforced; but it was otherwiſe decreed; for, not hearing any thing of the Bretons ſince he had ſeen them advancing

* Sir John Chambo,—ſir John Caſſilies. Q. Barnes calls the laſt Caſe.

in

in a large body towards the bridge, he thought they might have retreated; so that lord Thomas and his men continued their march, keeping the road to Poitiers, ignorant of what was passing.

Though the English fought so bravely at the bridge of Lussac, in the end they could not withstand the force of the Bretons and French, but were defeated, and the greater part made prisoners. Sir Edward Clifford stood firm, and would not quit the body of his nephew.

If the French had had their horses, they would have gone off with honour, and have carried with them good prisoners; but, as I have before said, their servants had gone away with them. Those of the English also had retreated, and quitted the scene of battle. They remained therefore in bad plight, which sorely vexed them, and said among themselves, 'This is a bad piece of business: the field is our own, and yet we cannot return through the fault of our servants. It is not proper for us who are armed and fatigued to march through this country on foot, which is quite against us; and we are upwards of six leagues from the nearest of any of our fortresses. We have, besides, our wounded and slain, whom we cannot leave behind.'

As they were in this situation, not knowing what to do, and had sent off two or three of the Bretons, disarmed, to hunt after and endeavour to find their servants, they perceived advancing towards them, sir Guiscard d'Angle, sir Louis de Harcourt, the lords de Partenay, de Tannay-bouton, d'Argenton, de Pinane, sir James de Surgeres,

Surgeres, and ſeveral others. They were full two hundred lances, and were ſeeking for the French; for they had received information that they were out on an excurſion, and were then following the traces of their horſes. They came forwards, therefore, with diſplayed banners fluttering in the wind, and marching in a diſorderly manner.

The moment the Bretons and French ſaw them, they knew them for their enemies the barons and knights of Poitou. They therefore ſaid to the Engliſh: 'You ſee that body of men coming to your aſſiſtance: we know we cannot withſtand them: therefore,' calling each by his name, 'you are our priſoners, but we give you your liberty, on condition that you take care to keep us company; and we ſurrender ourſelves to you, for we have it more at heart to give ourſelves up to you than to thoſe who are coming.' They anſwered, 'God's will be done.' The Engliſh thus obtained their liberty.

The Poitevins ſoon arrived, with their lances in their reſts, ſhouting their war-cries; but the Bretons and French, retreating on one ſide, ſaid, 'Hola! ſtop, my lords: we are priſoners already.' The Engliſh teſtified to the truth of this by adding, 'It is ſo: they belong to us.' Carnet was priſoner to ſir Bertrand de Caſſilies and ſir Louis de St. Julien to ſir John Chambo: there was not one, who had not his maſter.

Theſe barons and knights of Poitou were ſtruck with grief when they ſaw their ſénéſchal, ſir John Chandos, lying in ſo doleful a way, and not able to ſpeak.

ſpeak. They began grievouſly to lament his loſs, ſaying; 'Flower of knighthood! oh, ſir John Chandos! curſed be the forging of that lance which wounded thee, and which has thus endangered thy life.' Thoſe who were around the body moſt tenderly bewailed him, which he heard, and anſwered with groans, but could not articulate a word. They wrung their hands, and tore their hair, uttering cries and complaints, more eſpecially thoſe who belonged to his houſehold.

Sir John Chandos was diſarmed very gently by his own ſervants, laid upon ſhields and targets, and carried at a foot's pace to Mortemer, the neareſt fort to the place where they were. The other barons and knights returned to Poitiers, carrying with them their priſoners. I heard that James Martin, he who had wounded ſir John Chandos, ſuffered ſo much from his wounds that he died at Poitiers.

That gallant knight only ſurvived one day and night. God have mercy on his ſoul! for never ſince a hundred years did there exiſt among the Engliſh one more courteous, nor fuller of every virtue and good quality than him.

When the prince, princeſs, earls of Cambridge and Pembroke, and the other Engliſh knights in Guienne heard of this event, they were completely diſconcerted, and ſaid, they had now loſt every thing on both ſides of the ſea. Sir John was ſincerely regretted by his friends of each ſex; and ſome lords in France bewailed his loſs. Thus it happens through life. The English loved him for all the excellent qualities he was possessed of. The French hated him because they were afraid of him. Not but that I have heard him at the time regretted by renowned knights in France; for they said it was great pity he was slain, and that, if he could have been taken prisoner, he was so wise and full of devices, he would have found some means of establishing a peace between France and England; and was so much beloved by the king of England and his court that they would have believed what he should have said in preference to all others. Thus were the French and English great losers by his death, for never have I heard otherwise, but the English the most, for by his valour and prudence Guienne might have been totally recovered *.

---

* Sir John Chandos was buried at Mortemer. Underneath is his epitaph, from les Annales d'Aquitaine par Bouchet

Je Jehan Chandault, des anglois capitaine,
Fort chevalier, de Poictou sénéschal
Après avoir fait guerre tres lointaine
Au rois francois, tant à pied qu' â cheval
Et pris Bertrand de Guesclin en un val,
Les Poitevins, prés Lussac, me diffirent,
A Mortemer, mon corps enterrer firent,
En un cercueil elevé tout de neuf,
L'an mil trois cens avec seixante neuf

He founded and endowed the carmelite convent at Poitiers.

'He was never married. Elizabeth and Eleanor, two of his sisters, (the latter being the wife of si. Roger Collins) and Isabella, daughter to Margaret the third sister, at that time married to sir John Annesley, were found to be his next heirs.' BARNES.

Lord

Lord Thomas Percy was appointed ſénéſchal of Poitou after the death of ſir John Chandos. His eſtates of St. Sauveur le Vicomte fell to the king of England, who gave them to one of his own knights, by name ſir Aleyne Boxhull *, an uncommonly able man. The prince of Wales ſucceeded as heir to the other riches of ſir John Chandos, as he was never married, and therefore had no children, to the amount of four hundred thouſand francs †.

Shortly afterwards, thoſe captains who had been made priſoners at the bridge of Luſſac were ranſomed, and received their freedom on paying down the ſums agreed on, in which the king of France aſſiſted them. Sir Louis de St. Julien, ſir William des Bourdes and Carnet le Breton returned to their garriſons.

---

* Sir Aleyne Boxhull—was the 52d knight of the Garter, conſtable of the Tower of London, cuſtos of the parks of Clarendon, &c. He lies buried near St Erkenwalde's ſhrine in St. Paul's church, about the year 1380.

Sir Aleyne Boxhull had a commiſſion to reſtrain the exceſſes of Charles de Navarre in Normandy, and to put the caſtle in good repair, dated the 24th November, 1370.—Rymer.

† I ſhould imagine Froiſſart muſt mean that the prince inherited all he poſſeſſed in Aquitaine, &c. but his ſiſter's children were his heirs in England.

CHAP X.

THE LORD DE COUCY AND THE LORD DE POMMIERS ARE UNWILLING TO TAKE PART WITH EITHER SIDE IN THIS WAR.—THE LORDS DE MALEVAL AND DE MARNEIL TURN TO THE FRENCH.

AT this time, there were knights in France greatly hurt at ſeeing this war between the two kings carried on with increaſing vigour; and in particular, the lord de Coucy, who was much intereſted in it, as indeed he ought to be, for he held a very large eſtate in England, as well in his own right as in that of his wife, who was daughter of the king of England; which eſtate it would be neceſſary for him to renounce, if he wiſhed to ſerve the king of France, whoſe kinſman and countryman he was: he therefore thought it moſt profitable to diſſemble between the two kings, and to travel to foreign parts. He very wiſely took all his meaſures; and, having obtained leave of the king of France, he ſet out with few attendants, and went to Savoy, where he was honourably received by the earl, barons and knights of that country. When he had remained there as long as he judged proper, he departed, and, continuing his road, entered Lombardy, viſited the lords of Milan, the lords Galeas and lord Barnabo Viſconti, when at firſt he was made heartily welcome by them.

In

In like manner did ſir Aimemon de Pommiers, who was one of the prince's knights, quit the duchy of Aquitaine. He declared, that during this war, he would not bear arms for one ſide nor the other. This knight croſſed the ſea to Cyprus: he viſited the holy ſepulchre, and travelled to ſeveral other places.

At this period, ſir John de Bourbon * came to Paris. He held ſome lands of the prince; and the king of France would have gladly ſeen him return the homage to the prince, but the count de la Marche would not liſten to it. The lord de Pierre Buffiere, a limouſin knight at that time at Paris, followed his example. But two other barons and great lords in Limouſin unfortunately acted otherwiſe: ſir Louis de Maleval and ſir Raymond de Marneil his nephew, who being at Paris turned Frenchmen, and from their fortreſſes afterwards made a diſaſtrous war on the prince.

The king of England and his council were much vexed at this; for it appeared that the barons and knights of Guienne thus changed their ſides without any conſtraint, and of their own free will. The king therefore, by the advice of his council, ordered letters to be written and ſealed with his ſeal, which he ordered to be ſent by two or three of his knights into Poitou and Aquitaine, to publiſh them in all the cities, caſtles and principal towns.

---

* Sir John de Bourbon. 'He was ſon of ſir James de Bourbon who combated the free companies, chapter ccxxv, and was count de la Marche.'—Denys Sauvage—*Annot.* 120.

At this time, ſir Caponnel de Caponnal was delivered from his priſon at Agen, in exchange for one of the prince's knights, by name ſir Thomas Banaſter, who had been taken in a ſkirmiſh before Perigord. But the counſellor of ſtate who had been ſent with him remained priſoner in Agen, and ſir Caponnel returned to France. We will report the letter which the king of England ſent into Aquitaine.

CHAP XI.

THE FORM OF THE LETTER WHICH THE ENGLISH KING SENT INTO AQUITAINE.—CHATELHERAUT IS TAKEN BY THE FRENCH, AND BELLEPERCHE IS BESIEGED.

EDWARD, by the grace of GOD, king of England, lord of Ireland and of Aquitaine, to all who ſhall ſee or hear theſe preſent letters: Know, that we having conſidered the matter of the boundaries of our lordſhip of Aquitaine, as well as its extent under various lords, have had information relative to ſome oppreſſions done, or intended to have been done, by our very dear ſon the prince of Wales, to this lordſhip aforeſaid: for which cauſe we hold it a duty to endeavour to obviate and remedy any ſuch improper acts, and to conciliate all hatred and rancour that may have arisen between us and our loyal friends and subjects. We therefore announce, pronounce and ordain, out of our deliberate and perfect good will, and by the resolutions of our council for this cause assembled, that our very dear son the prince of Wales desist from all sorts of exactions, done or about to be done; and that he restore and make restitution to all of each sex who may have been oppressed by him, or by his officers in Aquitaine, with all costs, fees and expenses that they may have incurred under the name of these taxes, aids or fouages.

And if any of our feal subjects and friends, as well prelates as other members of the church, universities, barons, knights, townships, inhabitants of cities and large towns have turned, or may be willing to turn, through bad information or weak advice, to the party of our adversary the king of France, we pardon this misdeed, if, after having read this letter, they shall return to us within one month from the date hereof. And we entreat those our loyal and trusty friends, that they so comport themselves not to draw on them any reproach as to their faith and homage, which thing would greatly displease us, and with sorrow should we perceive it. If our very dear son the prince of Wales, or any of his dependants complain of being hurt or oppressed, either now or in former times, we will have such oppressions amended; so that in reason it may be sufficient to encourage love, peace and concord between us and those within our boundaries in our aforesaid lordship. And, in order that these things may be publicly known, we will that each person have a copy of this present letter, the conditions of which we have solemnly sworn to observe, and not break through, upon the body of JESUS CHRIST, in the presence of our very dear son John duke of Lancaster, William earl of Salisbury, the earl of Warwick, the earl of Hereford, Walter Manny, the bastard of Percy, lords Neville, Bourchier and Stafford, Richard Pembridge, Roger Beauchamp, Guy Brian, the lords Mohun and Delaware, Aleyne Boxhul and Richard Sterry, knights. Given at our palace of Westminster, the fifth day of November, in the forty-fourth year of our reign*.

This letter was carried by two of the king of England's knights into the principality and duchy of Aquitaine, proclaimed and published every where. Copies of it were promptly and secretly sent to Paris, to the viscount de la Rochechouart, the lords de Maleval and de Marneil, as well to several others of the French nation as to those who had turned to that interest.

Notwithstanding the letter they had proclaimed in the country of Aquitaine and elsewhere, I never heard that it had any effect, or that any one was prevented by it from following his own inclinations; but that more turned to the party of

* This letter is not in Rymer.

France,

France, and the French daily advanced in their conquefts.

As foon as fir Louis de St. Julien was returned to la Roche-pofay, fir William des Bourdes to his garrifon of la Haye in Touraine, and Carnet le Breton* to St. Savin, they fecretly planned a new expedition of men at arms, and companions well mounted on whom they could depend. They fet off to fcale the walls of the town of Chatelheraut, and, arriving there at early morn, would have made prifoner fir Louis de Harcourt, who was fleeping at his hôtel in the town, not any way fufpecting fuch an enterprife, if he had not fled with his bed-clothes, without fhoes or ftockings, from houfe to houfe, and from garden to garden, in great dread of being taken by the French, who had fcaled the walls of the town, until at laft he arrived at the bridge of Chatelheraut, which his people had fortified: there he faved himfelf, and remained a confiderable time.

The Bretons and French, however, were mafters of the whole town, and placed a ftrong garrifon in it, of which Carnet was captain. This garrifon advanced daily to engage with thofe who ftill kept

* His name was Jean de Keranlouet. In the proofs attached to the Hiftoire de la Bretagne, are feveral acquittances from Jean de Keranlouet, in which he is ftiled, *Ecuyer, Huiffier d'Armes du Roi nôtre Sire, Capitaine de la Ville de la Roche-pofay,* for his own pay as well as for his foldiers. He was to conduct four hundred combatants into Guienne 1371; and alfo to march to the affiftance of Moncontour.

possession

posseſſion of the bridge; and many a gallant ſkirmiſh and feat of arms were performed.

Duke Louis de Bourbon was much enraged that the Engliſh and free companies ſhould keep poſſeſſion of his country, the Bourbonois, and that Ortigo, Bernard de Wiſt and Bernard de la Salle, ſhould hold his caſtle of Belleperche, and detain his mother priſoner in it: he reſolved, therefore, to ſet on foot an expedition of men at arms, and lay ſiege to the caſtle of Belleperche, which, he declared, he would not quit until he had re-taken it. He ſpoke of it to the king of France, who inſtantly promiſed to aſſiſt him in the ſiege with men and money. He left Paris, having ordered his rendezvous at Moulins in the Bourbonois, and at St. Pourſaint*, whither there came a numerous body of men at arms and able combatants.

The lord de Beaujeu came to ſerve him, with three hundred lances: the lords de Villars and de Roucillon, with one hundred; and numbers of barons and knights from Auvergne and Forêts, of which he was lord paramount, through the lady his wife, the daughter of that gallant lord Beroald count dauphin.

The duke arrived and fixed his quarters before the caſtle of Belleperche, where he built a large and ſtrong redoubt, in which his men might be ſheltered every night, and ſkirmiſh with the garriſon during the day. He had alſo brought and

* St. Pourſaint,—a town in Auvergne, dioceſe of Clermont.

pointed

pointed against the castle four large machines, which kept continually throwing, night and day, stones and logs of wood, so that they broke through the roofs of all the houses, and beat down the greater part of the towers.

The mother of the duke of Bourbon, who was a prisoner within the castle, was much alarmed, and sent frequently to entreat her son to abstain from this mode of attack, for these machines annoyed her exceedingly; but the duke, who knew for certain that these requests came from his enemies, replied that he would not desist happen what would.

When the garrison found themselves so much harassed, and that the French force was daily increasing; for sir Louis de Sancerre, marshal of France, had just arrived with a large body of men at arms; they resolved to send and acquaint sir John Devereux, sénéschal of Limousin, who resided at la Souteraine*, two short days journey from them, of their distress, and who knew that, when these lords of Poitou and Gascony had made an excursion from Quercy, it was upon the faith, that if they should take any castles in France, and were besieged in them, they would be assisted.

They wrote their letters, and sent them off in the night by one of their servants to the castle of sir John Devereux. Sir John recognized the messenger by the tokens he mentioned, and, having

* La Souteraine,—a town in Limousin, about two leagues from Limoges.

read

read the letters, ſaid, ‘ that he would moſt willingly acquit himſelf of his engagement, and that the more effectually to do ſo, he would immediately wait on the prince and the lords who were with him, at Angoulême, and exert himſelf ſo that the garriſon of Belleperche ſhould be reinforced.’

Sir John Devereux ſet out, after having given proper directions reſpecting his caſtle and garriſon to his officers, and, being arrived at Angoulême, found there the prince, the earl of Cambridge, the earl of Pembroke, ſir John Mountagùe, ſir Robert Knolles, lord Thomas Percy, ſir Thomas Felton, ſir Guiſcard d'Angle, the captal de Buch and many others. He explained to them, how theſe free companies in the caſtle of Belleperche were beſieged and much ſtraitened by the French under the duke de Bourbon and the count de St. Pol*. The lords, on hearing this ſtatement, replied with great cheerfulneſs, that they muſt be relieved, according to the promiſes which had been made them.

This buſineſs was intruſted to the earls of Cambridge and Pembroke; and the prince iſſued a ſummons to all his vaſſals, who, in ſight of it, were to aſſemble in the town of Limoges. Upon which, knights, ſquires, free companies, and men

* Denys Sauvage thinks it ought to be the count de Sancerre, as the count de St. Pol's name has not been mentioned before. I ſhould be of this opinion, if every copy I have, printed and MS. did not ſay St. Pol.

at arms, marched to that place, according to their orders; and, when they were mustered, they amounted to upwards of fifteen hundred lances and about three thousand others. They marched to Belleperche, where they encamped themselves opposite to the French.

The French kept themselves close in their redoubt, which was as strong and as well fortified as a good town might be. The English foragers were at a loss where to seek for provisions, so that, whenever it was possible, some were brought to them from Poitiers.

Sir Louis de Sancerre, marshal of France, gave exact information of the number and condition of the English to the king of France, and to those knights who had remained at Paris: he sent also a proclamation, which he had affixed to the gates of the palace. It ran in these words:

'Ye knights and squires who are anxious of renown, and seek for deeds of arms, I inform you for a truth, that the earl of Cambridge and the earl of Pembroke are arrived with their troops at Belleperche, with the intention of raising the siege which we have so long made: we have so much straitened the garrison of the castle that it must immediately surrender, or our enemies beat us in a pitched battle. Come therefore hither, directly, for you will have opportunities of exhibiting your prowess in arms; and know that the English are encamped so much apart, and in such positions, that they may be wonderfully annoyed.'

Upon

Upon this exhortation and requeſt of the marſhal, ſeveral good knights and ſquires of France advanced to thoſe parts, and I know myſelf that the governor of Blois, named Alart de Touſtanne, went thither with fifty lances; as did alſo the count de Porcien, and his brother ſir Hugh de Porcien.

CHAP. XII.

THE EARLS OF CAMBRIDGE AND PEMBROKE CARRY OFF THE MOTHER OF THE DUKE OF BOURBON WITH THE GARRISON OF BELLEPERCHE.—THE DUKE OF BOURBON TAKES POSSESSION OF THAT CASTLE.

WHEN the earls of Cambridge and Pembroke had remained before the French army at Belleperche fifteen days, and did not ſee any ſigns of the French quitting their redoubt to fight with them, they called a council, in which they reſolved to ſend to them a herald, to know what they meant to do. Chandos the herald was ordered on this buſineſs, and it was repeated to him what he was to ſay: he therefore went to them, and ſaid; ‘ My maſters and lords ſend me to you, and inform you by my mouth, that they are quite aſtoniſhed you have allowed them to remain fifteen days here, and have not ſallied out of

yo

your fort to give them battle. They therefore tell you, that if you will come forth to meet them, they will permit you to choose any plot of ground for the field of battle; and let God give the event of it to whomsoever he pleases.'

The duke of Bourbon made to this the following reply: 'Chandos, you will tell your masters, that I shall not combat as they may wish or desire. I know well enough where they are; but for all that, I will not quit my fort nor raise the siege, until I shall have re-conquered the castle of Belleperche.' 'My lord,' answered the herald, 'I will not fail to report what you have said.'

The herald set out, and on his return gave the duke's answer, which was not very agreeable. They called another council, and when it was over, gave to Chandos a proposal, for him to carry to the French. He did so, and said; 'Gentlemen, my lords and masters let you know, that since you are not willing to accept the offer they have made you, three days hence, between nine and twelve o'clock in the morning, you, my lord duke of Bourbon, will see your lady-mother placed on horseback, and carried away. Consider this, and rescue her if you can.'

The duke answered; 'Chandos, Chandos, tell your masters, they carry on a most disgraceful war, when they seize an ancient lady from among her domestics, and carry her away like a prisoner. It was never seen formerly, that in the warfare between gentlemen, ladies or damsels were treated as prisoners. It will certainly be very unpleasant

to

to me to see my lady-mother thus carried off: we must recover her as soon as we can: but the castle they cannot take with them: that, therefore, we will have. Since you have twice come hither with propositions, you will bear this from me to your masters, that if they will draw out fifty men, we will draw out the same number, and let the victory fall where it may.' 'My lord,' replied the herald, 'I will relate to them every thing you have told me.'

At these words, Chandos left them, and returned to the earls of Cambridge and Pembroke and the other lords, and told them the offer the duke of Bourbon had sent them. They were advised not to accept it. Preparations were therefore made for the departure of the army, and to carry off with them the lady and the garrison, which had been exceedingly harrassed by the machines of the enemy.

When the appointed day arrived, they ordered their trumpets to sound at early morning: upon which every one armed himself and drew up, both horse and foot, in order of battle, as if they expected a combat, with their banners and pennons flying before them. In this manner were they arrayed; and on this day sir John Montague, nephew to the earl of Salisbury, displayed his banner. They had ordered their trumpets and minstrels to sound very loud; and at nine o'clock the garrison and madame de Bourbon came out of the castle of Belleperche. They mounted her on a

palfrey

palfrey handsomely equipped for her. She was accompanied by her ladies and damsels.

The English army marched away at mid-day. Sir Eustace d'Ambreticourt and sir John Devereux* attended upon madame de Bourbon; and in this manner they returned to the principality, where the lady remained a considerable time a prisoner to the free companions at la Roche Vaucloix in Limousin†.

This capture never pleased the prince, who, whenever it was mentioned, said, that if any others than the free companies had taken the duchess, she should instantly have had her liberty: and when the captains of these free companies spoke to him on the subject, he told them to

* Sir John Devereux—banneret—76th knight of the Garter, a baron from the 8th to the 16th Richard II.—See Dugdale.—Steward of the household to Richard II. constable and governor of the cinque ports. Died suddenly 16th Richard II. Buried Grayfriars, London.

' Sir Nicholas Lovaine held Penshurst 44th Edward III. and married Margaret, eldest daughter of John Vere, earl of Oxford,—.e-married to Henry lord Beaumont, and after to sir John Devereux, knight of the Garter, lord warden of the cinque ports, steward of the household 11th Richard II., in whose 16th year he had licence to embattle his mansion-house at Penshurst, and his daughter and heiress was married to William lord Fitzwalter, but he only enjoyed this manor in right of his wife.'—*Anstis MSS from Philpot's Kent*, p. 270.

† In the curious life of the duke de Bourbon, printed at Paris 1612, from old MSS. the account of this siege is very differently related, and entirely to the honour of the French. The duchess is there said to be carried prisoner to the tower of Bron, near to Brouage on the sea-coast.

make ſome ſort of an exchange, for him to get back his knight, ſir Simon Burley *, whom the French had taken.

You may ſuppoſe the duke of Bourbon was greatly incenſed when he ſaw his lady-mother carried away from the caſtle of Belleperche in the Bourbonois. Soon after her departure, he marched from the redoubt, and ſent his men to take poſſeſſion of his own caſtle of Belleperche, which the Engliſh had left quite empty.

Thus ended this grand expedition, and each withdrew to his uſual place of reſidence. The French, who were under the duke of Bourbon retired to the garriſons from whence they had come. The duke returned with his knights and ſquires to the king of France, who received him with great joy, and entertained him handſomely, The earl of Cambridge went to his brother at Angoulême; and the earl of Pembroke and his troops to Mortagne in Poitou. Thoſe free companies and men at arms who had been in Belleperche went into Poitou and Saintonge, ſeeking for proviſions, and committing many diſgraceful acts, from which they had not the inclination to refrain themſelves, nor power to reſtrain others.

Sir Robert Knolles, ſhortly after this, left the prince, and returned to his caſtle of Derval in Brittany, where he had not been a month, before

* Sir Simon Burley—knight—was 75th knight of the Garter, warden of the cinque ports, governor of Windſor and Dover caſtles. Beheaded 1388. See Hollingſhead.

the king of England ſent him poſitive orders to ſet out, without delay, and croſs the ſea to him in England, as he would find his profit in it. Sir Robert very willingly obeyed this ſummons: having made his preparations, he embarked and landed in Cornwall, at St. Michael's Mount, and thence continued his road until he arrived at Windſor, where he found the king, who was right glad to ſee him, as were all the Engliſh barons; for they thought they ſhould have much need of him, as he was ſo great a captain and leader of men at arms.

CHAP. XIII.

THE FOUR BROTHERS OF FRANCE HAVE A MEETING.—THEIR PREPARATIONS FOR THE WAR.—THE MOTHER OF THE DUKE OF BOURBON OBTAINS HER LIBERTY.—A TREATY ENTERED INTO BETWEEN THE KINGS OF FRANCE AND NAVARRE.

AT this time the duke of Anjou ſet out from Toulouſe, and marched in great array through the kingdom of France: he continued his route until he arrived in Paris, where he found the king and his other brothers the dukes of Berry and Burgundy, who received him with infinite pleaſure.

 The

The four brothers, during the time they were together in Paris, held many councils and consultations on the ſtate of the kingdom, and in what manner they ſhould beſt act during the enſuing ſummer. It was determined to raiſe two large armies, and make an incurſion to Aquitaine. The duke of Anjou was to command one of theſe armies, which ſhould enter Guienne by la Réole and Bergerac: the duke of Berry the other towards Limoges and Quercy, when theſe two armies were to unite and march to Angoulême, to beſiege therein the prince of Wales. It was alſo propoſed and determined in theſe conſultations to recal that valiant knight ſir Bertrand du Gueſclin, who had ſo gallantly and loyally fought for the crown of France, and entreat him to accept the charge of conſtable of France.

When king Charles, his brothers and his council, had completely arranged their future plans, and had enjoyed themſelves together for ſome time, the duke of Anjou, early in May, took his leave of them, to return the firſt to his government, for he had the longeſt journey to make. He was eſcorted by the barons and knights of France, being much beloved by them, and purſued his journey until he came to Montpellier, where he tarried upwards of a month, and then returned to Toulouſe.

He directly collected as many men at arms as he was able, wherever he could hear of them, and ſoon had a large force from thoſe who had kept the field guarding the frontiers of the Engliſh in

Rouergue

Rouergue and Quercy: for le petit Mechin, Naudon de Pans, Perrot de Savoye, le bourg Camus, Anthoine le Negre, Lanuit, Jaques de Bray and numbers of their companions had remained all the year at Cahors, where they had ravaged and ruined the country.

On the other hand, the duke of Berry went to Bourges in Berry, where he had issued a grand summons to all knights and squires of France, and Burgundy.

The duke of Bourbon had gone into his own country, where he had given orders concerning this intended expedition, and had collected a large body of knights and squires from the country of Forêts and the Bourbonois. His brother, count Peter d'Alençon made preparations in another part, and with good effect.

Sir Guy de Blois, at this period, was returned from Prussia, where he had been made a knight, and displayed his banner in an enterprize against the enemies of God. As soon as this gallant knight arrived in Hainault, and was informed of the expedition which his cousins of France were about to undertake in Aquitaine, he made immediate preparations for joining it; and, setting out from Hainault with all his array, he arrived at Paris to present himself to the king. He was gladly received by him, and ordered to join the duke of Berry with a command of knights, squires and men at arms in the expedition. Sir Guy de Blois, therefore, left the city of Paris, and rode to Orleans in his way to Berry.

In like manner as the king of France had arranged his armies, so did the king of England by two armies and two expeditions. It was ordered that the duke of Lancaster should march with four hundred men at arms and as many archers into Aquitaine, to reinforce his brothers; for it was thought that the greatest force of the enemy would be sent to that country. The king and his council determined that another army of men at arms and archers should enter Picardy under sir Robert Knolles, who was perfectly capable of such a command, having learnt it under the most able masters for a considerable time.

Sir Robert, at the request of the king, willingly undertook this expedition: he promised to cross the sea to Calais, to pass through the whole kingdom of France, and to fight with the French, if they were bold enough to meet him in the field. Of this he seemed quite certain, and made wonderful preparations for himself, as well as for all those who were to accompany him.

The mother of the duke of Bourbon about this time obtained her liberty, being exchanged for sir Simon Burley, the prince of Wales's knight. Sir Eustace d'Ambreticourt was very instrumental in bringing this business to an end, for which the duke of Bourbon and the queen of France testified their obligations to him.

There had been for a considerable time, long negociations carried on between the king of France and the king of Navarre, who resided at Cherbourg. The ministers of both kings managed the

the business in such a manner that they informed the king of France he had not any reason for waging war against his brother-in-law the king of Navarre. They added, that for the present he had enough on his hands with his war with England, and that he had better leave things as they then were, lest greater evils might arise, for, if the king of Navarre should consent to admit the English into his forts in Coutantin, they would harrass the country of Normandy most grievously, which was a thing to be well considered and attended to.

Upon receiving this information and advice, the king of France consented to a peace. He went to the town of Rouen, where all the treaties were drawn up and confirmed. The archbishop of Rouen, the count d'Alençon, the count de Sallebruche, sir William des Dormans * and sir Robert Lorris waited on the king of Navarre, whom they found at Vernon. He made for them grand dinners and magnificent feasts; after which they conducted him to the king of France at Rouen, when these treaties and alliances were again read, sworn to, confirmed and sealed. It seems that the king of Navarre, by the articles of this peace was to renounce whatever engagements he may have entered into with the king of England, and that he himself, on his return to Navarre, was to declare war against him. For greater security of the affection between him and the king

* Sir William des Dormans—was chancellor of France.

of France, he was to leave in his hands his two ſons, Charles and Peter, as hoſtages. Upon this treaty being concluded, the two kings left Rouen, and came to Paris, where there were again great feaſts. When they had ſufficiently enjoyed and amuſed themſelves, they took leave of each other. The king of Navarre quitted the king of France in the moſt amicable manner, leaving his two children with their uncle. He ſet out for Montpellier, and returned through that country to Foix, and from thence to his own kingdom of Navarre.

We will now return to what was paſſing in Aquitaine.

CHAP XIV.

SIR BERTRAND DU GUESCLIN LEAVES SPAIN AND ARRIVES AT TOULOUSE, WHERE THE DUKE OF ANJOU RECEIVES HIM WITH GREAT JOY.—THEY TAKE TOGETHER SEVERAL CASTLES FROM THE ENGLISH.

YOU know, as we have before mentioned it, that the duke of Anjou had been in France, and that, according to arrangements then made, upon his return to Languedoc, he was to invade, with his whole force, Guienne, for he never loved the prince of Wales nor the Engliſh, and indeed made no pretenſions to that effect. Before he left Paris, the king of France, by his deſire, had ſent letters

letters and ambaſſadors to the king of Caſtile, to requeſt he would ſend back ſir Bertrand du Gueſclin, for by ſo doing he would very much oblige him At the ſame time, the king and duke of Anjou wrote moſt friendly letters to ſir Bertrand himſelf.

The envoys made haſte on their journey, and found king Henry with ſir Bertrand in the city of Léon in Spain, to whom they delivered their letters and the meſſage from the king of France.

The king of Spain never wiſhed to detain ſir Bertrand, nor would have forgiven himſelf for ſo doing. Sir Bertrand therefore made his preparations in haſte, and, taking leave of king Henry, ſet out with his attendants, and continued his road until he came to Toulouſe. where the duke of Anjou was. He had already there aſſembled a very large force of men at arms, knights and ſquires, and waited for nothing but the arrival of ſir Bertrand du Gueſclin; ſo that upon his coming the duke of Anjou and all the French were mightily rejoiced. Orders were given to march from Toulouſe, and invade the territories of the prince.

The duke of Lancaſter at this time was arrived at Southampton, with four hundred men at arms and an equal number of archers. He embarked them and every neceſſary proviſion and ſtores on board ſhips, with the intent of ſailing for Bourdeaux, provided they might have a favourable wind.

With the duke, and under his command, were the lord Roos (of Hamlake), ſir Michael de la Pole,

Pole *, ſir Robert le Roux †, ſir John de St. Lo, and ſir William Beauchamp ‡.

The duke of Anjou left the city of Toulouſe with a great and well ordered array. He was attended by the count d'Armagnac, the lord d'Albret, the count de Perigord, the count de Comminges, the viſcount de Carmaing, the count de Liſle, the viſcount de Bruniguel, the viſcount de Narbonne, the viſcount de Talar, the lord de la Barde, the lord de Pincornet, ſir Bertrand Tande, the ſénéſchal of Toulouſe, the ſénéſchal of Carcaſſonne, the ſénéſchal of Beaucaire and ſeveral others, amounting in the whole to upwards of two thouſand lances, knights and ſquires, and ſix thouſand footmen, armed with pikes and ſhields. Sir Bertrand du Gueſclin was appointed to the command of all this force.

They directed their march through the Agénois; and being joined by more than a thouſand combatants from the free companies, who had waited for them all the winter in Quercy, they made for Agen.

The firſt fort they came to was that of Moiſſac ‖. The whole country were ſo frightened at the arrival of the duke of Anjou, and the large army he had brought, that they trembled before him, and

---

* Sir Michael de la Pole, afterwards earl of Suffolk, and favourite of Richard II.—See Dugdale.

† Sir Robert le Roux,—Barnes calls ſir Robert Ros.

‡ Sir William Beauchamp,—Lord Abergavenny.—DUGDALE.

‖ Moiſſac,—a town in Quercy, 12 leagues from Agen.

neither

neither towns nor castles had any inclination to hold out against him. When he arrived before Moissac, the inhabitants instantly surrendered and turned to the French. They then advanced to Agen, which followed this example. They afterwards marched towards Tonneins * on the Garonne; and the French went on unmolested, following the course of the river Garonne, in order to have plenty of forage: they came to Port St. Marie †, which immediately surrendered. The French placed men at arms and garrisons in all these towns. The town and castle of Tonneins did the same, in which they placed a captain and twenty lances to guard it. They afterwards took the road to Montpezat ‡ and Aiguillon ‖, burning and destroying all the country.

When they came before Montpezat, which is a good town and has a strong castle, those within were so much frightened by the duke of Anjou that they directly opened their gates. The French then advanced to the strong castle of Aiguillon, where they only remained four days; for then the garrison surrendered to the duke, not being such men as sir Walter Manny commanded, when he defended it against John duke of Normandy, afterwards king of France. The inhabitants of Ber-

* Tonneins,—a town of Agénois on the Garonne, 41 leagues from Toulouse.

† Porte St. Marie, on the Garonne, below Agen

‡ Montpezat,—a village in Guienne, near Tonneins.

‖ Aiguillon,—a town of Guienne, one league from Tonneins.

gerac were very much aſtoniſhed at their having ſo done: for the governors, at this time, of Bergerac, were the captal de Buch and ſir Thomas Felton, who had with them one hundred lances, Engliſh and Gaſcons.

CHAP. XV.

THE DUKE OF BERRY INVADES LIMOUSIN.

JUST as the duke of Anjou and his army had invaded the territories of the prince by the way of Toulouſe and Agen, ſo did the duke of Berry with his army enter the Limouſin. He had full twelve hundred lances and three thouſand footmen, who conquered towns and caſtles, and burnt and deſtroyed the country they marched through.

With the duke of Berry were, the duke of Bourbon, the count d'Alençon, ſir Guy de Blois, ſir Robert d'Alençon count du Perche, ſir John d'Armagnac, ſir Hugh Dauphin, ſir John de Villemur, the lords de Beaujeu, de Villars, de Senac, ſir Geoffry de Montagu, ſir Louis de Maleval, ſir Raymond de Marneil, ſir John de Boulogne, his uncle ſir Geoffry de Boulogne, the viſcount d'Uzes, the lords de Sully, de Talenton, de Confant, Dappechere, Dacon, ſir John Damenue,

menue, Ymbaut de Peſchin, and many other good barons, knights and ſquires.

This army entered Limouſin, where they did infinite miſchief, and advanced to beſiege the city of Limoges. In this city were a body of Engliſh, whom ſir Hugh Calverley, the ſéneſchal of Limouſin had placed there; but he was not the maſter, for the biſhop of the city governed it, in whom the prince of Wales put much confidence, looking upon him as his ſteady friend.

The prince of Wales, who kept his court at Angoulême, had received information of theſe two grand expeditions of the dukes of Anjou and of Berry, and how they had invaded his principality at two different places. It was alſo told the prince, that as far as could be imagined, they were marching to form a junction near Angoulême, to beſiege him and the princeſs therein, and adviſed him to conſider of it.

The prince, who was valour itſelf, and full of reſources, replied, that 'his enemies ſhould never find him ſhut up in town or caſtle, and that he would immediately march and take the field againſt them.'

Clerks and knights were inſtantly employed to write and ſend off letters to loyal friends and ſubjects in Poitou, Saintonge, la Rochelle, Rouergue, Quercy, Goire, Bigorre and Agénois, commanding them, with as many men as they could bring, to meet him at the town of Cognac. His rendezvous was fixed there, and he ſoon left Angoulême,

lême, attended by the princeſs and his young ſon Richard.

But during the time this ſummons was ſent, and every one making his preparations, the French kept advancing, burning and ravaging the country. They came before Linde, a good town ſituated upon the river Dordonne, one league from Bergerac: a valiant knight of Gaſcony, named ſir Thonius de Bateſol *, was the governor of it.

The duke of Anjou, the count d'Armagnac, the lord d'Albret, the count de Perigord, the viſcount de Carmaing, and all the other barons with their men, came thither and formed the ſiege in a regular manner, ſaying they would not depart without having taken it.

This town was large, ſtrong and well provided with all ſorts of proviſion and artillery; for the captal de Buch and ſir Thomas Felton had been there a fortnight before, and had reinforced it. They thought that Linde was very capable of holding out, if thoſe within were determined, conſidering the aſſiſtance they might draw from Bergerac, ſhould there be occaſion. But the inhabitants were ſo wonderfully inclined to the French, that they entered into a negotiation with the duke of Anjou, and liſtened to his promiſes, which made them preſs the governor, ſir Thonius, that he alſo conſented to be a true Frenchman, upon

* Sir Thonius de Bateſol. It is ſo in all my printed copies, but otherwiſe in the MSS. One has *Thomas*. Q. if it ſhould not be ſo.

conſideration

consideration of receiving a large sum of money, and having a good annuity from the duke for his life.

Every thing being thus settled, the town was to be delivered up to the French. This treaty was, however, known at Bergerac the evening preceding the day of surrender. The earl of Cambridge had just arrived there with two hundred lances, and was present when this information was given. The captal and sir Thomas Felton were thunderstruck at the intelligence, and said they would be present at this surrender. Having ordered their troops, they set out from Bergerac after midnight, and rode towards the town of Linde. They came there by day-break, and, ordering one of the gates to be opened, pushed forward without stopping until they arrived at the other gate, through which the French were to enter: indeed, they were already assembled there in crowds, for sir Thonius was about to allow them to enter the gate. On seeing which, the captal, grasping his sword, dismounted, as did all his troops, and, advancing to sir Thonius, said: 'Sir Thonius, thou wicked traitor, thou shalt be the first dead man; and never more shalt thou commit another treason.' Upon which he thrust his sword into him, and with so much force that it went through his body and came out upwards of a foot on the other side, and struck him down dead.

The

The French, on ſeeing the banners of the captal de Buch and ſir Thomas Felton, immediately retreated, having failed in their attempt.

Thus did the town continue Engliſh, but was in great danger of being burnt, and the inhabitants ſlain, becauſe they had conſented to this treaty. They excuſed themſelves wiſely and prudently, ſaying that what they had done and conſented to was through fear, and principally through their governor, who had brought this buſineſs about. The lords appeared to believe all this, and the inhabitants remained in peace; but the captal and ſir Thomas Felton continued in the town as long as the duke of Anjou lay before it, and until he had taken another road.

We will now ſpeak a little of the ſtate and condition of England, for that is now neceſſary, and of the invaſion of France by ſir Robert Knolles.

CHAP. XVI.

A TRUCE IS ESTABLISHED BETWEEN ENGLAND AND SCOTLAND.—SIR ROBERT KNOLLES OVERRUNS, BURNS AND RAVAGES THE WHOLE COUNTRIES OF PICARDY AND THE VERMANDOIS.

WHEN ſir Robert Knolles was about to leave England, there were many councils held between the Engliſh and Scots. They were ſo well

well conducted by the able ministers of both kingdoms that a truce was established between each king, kingdom, subjects, and adherents, for nine years.

The Scots, by this treaty, might arm and hire themselves out like to others for subsidies, taking which side they pleased, either English or French: by which means sir Robert increased his army with one hundred lances*.

When sir Robert and all who were to accompany him were ready, and had arrived at Dover, they passed the sea, he himself crossing the last, and landed at Calais, where, on his disembarking, he was received with great joy by the governor, sir Nicholas Stambourn, and his brother soldiers.

When they had refreshed themselves for seven days, and had formed their plans with respect to the parts of France into which they should carry their attack, they ordered their baggage and stores to advance, and took the field in a very handsome manner. They were about fifteen hundred lances and four thousand archers, including the Welshmen. Sir Robert was accompanied, according to

* Mezeray says, this truce was for three years—Buchanan, fourteen,—Froissart, nine.—*Note in Barnes*, p. 800.

I cannot find this truce in the Fœdera. On the contrary, there is an offensive and defensive treaty with the king of France, dated at Edinburgh castle, 28th October, 1371, in which it expressly mentions that no truce is to be entered into, without including both France and Scotland, by either of the parties.—For more particulars, see Rymer.

 the

the king's orders, by ſir Thomas Grantſon*, ſir Aleyne Boxhull, ſir Gilbert Gifford, the lord de Salvatier†, ſir John Bourchier‡, ſir William de Merville§, ſir Geoffry Urſwell‖, and many other knights and ſquires, expert and able men at arms, who marched this firſt day pretty near to Fiennes¶.

Sir Moreau de Fiennes, who at that time was conſtable of France, reſided in his caſtle with a great number of men at arms, knights and ſquires, all prepared and ready to receive the Engliſh. On the morrow, when they advanced towards the caſtle and drew up to the attack, they found they ſhould not gain any thing, ſo they marched off through the county of Guines, and entered that of Faukenbourg, burning every thing on their road, and came before the city of Terouenne, but did not attack it; for it was ſo well garriſoned with

---

* Sir Thomas Grantſon,—82d knight of the Garter—See Grandiſon in Dugdale

† 'Le ſire de Salvatier' Q.

‡ Sir John Bourchier,—86th knight of the Garter—a baron.—See Dugdale

§ De Merville. Q. if not Neville. I believe it to be ſir William Neville, one of the ſons of Ralph lord Neville, of Raby—See Dugdale.

Barnes names ſir *Hugh* Meinel, ſir Walter Fitzwalter, and ſir John Menſtreworth.

‖ I have called this perſon *Urſwell*, after Barnes, but, as Froiſſart writes it *Overcelay*, it is probably one of the Worſley family. It may alſo be ſir Hugh Wrotteſley, ſpelled *Wortheſley* in Mills, who was 19th knight of the Garter, and perhaps with more probability.

¶ Fiennes,—a village in the Boulonnois, generality of Amiens.

men

men at arms that it would have been only loſt trouble. They continued their march through the country of the Terouennois, to enter Artois; and, as they only advanced three or four leagues a day on account of their baggage and infantry, they took up their quarters in the large villages at the early hour of mid-day or noon. Thus did they advance with their whole army until they came before the city of Arras. The lords and principal captains were lodged in the town of Mount St. Eloy, near Arras, and their army in the environs; whence they pillaged and ravaged all the country round, as far as they dared to extend themſelves.

The king of France had at this ſeaſon ordered a number of men at arms to the different cities, fortreſſes, large towns, caſtles, bridges, and fords, to guard and defend thoſe which ſhould be attacked, and which they were not to quit on any account.

When ſir Robert Knolles had refreſhed himſelf and army for two days, he quitted St. Eloy, and marched from before Arras in good array. Sir William de Merville and ſir Geoffry Urſwell, who were the marſhals of the army, could not reſiſt a wiſh to ſee thoſe of Arras a little nearer. They quitted, therefore, the battalion, and advanced with about two hundred lances and four hundred archers, as far as the barriers of the ſuburbs of Arras, which they found well guarded by men at arms and croſs-bows. The lord Charles de Poitiers was at that time in the town with madame d'Artois, but he made not any attempt to sally out on the English or otherwise attack them.

The English, having finished their course, had halted a short time at the barriers, and, seeing no appearance of any one coming to them, they set out on their return to the main army, who were waiting for them drawn up in a line of battle. However, before they departed, they wished to leave a remembrance behind, and set fire to the suburbs of Arras, in order to entice the inhabitants out of the town, who had not any good will to do so. This fire did much mischief, for it burnt a large monastery of preaching friars, cloisters and all that was without the town.

After this, the English continued their march, taking the road to Bapaume*, burning and ravaging the whole country. The army was constantly in motion, and, having entered the Vermandois, arrived at Roye†; which town they burnt, and then marched towards Ham‡ in Vermandois. All the inhabitants of the flat country had retired into this town, and into St. Quentin and Peronne, carrying with them every thing portable. The English found nothing but barns full of unthreshed corn, for it was now after August.

They advanced by easy marches, without any labour or fatigue, until they came to a rich coun-

* Bapaume,—a strong town of Artois, six leagues from Arras.

† Roye,—a strong town in Picardy, eighteen leagues from Arras

‡ Ham,—a town in Picardy, on the Somme, six leagues from Roye.

try,

try, where they halted for two or three days. During this time, ſir Robert Knolles ſent parties to a town or caſtle which commanded the ſurrounding country, and the marſhals, having obtained a parley with the governors, aſked, ' How much will you give us in ready money for all this country, if we will not deſpoil it ?' A treaty and compoſition was entered into with ſir Robert, and a large ſum of florins paid down. This country was reſpited from being burnt. Sir Robert gained by this treaty a ſum amounting to one hundred thouſand francs, for which he was afterwards ill at court, and accuſed to the king of England for not having done his duty faithfully, as I ſhall fully relate in the continuance of this hiſtory.

The lands of the lord de Coucy were unmoleſted; and never did the Engliſh hurt man or woman, nor take from them a farthing, who ſaid, ' I belong to the lord de Coucy.' They marched unto the good town of Noyon*, which was well provided with men at arms, and halted in the neighbourhood: they made their approaches very near, to ſee if it were poſſible for them to carry it by aſſault, but found it well fortified, and able to defend itſelf ſhould there be occaſion. Sir Robert was lodged in the abbey of Orcamp†, and his men in the neighbourhood. They advanced one day in order of battle to the walls of the city,

* Noyon,—now a village in Picardy, dioceſe of Amiens.

† Orcamp, or St. Anne,—a village in Picardy, near Noyon.

to ſee if the garriſon and inhabitants would iſſue forth, but in vain.

There was a Scots knight in the Engliſh army who performed a moſt gallant deed of arms. He quitted his troop, with his lance in its reſt, and mounted on his courſer, followed only by his page; when, ſticking ſpurs into his horſe, he was ſoon up the mountain and at the barriers. The name of this knight was ſir John Aſſueton*, a very valiant and able man, perfectly maſter of his profeſſion. When he was arrived at the barriers of Noyon, he diſmounted, aud, giving his horſe to his page, ſaid, 'Quit not this place.' then, graſping his ſpear, he advanced to the barriers, and leaped over them. There were on the inſide ſome good knights of that country, ſuch as ſir John de Roye, ſir Launcelot de Lorris, and ten or twelve others, who were aſtoniſhed at this action, and wondered what he would do next: however, they received him well. The Scots knight, addreſſing them, ſaid; 'Gentlemen, I am come to ſee you; for, as you do not vouchſafe to come out beyond your barriers, I condeſcend to viſit you. I wiſh to try my knighthood againſt yours, and you will conquer me if you can.' After this, he gave many grand ſtrokes with his lance, which they returned him. He continued in this ſituation alone againſt them all, ſkirmiſhing and fighting moſt gallantly, upwards of an hour. He wounded one or two of their knights; and

* Sir John Aſſueton. Probably Seton.

they

they had ſo much pleaſure in this combat, they frequently forgot themſelves. The inhabitants looked from above the gate and tops of the walls with wonder. They might have done him much hurt with their arrows, if they had ſo willed: but no: the French knights had ſtrictly forbidden it. Whilſt he was thus engaged, his page came cloſe to the barriers, mounted on his courſer, and ſaid to him aloud, in his own language, 'My lord, you had better come away: it is time, for our army is on its march.' The knight, who had heard him, made ready to follow his advice; and, after he had given two or three thruſts to clear his way, he ſeized his ſpear, and leaped again over the barriers without any hurt, and, armed as he was, jumped up behind the page on his courſer. When he was thus mounted, he ſaid to the French, 'Adieu, gentlemen: many thanks to you,' and, ſpurring his ſteed, ſoon rejoined his companions. This gallant feat of ſir John Aſſueton was highly prized by all manner of perſons.

CHAP. XVII.

THE GARRISON OF NOYON MAKE THE ENGLISH PRISONERS WHO HAD SET FIRE TO PONT L'EVEQUE.—THE KING OF FRANCE SENDS FOR SIR BERTRAND DU GUESCLIN.

SIR Robert Knolles and his army, on their departure from the town of Noyon, ſet fire to Pont l'Evêque on the river Oiſe, where there were ſeveral handſome hôtels. Thoſe knights and ſquires in the town of Noyon were exceedingly angry at this proceeding, and, underſtanding that ſir Robert and his forces had proceeded, left the city of Noyon with about fifty lances, and came ſo well in time to the town of Pont l'Evêque, that they found there thoſe who had burnt it, and others occupied in the pillage. They were attacked moſt furiouſly, and the greater part of them ſlain or made priſoners. The French took more than ſixty horſes, and reſcued many priſoners whom the enemy intended carrying off. Several good houſes would have been burnt if they had not come there ſo opportunely. They returned to Noyon with upwards of fifteen Engliſh priſoners, whom they beheaded.

The Engliſh continued their march in battle-array, intending to enter the Laonnois, and to croſs crofs the rivers Oife* and Aine†. They committed no devaftation in the county of Soiffons, becaufe it belonged to the lord de Coucy. True it is, they were followed and watched by fome lords of France, fuch as the vifcount de Meaux, the lord de Chauny, lord Raoul de Coucy, lord William de Melun, fon of the count de Tancarville, and their forces; fo that the Englifh, not daring to quit their line of march, kept in a compact body. The French did not attack them, but every night took up their quarters in caftles or ftrong towns, whilft the Englifh encamped in the open plains, where they found provifion in plenty, and new wine, with which they made very free. Thus did they advance, burning, ravaging, and oppreffing all the country, when they croffed the river Marne‡, and entered Champagne, and then paffed the Aube§, returning to the country about Provins‖; when they feveral times paffed the Seine, and made appearances of marching towards Paris; for they had heard that the king of France had collected a large force of men at arms under the command of the count de St. Pol and the lord de Cliffon, with whom they were very

* Oife,—a river in Picardy,—rifes in Hainault.

† Aifne or Aine,—a river which rifes in Champagne, and joins the Oife a little above Compiegne

‡ Marne,—a large river which rifes near Baffigny.

§ Aube,—a confiderable river in Champagne. It rifes at Auberive, near Langres.

‖ Provins,—an ancient town of Brie, on the Morin, which runs into the Marne, 22 leagues from Paris.

eager

eager to engage, and for that end made every preparation as if they only wiſhed for the combat.

Upon this, the king of France wrote to ſir Bertrand du Gueſclin, who was in Aquitaine with the duke of Anjou, to order him, as ſoon as he ſhould have read the letters, to ſet out for France, as he intended to employ him in another part of his kingdom.

Pope Urban V. came back about this time to Avignon, after having reſided nearly four years at Rome. He returned in the hope of making peace between the two kings; for this renewal of war was very diſpleaſing to him. All thoſe of Avignon and the country around it were very happy at the return of the pope, as they thought it would be more advantageous for them.

We will now ſay how the prince of Wales carried on his affairs.

CHAP. XVIII.

THE PRINCE OF WALES ASSEMBLES HIS ARMY AT COGNAC, WHERE HE MEETS HIS BROTHER THE DUKE OF LANCASTER.—THE DUKES OF ANJOU AND BERRY BREAK UP THEIR EXPEDITION, LIMOGES HAVING TURNED TO THE FRENCH.

YOU have before heard of the prince of Wales fixing his rendezvous at Cognac, with the intent of advancing to combat the duke of Anjou,

Anjou, who was burning and despoiling his territories. The barons, knights and squires of Poitou and Saintonge, and all who were vassals to the prince hastened to obey his summons. The earl of Pembroke quitted his garrison, with a hundred lances, and came to meet him.

The duke of Lancaster and his army arrived about this time at Bourdeaux, at which the country rejoiced much. He made not any long stay there; for, hearing that the prince was about to march against his enemies, he departed, and met, one day's march from Cognac, the earl of Pembroke, who was likewise going thither. They were very happy to see each other, and rode together to Cognac, where they found the prince, princess and earl of Cambridge, who were greatly pleased at their arrival. Men at arms daily came in from Poitou, Saintonge, la Rochelle, Bigorre, Gorre, Gascony and the surrounding countries under the obedience of the prince.

The duke of Anjou, the count d'Armagnac, the lord d'Albert, and the counts, viscounts, knights and squires of that army, who, as before has been related, conquered cities, towns and fortresses to the number of more than forty, by merely shewing themselves before them, and who had advanced within fifteen leagues of Bourdeaux, burning and ravaging the country round Bergerac and Linde, hearing that the prince had summoned his forces to meet him at Cognac, and that the duke of Lancaster was arrived with a strong body of men at arms and archers

archers from England, called a council to consider what measures would be now most proper for them to pursue. It was at this time that the king of France had sent back sir Bertrand du Guesclin to the duke of Berry, who was besieging the city of Limoges, and had pressed it so hard that it was upon the point of surrendering, but upon good terms. Sir Bertrand was summoned to attend this council of the duke of Anjou, as was right, and many were the debates at it. At last, after well considering the business, the duke of Anjou was advised, for the present, to break up this expedition, to order his men to different garrisons, and to carry on the war from thence, as he had done sufficient in the open field. It was therefore highly behoving the lords of Gascony who were present, such as the Count d'Armagnac, the count de Perigord, the lord d'Albert and others, to retire to their own country to guard aud defend it; for they knew not what the prince might be inclined to do with so large an army. They then separated, each going on his own business. The duke of Anjou returned to the city of Cahors: his men and the free companies spread themselves over the country which they had conquered, and quartered themselves in different garrisons. The count d'Armagnac and the other lords went to their homes, and amply stored their towns and castles with all sorts of provision and artillery, as if they expected a war: they ordered out their vassals, and trained them to defend their country should need be.

We

We will now ſpeak of ſir Bertrand du Gueſclin, who, on his departure from the duke of Anjou, marched with his men to the ſiege of Limoges, where the duke of Berry, the duke of Bourbon and the great knights of France were employed. The French were in high ſpirits on the arrival of ſir Bertrand, and it was a grand piece of news both within as well as without the city. He immediately followed up ſome treaties which had been before opened between the biſhop and citizens with the duke of Berry, and managed that they were concluded by the biſhop and citizens turning to the French. The dukes of Berry and Bourbon, ſir Guy de Blois and the lords of France entered the town with great ſtate, when they received from the inhabitants their homage and fealty. After they had reſted themſelves for three days, they followed the ſame reſolutions as had been determined upon in the council held by the duke of Anjou, and each man retired to his own country to guard his towns and caſtles againſt ſir Robert Knolles, who ſtill kept his ground in France, and alſo becauſe they had done enough by taking ſuch a city as Limoges. The lords then ſeparated, but ſir Bertrand remained in Limouſin with two hundred lances, which he poſted in the caſtles of the lord de Maleval, who had turned to the French.

When the duke of Berry left Limoges, he ordered into the city, at the requeſt of the biſhop, ſir John de Villemur, ſir Hugh de la Roche and Roger de Beaufort, with one hundred men at

arms

arms. He then retreated to Berry, and the duke of Bourbon to the Bourbonois. The other lords who had come from diſtant parts went to their different countries.

We will now return to the prince.

CHAP. XIX.

THE PRINCE OF WALES, ANXIOUS TO RECOVER LIMOGES, LAYS SIEGE TO IT, AND UNDERMINES IT.

WHEN intelligence was brought to the prince that the city of Limoges had become French, that the biſhop, who had been his companion and one in whom he uſed to place great confidence, was a party to all the treaties, and had been much aiding and aſſiſting in the ſurrender, he was in a violent paſſion, and held the biſhop and all other churchmen in very low eſtimation, in whom formerly he had put great truſt. He ſwore by the ſoul of his father, which he had never perjured, that he would have it back again, that he would not attend to any thing before he had done this, and that he would make the inhabitants pay dearly for their treachery.

When the greater part of his forces were arrived, he muſtered them: they amounted to twelve hundred lances, knights and ſquires, a thouſand archers

archers and a thousand footmen. They marched from the town of Cognac. Sir Thomas Felton and the captal de Buch remained at Bergerac, to guard that frontier against the French and the free companies who were dispersed over that part of the country.

With the prince were, his brothers of Lancaster and Cambridge, sir Guiscard d'Angle, sir Louis de Harcourt, the lords de Pons, de Partenay, de Pinane, de Tannaybouton, sir Percival de Coulonge, sir Geoffry d'Argenton, Poitevins: of Gascons there were, the lords de Montferrant, de Chaumont, de Longueren, sir Aimery de Tharse, the lords de Pommiers, de Muciden, de l'Esparre, the souldich de la Trane*, the lord de Gironde and several more: of English there were, lord Thomas Percy, the lord Roos, sir William Beauchamp, sir Michael de la Pole, sir Stephen Cossington, sir Richard de Pontchardon, sir Baldwin de Franville, sir Simon Burley, the earl of Angus, sir John Devereux, sir William Neville, and more whom I cannot name: of Hainaulters, were sir Eustace d'Ambreticourt: of the free companies, sir Perducas d'Albret, Naudon de Bagerant, Lanuit, the bourg de l'Esparre, the bourg de Breteuil, Espiote, Bernard de Wist, and others.

All these men at arms were drawn out in battle-array, and took the field, when the whole coun-

* The souldich de la Trane. See Ashmole, vol ii. where there is a long account of him, and mention also is made of the lords de Montferrant and de l'Esparre.

try

try began to tremble for the conſequences. At that time the prince of Wales was not able to mount his horſe, but was, for his greater eaſe, carried in a litter. They followed the road to the Limouſin, in order to get to Limoges, where in due time they arrived and encamped all round it. The prince ſwore he would never leave the place until he had regained it.

The biſhop of the place and the inhabitants found they had acted too wickedly, and had greatly incenſed the prince; for which they were very repentant, but that was now of no avail, as they were not the maſters of the town. Sir John de Villemur, ſir Hugh de la Roche and Roger de Beaufort, who commanded in it, did all they could to comfort them by ſaying, 'Gentlemen, do not be alarmed: we are ſufficiently ſtrong to hold out againſt the army of the prince: he cannot take us by aſſault, nor greatly hurt us, for we are well ſupplied with artillery.'

When the prince and his marſhals had well conſidered the ſtrength and force of Limoges, and knew the number of gentlemen that were in it, they agreed they could never take it by aſſault, but ſaid they would attempt it by another manner.

The prince was always accuſtomed to carry with him, in his expeditions, a large body of miners: theſe were immediately ſet to work, and made great progreſs. The knights who were in the town ſoon perceived they were undermining them, and on that account began to

counter-

countermine to prevent the effect. But we will now leave the prince a little, to return to ſir Robert Knolles.

CHAP. XX.

SIR ROBERT KNOLLES, IN CONTINUING HIS INCURSIONS THROUGH DIFFERENT PROVINCES OF FRANCE, ADVANCES NEAR TO PARIS.— A KNIGHT OF HIS ARMY, IN RETURNING FROM A VAINGLORIOUS EXPEDITION, IS SLAIN BY A BUTCHER OF PARIS.

SIR Robert Knolles, as has been before related, had entered France with a large body of men, and was marching by ſhort ſtages through that kingdom with a magnificence for which the people and the rich provinces paid dearly. The Engliſh, as they advanced and retreated, did infinite miſchief, at the ſame time ſhewing as if they only wiſhed for a battle.

Having paſſed through the countries of Artois, Vermandois, the biſhoprick of Laon, the archbiſhoprick of Rheims in Champagne, they returned into Brie, and from thence came near to Paris, and quartered themſelves for a day and two nights in the villages around it.

King Charles of France was at that time in the city, and he could ſee from his palace of St. Pol the

the fire and ſmoke which the enemy were making in the Gâtinois. There were alſo in the city the conſtable of France ſir Moreau de Fiennes, the count de St. Pol, the count de Tancarville, the count de Saltzburg, the viſcount Meaux, ſir Raoul de Coucy, the ſénéſchal of Hainault, ſir Odoart de Renti, ſir Enguerrand d'Audin, the lord de Château-julien, ſir John de Vienne, the lord de la Riviere, and many more great knights and valorous men of France: but not one of them ſallied forth, for the king had ſtrictly forbidden them ſo to do. The lord de Cliſſon, who was of the king's cabinet council, and more liſtened to than the reſt, ſaid every thing he could to prevent any knight from quitting the town, adding, among other things, 'Sire, why ſhould you employ your men againſt theſe madmen? Let them go about their buſineſs. They cannot take your inheritance from you, nor drive you out of it by ſmoke.'

The count de St. Pol, the viſcount de Rohan, ſir Raoul de Coucy, the lords de Canin, de Creſques, ſir Odoart de Renti and ſir Enguerrand d'Audin, were at the barriers of St. James's gate. Now it happened one Tueſday morning, when the Engliſh began to decamp, and had ſet fire to all the villages wherein they were lodged, ſo that the fires were diſtinctly ſeen from Paris, a knight of their army, who had made a vow the preceding day that he would advance as far as the barriers and ſtrike them with his lance, did not break his oath, but ſet off with his lance in his hand, his target on his neck, and completely armed except

his

his helmet, and, ſpurring his ſteed, was followed by his ſquire on another courſer carrying the helmet. When he approached Paris, he put on the helmet, which his ſquire laced behind. He then galloped away, ſticking ſpurs into his horſe, and advanced prancing to ſtrike the barriers. They were then open; and the lords and barons within imagined he intended to enter the town, but he did not mean any ſuch thing, for, having ſtruck the gates according to his vow, he checked his horſe and turned about. The French knights who ſaw him thus retreat cried out to him, 'Get away! get away! thou haſt well acquitted thyſelf.' As for the name of this knight, I am ignorant of it, nor do I know from what country he came; but he bore for his arms gules à deux fouſſes noir, with une bordure noire non endentée.

However, an adventure befel him, from which he had not ſo fortunate an eſcape. On his return, he met a butcher on the pavement in the ſuburbs, a very ſtrong man, who had noticed him as he had paſſed him, and who had in his hand a very ſharp and heavy hatchet with a long handle. As the knight was returning alone, and in a careleſs manner, the valiant butcher came on one ſide of him, and gave him ſuch a blow between the ſhoulders that he fell on his horſe's neck: he recovered himſelf, but the butcher repeated the blow on his head ſo that the axe entered it. The knight, through exceſs of pain, fell to the earth; and the horſe galloped away to the ſquire, who was waiting for his maſter in the fields at the ex-

 tremity

tremity of the ſuburbs. The ſquire caught the courſer, but wondered what was become of his maſter; for he had ſeen him gallop to the barriers, ſtrike them, and then turn about to come back. He therefore ſet out to look for him; but he had not gone many paces before he ſaw him in the hands of four fellows, who were beating him as if they were hammering on an anvil: this ſo much frightened the ſquire that he dared not advance further, for he ſaw he could not give him any effectual aſſiſtance: he therefore returned as ſpeedily as he could.

Thus was this knight ſlain: and thoſe lords who were poſted at the barriers had him buried in holy ground. The ſquire returned to the army, and related the misfortune which had befallen his maſter. All his brother-warriors were greatly angered thereat; and they marched to take up their quarters for the night, between Montlehery * and Paris, upon a ſmall river, where they encamped at an early hour in the day.

---

* Montlehery,—a town in the iſle of France, ſeven leagues from Paris.

CHAP. XXI.

SIR BERTRAND DU GUESCLIN TAKES THE FORTRESS OF ST. YRIER IN LIMOUSIN.—THE PRINCE OF WALES RE-CONQUERS LIMOGES.

DURING the time ſir Robert Knolles was employed in his expedition, and the prince of Wales with his two brothers were at the ſiege of Limoges, ſir Bertrand du Gueſclin with his company, amounting to about two hundred lances, marched through a part of Limouſin, but did not encamp in the open plain for fear of the Engliſh. He retreated every night into ſome of the ſtrong places which had lately turned to the French: in that number were the caſtles of ſir Louis de Maleval and ſir Raymond de Marneil, and ſeveral others: from thence he made daily excurſions to conquer other towns and caſtles.

The prince knew well all this; for he received every day information of what was paſſing, as well as complaints on the ſubject; but he would not break up his ſiege, for he had too much at heart the loſs of Limoges.

Sir Bertrand entered the viſcounty of Limoges, a territory which was dependant on lord John de Montfort, duke of Brittany, in the name of the widow of lord Charles de Blois, to whom it had formerly belonged. He made war upon it without any oppoſition, for the duke of Brittany did not imagine Sir Bertrand would carry the war into any part of his property. He came before St. Yrier *, where there were not any gentlemen that knew how to defend it; and the inhabitants were so frightened, they surrendered themselves under the obedience of the duchess dowager of Brittany, in whose name the war was made. The Bretons formed St. Yrier into a considerable garrison; by which means they took many other towns in Limousin. But let us return to the prince.

The prince of Wales remained about a month, and not more, before the city of Limoges: he would not allow of any assaults or skirmishing, but kept his miners steadily at work. The knights in the town perceived what they were about, and made countermines to destroy them; but they failed in their attempt. When the miners of the prince (who, as they found themselves countermined, kept changing the line of direction of their own mine) had finished their business, they came to the prince, and said, 'My lord, we are ready, and will throw down, whenever you please, a very large part of the the wall into the ditch, through the breach of which you may enter the town at your ease and without danger.'

This news was very agreeable to the prince, who replied, 'I wish then that yould prove your words to-morrow morning at six o'clock.' The miners set fire to the combustibles in the mine; and on the morrow morning, as they had foretold

* St. Yrier,—a village in Limousin, election of Tulles.

the

the prince, they flung down a great piece of wall, which filled the ditches.

The English saw this with pleasure, for they were all armed and prepared to enter the town. Those on foot did so, and ran to the gate, which they destroyed as well as the barriers, for there were no other defences; and all this was done so suddenly that the inhabitants had not time to prevent it.

The prince, the duke of Lancaster, the earls of Cambridge and of Pembroke, sir Guiscard d'Angle and the others, with their men, rushed into the town. You would then have seen pillagers, active to do mischief, running through the town, slaying men, women and children, according to their orders. It was a most melancholy business, for all ranks, ages and sexes cast themselves on their knees before the prince, begging for mercy, but he was so inflamed with passion and revenge that he listened to none, but all were put to the sword, wherever they could be found, even those who were not guilty: for I know not why the poor were not spared, who could not have had any part in this treason; but they suffered for it, and indeed more than those who had been the leaders of the treachery.

There was not that day in the city of Limoges any heart so hardened, or that had any sense of religion, who did not deeply bewail the unfortunate events passing before their eyes; for upwards of three thousand men, women and children were to death that day. God have mercy on their ſouls! for they were veritable martyrs.

A company of Engliſh, in entering the town, haſtened to the palace of the biſhop, whom they there found and took priſoner, carrying him, without any regard to his dignity, to the prince of Wales, who, eyeing him indignantly, told him that his head ſhould be cut off, and ordered him out of his preſence.

We will now ſpeak of thoſe knights who were in the town, ſir John de Villemur, ſir Hugh de la Roche, and Roger de Beaufort, ſon to the count de Beaufort, governors of the city. When they perceived the tribulation which was overpowering them, they ſaid; 'We ſhall be all ſlain for a certainty, if we do not gallantly defend ourſelves: let us therefore ſell our lives as dearly as good knights ought to do.' Upon this, ſir John de Villemur ſaid to Roger de Beaufort, 'You muſt be knighted.' Roger replied, 'Sir, I have not as yet ſignalized myſelf ſufficiently for that honour, but I thank you much for your good opinion in ſuggeſting it to me.' No more was ſaid, for they had not time to hold further converſation.

They collected in a body, and, placing themſelves before an old wall, ſir John de Villemur and ſir Hugh de la Roche diſplayed their banners, and drew up in good order. They might be, in the whole, about fourſcore.

The duke of Lancaſter and the earl of Cambridge, with their men, advanced upon them, and diſmounted, to be on an equality with the enemy.

They

They attacked them with hearty good will. You may easily imagine that this handful of men could not resist the English, but were all slain or made prisoners.

The duke of Lancaster was engaged for a long time with sir John de Villemur, who was a hardy knight, strong and well made. The earl of Cambridge singled out sir Hugh de la Roche, and the earl of Pembroke Roger de Beaufort, who was but a simple esquire. These three Frenchmen did many valorous deeds of arms, as all allowed, and ill did it betide those who approached too near. The prince, coming that way in his carriage, looked on the combat with great pleasure, and enjoyed it so much that his heart was softened and his anger appeased. After the combat had lasted a considerable time, the Frenchmen, with one accord, viewing their swords, said, 'My lords, we are yours: you have vanquished us: therefore act according to the law of arms.' 'By God,' replied the duke of Lancaster, 'sir John, we do not intend otherwise, and we accept you for our prisoners.' Thus, as I have been informed, were these three knights taken. But the business was not here ended, for the whole town was pillaged, burnt, and totally destroyed. The English then departed, carrying with them their booty and prisoners. They marched to Cognac, where the princess had remained, and there the prince disbanded his forces, not intending to do any thing more that season; for he did not feel himself at his ease, as every exertion aggravated his disorder, which

which was increaſing, to the great diſmay of his brothers and all thoſe about him.

I muſt inform you how the biſhop of Limoges eſcaped with impriſonment, who had been in imminent danger of his life. The duke of Lancaſter aſked him of the prince, who conſented, and ordered him to be given up to the duke, for him to do with him according as he willed. The biſhop having good friends, they ſent information of his ſituation to the pope, who had lately arrived at Avignon; and fortunate was it for the biſhop they did ſo, otherwiſe he would have been a dead man. The pope wrote ſuch preſſing and kind letters to the duke of Lancaſter, to requeſt he would give him the biſhop, that he was unwilling to refuſe, and ſent him to the pope, who felt himſelf exceedingly obliged for it.

We will now ſay what was going forward in France.

CHAP. XXII.

SIR BERTRAND DU GUESCLIN IS MADE CONSTABLE OF FRANCE.

THE king of France was informed of the conqueſt and deſtruction of Limoges, and how the prince and his army had left it empty and deſerted, which vexed him much on account of the

the diſtreſs and loſs of the late inhabitants. It was therefore thought adviſable in a council of nobles and prelates, as well as by the common aſſent of the whole kingdom, to elect a chief or commander, called a conſtable (for ſir Moreau de Fiennes wiſhed to reſign the office) who was a valiant and enterpriſing man, and one to whom all knights and ſquires would pay proper deference. After all things had been well conſidered, they unanimouſly elected ſir Bertrand du Gueſclin (provided he would undertake the office), as the moſt valiant, the beſt informed, the moſt virtuous and fortunate in conducting affairs for the crown of France of all thoſe who were bearing arms in its defence.

The king wrote to him by meſſengers, for him to come to Paris. Thoſe ſent found him in the viſcounty of Limoges, taking caſtles and forts, which he put under the obedience of madame de Bretagne, widow of the late lord Charles de Blois. He had lately taken a town called Brantome*, whoſe inhabitants had ſurrendered themſelves to him, and was then on an expedition againſt another.

When the king's meſſengers came to him, he received them handſomely, as he knew well how to do. They gave him their letter, and delivered their meſſage word for word. When ſir Bertrand thus ſaw himſelf ſpecially ordered, he was unwilling to make any more excuſes for not

* Brantome,—a town in Perigord, dioceſe of Perigueux.

waiting

waiting on the king of France to know his will: he ſet out as ſoon as poſſible, having ordered all his men into the garriſons which he had conquered, and appointed his nephew, ſir Oliver de Mauny, commander over them.

He rode on to Paris, where he found the king ſurrounded by a number of the lords of his council. He was received by all with great pleaſure; and the king told him of his being choſen conſtable of France. On hearing which, ſir Bertrand modeſtly and ſagely excuſed himſelf, ſaying, 'he was not worthy of it: that he was but a poor knight and ſimple batchelor, in compariſon with the great lords and valorous men of France, however fortune might have been favourable to him.' The king replied, 'that his excuſes would be of no avail; that he muſt conſent to accept this dignity, for it had been ſo determined by the deciſion of the whole of the council of France, and that he would not break through ſuch a reſolution.' Sir Bertrand uſed other arguments to excuſe himſelf, adding 'Dear lord and noble king, I cannot, I dare not, whatever I may wiſh, oppoſe what may be your good pleaſure: but in truth I am too poor a man, and of low extraction, for the office of conſtable, which is ſo grand and noble that it is proper for thoſe (who wiſh to exerciſe it juſtly and honourably) to command and keep a ſtrict eye more upon the great than the poor. Now Sir, here are my lords your brothers, your nephews and your couſins, who will have different commands in your armies, and in various expeditions; and how ſhall

I dare

I dare to order them? Certainly, my dear lord, envy and jealouſy are ſo much abroad, I ought to be on my guard againſt them: I therefore entreat you will not inſiſt on my taking this office, but give it to ſome other who will readily accept of it, and who knows better than I do how to execute it.' The king made anſwer; 'Sir Bertrand, that excuſe will not ſerve you; for I have neither brother, nephew, couſin, count nor baron in my realm but who will obey your orders; and ſhould any one act otherwiſe, he would ſo anger me that he ſhould ſoon feel the effects of it: I therefore beg of you to accept this office with a good will.'

Sir Bertrand, finding that no excuſe nor any thing he could ſay would be liſtened to, accepted the king's offer, but it was much againſt his inclination. He was inveſted with the office of conſtable; and the king, to ſhew him greater affection, made him be ſeated at his table, and gave him, beſides this office, many rich gifts and large domains in land, for him and his heirs. The duke of Anjou was very active in forwarding this promotion.

CHAP. XXIII.

SIR BERTRAND DU GUESCLIN AND THE LORD DE CLISSON DEFEAT THE FORCES OF SIR ROBERT KNOLLES AT PONT-VALIN*.

SOON after ſir Bertrand du Gueſclin had been inveſted with the dignity of conſtable, he told the king he wiſhed to form an expedition againſt ſir Robert Knolles and his forces, who were at that time on the borders of Maine and Anjou. This was very agreeable to the king, who ſaid to him, ‘ Take any number of men at arms you pleaſe, and whatever elſe you may think right.’

The conſtable made every neceſſary preparation, and collected a large body of men at arms, Bretons and others, and marched towards Maine, taking with him the lord de Cliſſon. The conſtable came to the city of Mans, where he fixed his head-quarters, and the lord de Cliſſon in another town hard by: they might be about five hundred lances.

Sir Robert Knolles and his army were ſtill in that part of the country, but they did not agree very well together; for there was an Engliſh knight among them, called ſir John Menſtreworth,

* Pont-Valin,—a town in Anjou, election of la Flèche.

worth*, who always objected to what others proposed, and said they only wasted their time in these expeditions, and wore down and fatigued the men without doing any thing essential, or making any conquest. This knight, who commanded a large force, and had some able men at arms with him, left the others. Sir Robert Knolles and sir Aleyne Boxhull, however, kept together, and were quartered pretty near to Mans. Sir Thomas Grantson, sir Gilbert Gifford, sir Geoffry Worsley, and sir William Neville, were quartered a good day's march in the rear.

When sir Robert Knolles and sir Aleyne Boxhull heard that the constable of France and the lord de Clisson were come into those parts, they were much rejoiced, and said, ' It will be well for us to collect our forces more together, and post ourselves to our advantage in this country, for sir Bertrand, in the novelty of office, is certainly come to look at us, and he would not have been happy if he had not made this expedition. We have already rode through the realm of France without meeting with any hindrance. Let us inform sir Hugh Calverly (who is at Saumur on the Loire), and sir Robert Cheney, sir Robert Briquet, and the other captains of companies who

---

* Sir John Menstreworth. Froissart calls him *Maistreurde*. I have followed Barnes, who adds that he was a traitor, sold to the French, and, having embezzled large sums destined for the pay of the army, was afraid to be called to an account for them.

are

are near us, of our ſituation and intentions, who will willingly haſten to join us. We may therefore fall upon this new conſtable, and the lord de Cliſſon, who is ſo much our enemy*; and we ſhall make a handſome finiſh to our campaign.'

Between ſir Robert Knolles, ſir Aleyne Boxhull, and ſir John Seton, there was not any difference of opinion; and they acted always in uniſon. They immediately ſent off meſſengers ſecretly to ſir Hugh Calverly, ſir Robert Briquet, and the others, with letters to inform them how they were ſituated, and to propoſe that they ſhould join in an attack upon the French. They ſignified the ſame to ſir Thomas Grantſon, ſir Gilbert Gifford, ſir Geoffry Worſley and the others, deſiring them

---

* *The lord de Cliſſon, ſo much our enemy.* His quarrel with the duke of Brittany and the Engliſh, to whom he had always been attached, was cauſed by the duke's refuſal of a requeſt he made for the lordſhip of Gavre, which was very convenient to him, and near his caſtle of Blein.

When he aſked for it, the duke ſaid he had diſpoſed of it in favour of ſir John Chandos, to whom he had eſſential obligations. Cliſſon, enraged at this preference, ſwore he would never have an Engliſhman for his neighbour, ſet fire to the houſe, and had the ſtones carried to Blein, uſing them to fortify this caſtle. He conceived ſo mortal a hatred to the Engliſh that he embraced the party of the counteſs de Penthievre, on whom he had before made war, and accepted the lieuterancy of Brittany under her, and the guard of all the places ſhe had there. This change of conduct introduced him to the ſervice of Charles V. who admitted him to his councils, loaded him with gifts, and gave him the lieutenance general de Touraine.—*Memoires de Bertrand du Gueſclin, par Berville,* vol. ii. p. 210, note.

to

to advance to a place which they pointed out to them, for they were in hopes to engage the French who had come on this expedition. Upon receiving this intelligence, they all made ready with great cheerfulneſs to join their companies, amounting to about two hundred ſpears.

This matter, however, was not carried on ſo ſecretly but that ſir Bertrand and the lord de Cliſſon got wind of it, and knew alſo what was intended on the junction of their forces: they therefore armed themſelves during the night, and, marching with their men and garriſons, took the field. This ſame night, ſir Thomas Grantſon, ſir Geoffry Worſley, ſir Gilbert Gifford, ſir William Neville and the others, had left their quarters, and advanced towards ſir Robert Knolles and ſir Aleyne Boxhull to a ſpot where they expected to find them. But their march was ſhortened; for, directly at a place called Pont-valin, they were met by the French, who immediately charged them, and ſurrounded them, as they were full four hundred lances and the Engliſh about two hundred. The battle was ſharp and long, and well fought on both ſides. As ſoon as they met, they diſmounted, and attacked each other moſt valiantly with ſpears and ſwords. The French gained the victory over the Engliſh, who were all ſlain or made priſoners; for not an Engliſhman fled, except ſome of the pages or ſervants, who, mounting their maſters' courſers, made off as faſt as poſſible when they ſaw they were defeated. Among the priſoners were, ſir Thomas Grantſon,

 ſir

ſir Gilbert Gifford, ſir Geoffry Worſley, ſir William Neville, ſir Philip Courtenay, ſir Hugh Deſpencer, and many more knights and ſquires, who were all conducted to the city of Mans.

Intelligence of this was ſpeedily ſpread over the country, and ſoon known to ſir Robert Knolles, ſir Hugh Calverley and the others, who were much vexed thereat, and broke up their intended attack, through this unexpected event. Thoſe at Saumur, as well as in the other quarters, remained quiet. Sir Robert Knolles and ſir Aleyne Boxhull made a handſome retreat into Brittany, for they were not far diſtant. Sir Robert went to his caſtle of Derval, where he gave orders to all his men at arms and archers to go wherever they might find profit or honour, and ſeveral returned to England, whence they had come. Sir Aleyne Boxhull went to paſs the winter in his town of St. Sauveur le Vicomte, which the king of England had given to him.

After the defeat of Pont-valin, where a part of the Engliſh were ſlain and the remainder put to the rout, ſo that the expedition was ruined, ſir Bertrand du Gueſclin (whoſe entrance into the office of conſtable had been thus fortunately ſignalized, in a way to gain him great honour and reputation) came to Paris, accompanied by the lord de Cliſſon, and bringing with them the greater part of their priſoners, to whom they behaved very handſomely, allowing them to go at large on their parole for their ranſom. They neither ſhut them up in priſon, nor put on ſhackles and fetters, as

the

the Germans do in order to obtain a heavier ransom. Curses on them for it. These people are without pity or honour, and they ought never to receive quarter. The French entertained their prisoners well, and ransomed them courteously without being too hard with them.

The prince of Wales, the duke of Lancaster and all the English, who, after the conquest and vengeance taken on Limoges, had retired to Cognac, were much dismayed by the defeat at Pontvalin.

This year, about Christmas, pope Urban V. died at Avignon. He was a learned and wise man, and a good Frenchman. The cardinals assembled in conclave to choose a successor, when they unanimously elected the cardinal de Beaufort, who took the name of pope Gregory XI. The king of France was well pleased with this creation and divine election, for he knew him to be a loyal Frenchman and a prudent man. The duke of Anjou was at Avignon during the conclave, and took much pains that he should be elected pope.

CHAP. XXIV

SIR EUSTACE D'AMBRETICOURT IS MADE PRISONER AND RANSOMED.—SIR RAYMOND DE MARNEIL, A PARTISAN OF FRANCE, IS TAKEN, AND IN IMMINENT DANGER, BUT SAVED BY HIS KEEPER.

A VERY unfortunate adventure befel fir Euftace d'Ambreticourt much about this time. As he was riding one day through Limoufin, he came in the evening to the caftle of the lord de Pierre Buffiere, which he entered, thinking him a friend, a brother foldier and a good Englifhman. But Pierre Buffiere had given up his caftle to Thibaut du Pont, a man at arms from Brittany, and his company. Thibaut feized fir Euftace, who was not any way on his guard, made him his prifoner, and afterward ranfomed him for twelve thoufand francs, of which he paid down four thoufand, and left his fon, François d'Ambreticourt, his hoftage for the remainder to the duke of Bourbon, who had gone fecurity for him, and had taken great pains to obtain his liberty, becaufe fir Euftace had been very active in obtaining the freedom of the lady his mother, when fhe had been made prifoner by the free companies at Belleperche. After he had obtained his liberty, fir Euftace went and refided in Carentan, beyond the fords of St. Clement in lower Normandy, a very handfome town which the

the king of Navarre had given him, and where he died. God have mercy on his soul! for whilst he lived and remained in the world he was a most valiant knight.

Nearly at this period, sir Raymond de Marneil, who had changed his party from the English to the French, was returning to his own country from Paris, when he met with a disagreeable accident. On his road, he encountered a body of English, belonging to the forces of sir Hugh Calverley, commanded by a knight of Poitou, and came so suddenly among them that he could not escape: he was thus taken, and carried prisoner to the castle of the knight in Poitou. The capture of sir Raymond was known in England, and came to the king's knowledge, who immediately wrote to the knight, ordering him to send that enemy and traitor sir Raymond de Marneil directly to England, on whom he would wreak such vengeance that it should serve as an example to all others; and that he would pay him six thousand francs for his ransom. Sir Geoffry d'Argenton, who had taken sir Raymond, was not willing to disobey the orders of his sovereign and lord, and replied he would punctually follow his commands.

Sir Raymond de Marneil was informed that the king of England wished to have his person, and had sent orders to that effect; and also that sir Geoffrey was determined to obey them. He was therefore more alarmed than ever, and not without reason. He began to utter in his prison the most piteous moans, insomuch that the person who

 guarded

guarded him, and was an Englifhman, began to compaffionate him and gently to footh him.

Sir Raymond, who faw no rays of comfort in his diftrefs, fince he was to be fent to England, at laft opened his mind to his keeper. 'My friend,' faid he, 'if you will engage to deliver me from the peril in which I am, I will promife and fwear on my loyalty to divide half and half with you all my landed poffeffions, which you fhall have for your inheritance; and never as long as I live will I be wanting to you in whatever manner you may pleafe.' The Englifhman, who was poor, confidered that fir Raymond was in danger of his life, and as he had promifed him fuch a handfome recompenfe to fave it, he took compaffion on him, and faid he would do all he could to ferve him. Sir Raymond heard this with great joy, and fwore upon his honour to perform ftrictly what he had promifed, and even more if he infifted upon it. Upon which they confulted how they could beft bring this bufinefs to a happy end.

When night came, the Englifhman, who kept the keys of the tower of the caftle where fir Raymond lay, opened his prifon and a poftern-gate, from whence they iffued into the plain, and made for a wood, to prevent themfelves being overtaken. They were in greater diftrefs all the night than can be imagined, for they marched feven leagues on foot, and it had frozen fo hard, that their feet were all cut and torn. At laft, however, at the dawn they came to a French Fortrefs, where they were heartily received by the companions who guarded

it.

it. Sir Raymond related to them his adventures, and they all returned thanks to God for his fortunate escape. In truth, when the knight on the morrow found they had gone off, he sent horsemen every where round the country in search of them, but in vain.

In this manner did sir Raymond de Marneil escape from such imminent danger. He returned to Limousin, and told all his friends his great obligations to the English squire. The Englishman was much honoured by them, and sir Raymond wanted to divide his estate with him; but he refused to accept so much, and would only take two hundred livres a-year, adding that was fully sufficient for the support of himself in his situation.

CHAP. XXV.

THE PRINCE OF WALES, HAVING LOST BY DEATH HIS ELDEST SON, GIVES UP THE DUCHY OF AQUITAINE TO THE CARE OF THE DUKE OF LANCASTER.—FOUR KNIGHTS OF BRITTANY TAKE THE CASTLE OF MONT-PAON*.

AT this time, the eldest son of the prince and princess of Wales died in the city of Bourdeaux. They were exceedingly grieved at this

* Mont-paon,—a village of Rouergue, election of Milhaud.

event, and not without reaſon. The prince was adviſed to return to England, as perhaps he might there recover his health; and, as this advice was given him by his phyſicians and ſurgeons, he agreed to it. Preparations were made for his departure; and, I believe, the earls of Cambridge and Pembroke were ordered to return with him to bear him company.

When the prince was about to leave Aquitaine, and his veſſel was in the harbour of Bourdeaux, on the river Garonne, where he had arrived with the princeſs and the young Richard, his ſon, he iſſued from the city of Bourdeaux a ſpecial ſummons to all the barons and knights of Gaſcony and Poitou, and to all others over whom he was lord or who depended on him. When they were arrived, and aſſembled before him in his hall of audience, he addreſſed them by ſaying, 'that during the time he had been their prince, he had always maintained them in peace, proſperity and power, as far as depended on him, againſt all their enemies, but that now, in the hope of recovering his health, of which he had great need, he intended to return to England: he therefore beſought them earneſtly to put their faith in, and to ſerve and obey his brother, the duke of Lancaſter, as they had before ſerved and obeyed him: that they would find him a good and courteous lord, and he begged of them to aid and aſſiſt him in all his affairs.'

The barons of Aquitaine, Gaſcony, Poitou and Saintonge aſſented to his requeſt, and ſwore upon their faith and loyalty never to deſert him. They

per-

performed fealty and homage to the duke, declaring themselves willing to pay him all affection, service and obedience. This they swore in the prince's presence, and they all kissed him on the mouth*. After these affairs were settled, the prince did not tarry long in Bourdeaux, but embarked on board his vessel with the princess and his son, accompanied by the earls of Cambridge and Pembroke. There were in this fleet five hundred combatants, besides archers. They had favourable weather, and, meeting with no accident, arrived safely at Southampton. They were disembarked; and, after having refreshed themselves for two days, all mounted their horses, and took the road for Windsor, except the prince, who was carried in his litter. On their arrival, they found the king, who was then there. He received his children very kindly, and made many enquiries into the state of Guienne. After the prince had made some stay with the king, he took his leave, and retired to his manor of Berkhamstead, twenty miles from the city of London.

We will for the present leave the prince, and say what had passed in Aquitaine.

Soon after the departure of the prince from Bourdeaux, the duke of Lancaster ordered preparations for the funeral of his nephew Edward. It

* *All kissed him on the mouth.* Homage de bouche et des mains is done by a vassal with head uncovered, hands joined and a kiss received, which binds him to fight for his lord only in defence of the lands whereof he holds.—COTGRAVE.

was

was very grand and magnificent, and was attended by all the barons of Gascony and Poitou*.

Whilst all these things were going forward, and the funeral occupied every one's attention, and detained the Barons in Bourdeaux, there issued forth from the garrison of Perigord upwards of two hundred lances of Bretons, whom the duke of Anjou had sent and posted there. They were commanded by four valiant and hardy knights, whose names were, sir William de Longueval, sir Alain de la Houssaye, sir Louis de Mailly and the lord d'Arcy. These knights marched with their men to a handsome and strong castle called Mont-paon, of which a knight was lord. When these Bretons arrived, and had advanced up to the barriers, they manœuvred as if they intended an immediate assault, and completely surrounded it. Upon which sir William de Mont-paon, proving he had more of French courage than English, turned to them, and in short surrendered. He gave admittance to these knights and their companions into his castle, of which they took possession, and said they would defend it against all the world. They repaired and added to it whatever might have been wanting.

Intelligence of this was soon carried to Bourdeaux, when the duke of Lancaster told the barons

* He was buried in the Augustine Friars, London.

'Here was interred the bodie of Edward, the eldest sonne of Edward the black prince, by Joan his wife, surnamed The Faire Maide of Kent, who was born at Angolesme anno 1375, and died at seven years of age.'—*Weever's Funeral Monuments.*

they were inactive, for that the Bretons had made an incursion, and had taken Mont-paon, which was close to their borders. Indeed, when the duke and barons first heard of this, they were much ashamed, and made immediate preparations for marching towards that part; they set out from the city of Bourdeaux on a Wednesday after dinner.

With the duke of Lancaster there were, the lords de Pons and de Partenay, sir Louis de Harcourt, sir Guiscard d'Angle, sir Percival de Coulongne, sir Geoffry d'Argenton, sir James de Surgeres, sir Maubrun de Linieres, sir William de Montendre, sir Hugh de Vinoye, the lord de Crupenac, and many more knights and barons of Poitou and Saintonge. From Gascony were, the captal de Buch, the lord de Pommiers, sir Helie de Pommiers, the lords de Chaumont, de Montferrant, de Langeron, the souldich de la Trane, sir Bernardet de l'Abret, the lord de Gironde, sir Aimery de Testu, and several others. Of the English were, sir Thomas Felton, lord Thomas Percy, the lord Roos, sir Michael de la Pole, the lord Willoughby, sir William Beauchamp, sir Richard de Pontchardon, sir Baldwin de Franville, the earl of Angus and many more. They were in all rather more than seven hundred spears and five hundred archers. They marched in good order to Mont-paon, where on their arrival sir William de Montpaon, seeing the duke of Lancaster and his army come to besiege him, felt very uneasy; for he knew that, if he were taken, he should die a disgraceful death, without hopes of mercy, as he had done too much

against

againſt him to expect any. He told his fears to the four knights, and said he ſhould make his eſcape and go to Perigord, but that they were maſters of his caſtle to do as they pleaſed with it. Upon this he directly departed, and went to the city of Perigord, which was very ſtrong, and left his caſtle under the guard of theſe four knights.

CHAP. XXVI.

THE FOUR KNIGHTS DEFEND THEMSELVES AGAINST THE DUKE OF LANCASTER.—THE DUKE, ON TAKING THE PLACE, ADMITS THEM TO RANSOM.

WHEN the duke of Lancaſter was arrived at Mont-paon, with all his barons, knights and men at arms, he immediately laid ſiege to it. They built themſelves ſubſtantial huts all round the caſtle, as if they were to remain there ſeven years. They were not, however, idle, but began the aſſault with great vigour, and had large quantities of wood and faggots cut down by the peaſants, and carried to the ditches, which they threw in and covered with large beams and earth; by which means they were ſo filled up that they could advance to the walls to ſkirmiſh with the garriſon, as was daily done, and there were many gallant conflicts.

The

The four breton knights in the caſtle were right good men at arms, and fought and defended themſelves ſo valorouſly, that they were deſerving of great praiſe. They were not diſmayed, however near the Engliſh or Gaſcons might advance, and never ſuffered them to return conquerors.

Not far diſtant, in the garriſon of St. Macaire*, which belonged to the Bretons, were John de Maleſtroit and Silveſtre Budes, the governors of it, who, hearing every day of the great feats of arms which were doing before Mont-paon, were anxious to be partakers of them. They converſed frequently on this ſubject, ſaying, 'Since we know that our companions are ſo near to us, and thoſe valiant men,' as ſuch a one and ſuch a one, naming them, 'have daily five or ſix attacks on their hands, and are continually fighting, whilſt we remain here doing of nothing, we certainly do not act well.' They were very eager to go and aſſiſt them; but, when they and their companions had all ſpoken, they began to conſider the danger there might be, if they ſhould leave the garriſon without one of the commanders, and this puzzled them how to act. Silveſtre Budes ſaid, 'By God, I will go.' 'Silveſtre,' replied John, 'you ſhall ſtay, and I will go.' This diſpute continued ſome time. At laſt they agreed on their oaths, before all their companions, to draw ſtraws, and that he who had the longeſt ſtraw ſhould go, and the other re-

---

* St Macaire,—A city of Guienne, on the Garonne, nine leagues from Bourdeaux.

main.

main. Upon which they drew ſtraws, and Silveſtre Budes had the longeſt, which created a great laugh among the company.

Silveſtre did not take it for a joke, but went and made himſelf ready; when, mounting his horſe, he ſet off with eleven men at arms, and rode for the caſtle of Mont-paon, where he arrived and entered in the evening. The knights and garriſon were much rejoiced at ſeeing him, for they had a high opinion of his courage.

As I have before ſaid, there were continued attacks every day made on Mont-paon; and the knights within defended themſelves ſo well that they acquired great honour, for until a large piece of the wall had been thrown down, they were not any way diſmayed.

The Engliſh had brought thither large machines and other engines of aſſault, which they could now place near to the walls where the ditches were filled up. There were alſo footmen covered with large ſhields, who worked with pick-axes, and laboured ſo earneſtly that one afternoon they flung down upwards of forty feet of the wall. The lords of the army directly ordered out a body of archers, who kept up ſo well-directed and ſharp an attack with their arrows that none could ſtand againſt them, nor even ſhow themſelves.

Upon this, ſir William de Longueval, ſir Alain de la Houſſaye, ſir Louis de Mailly and the lord d'Arcy, finding from this ſituation that they could not any longer hold out, ſent one of their heralds mounted on horſeback, through the breach, to

ſpeak

ſpeak with the duke of Lancaſter; for they wiſhed, if poſſible, to enter into a treaty. The herald advanced to the duke, way being made for him, and explained the buſineſs on which he was ſent. The duke, by the advice of thoſe about him, granted an armiſtice to the garriſon during the time of a parley; and the herald returned with this anſwer to his maſters. The four knights directly came forward upon the ditch, and the duke ſent ſir Guiſcard d'Angle to hold a parley with them.

Upon the ditch, therefore, they entered on a treaty, by aſking, ' In what ſort or manner does the duke intend to make us priſoners?' Sir Guiſcard, who had received his inſtructions, replied; ' Gentlemen, you have greatly diſpleaſed my lord; for you have detained him here ſeveral weeks*, which has fretted him very much, and cauſed the loſs of ſeveral of his men: for which reaſons, he will not receive you, nor grant you mercy, but will have you ſurrender yourſelves ſimply to him. He alſo inſiſts on ſir William de Mont-paon being firſt given up, for him to be dealt with according to his deſerts as a traitor.'

Sir Louis de Mailly replied; ' Sir Guiſcard, in regard to ſir William de Mont-paon, whom you require from us, we ſwear truly and loyally that

* *Several weeks.* All my copies differ as to the number of weeks: ſome eleven, ſome ſix weeks: I have therefore ſaid ſeveral weeks, as it appears very uncertain. but I ſhould rather incline to the ſmaller number.

we are ignorant what is become of him, for he did not remain in this town a moment after you had begun to besiege it. But it will be very hard for us to surrender ourselves in the manner you insist on, who are soldiers sent here for pay, just as your commanders may send you, or you may be obliged to it by personal service; and, before we accept of such a bargain, we will sell our lives so dearly that report shall speak of it a hundred years hence. Return, therefore, to the duke of Lancaster, and tell him to accept of us in a courteous manner, upon certain terms of ransom, as he would wish should be done to any of his own party, should they happen to be so unfortunate.'

Sir Guiscard answered, that he would very willingly do so to the utmost of his power. With these words, he returned to the duke, and took with him the captal de Buch, the lords de Rosen and de Mucident, the better to forward the business. When these lords were come into the duke's presence, they remonstrated with him so eloquently, and with such good success, that he granted their request, and received the four knights, with Silvestre Budes, and their men, in mercy as prisoners.

Thus had he once more possession of the castle of Mont-paon, and received the homage of the inhabitants of the town. He placed there two gascon knights as governors, with forty men at arms and as many archers, and had all the walls

completely

completely repaired by masons in the neighbourhood: he victualled the place, and supplied it well with all sorts of artillery.

CHAP XXVII.

THE DUKE OF LANCASTER DISBANDS HIS ARMY, AND RETURNS TO BOURDEAUX.—THE LORD DE PONS TURNS TO THE FRENCH PARTY.

AFTER the conquest of Mont-paon, when the duke of Lancaster had reinforced it with good men at arms and captains, he broke up his camp, and disbanded his army. Each therefore went to his own home, and the duke returned to Bourdeaux. The Poitevins retreated to their country, and the Gascons to their towns and castles; but the free companies dispersed themselves over the whole principality, where they did as much mischief to friends as enemies. The duke winked at this, and suffered them to act as they pleased, because he thought he might soon have a fresh occasion for their services; more especially as the war at that moment was much more oppressive in Poitou, without comparison, than any where else.

The French kept a large garrison in the castle of Montcontour, four leagues distant from Thouars, and six from Poitiers, which was commanded by sir Peter de Guerfille and Jourdain de Coulongne. They daily harassed the country, either about Thouars or about Poitiers, and greatly damaged and pillaged the inhabitants. On the other ſide, Carnet le Breton held Chatelheraut, with ſeven hundred Bretons, who much ruined the country. The garriſons from la Roche-poſay and St. Salvin were out almoſt every day, ſo that the barons and knights of Poitou attached to the Engliſh dare'd not venture abroad but in large parties, for fear of the French who had thus forced themſelves into their country.

Soon after the return from Mont-paon, and when the lords of Poitou had retired to their own country, which was one of the frontiers to France, many ſecret negotiations were ſet on foot by the lord Louis de St. Julien, the viſcount de la Rochechouart, and ſeveral others in the French intereſt, who, with large ſums received from the king of France, laboured day and night, to gain over the lords of Poitou to his party. Theſe negotiations were ſo ſucceſsful that the lord de Pons turned to the French, in ſpite of the entreaties of the lady his wiſe, and of all the inhabitants of the town of Pons in Poitou. Notwithſtanding, however, the lord de Pons changed his ſide, the lady remained attached to the Engliſh. All the barons and knights in Poitou in the Engliſh intereſt were violently enraged, for the lord de Pons was a powerful baron.

The duke of Lancaſter was much grieved at this, and, wiſhing every curſe to attend the lord, felt himſelf obliged to the lady and to thoſe of the town who had not deſerted him. Sir Aimemon de Bours, a good and valiant knight, was ordered to aſſiſt [illegible] [illegible]d courage; for the lord

lord de Pons advanced every day to the gates of the town, doing no damage to any one; but sometimes he was driven back, and retreated with loss.

CHAP. XXVIII.

THE ENGLISH TAKE THE CASTLE OF MONTCONTOUR.

THUS were the English affairs in Poitou entangled; the lords and knights opposed to each other; when the strong oppressed the weak, and none received either law, justice or right. The castles and strong places were intermixed; some being French, others English, who each made excursions on the other, and pillaged on all sides without mercy.

Some of the barons and knights of Poitou of the English party, having considered that the garrison of Montcontour was more active in harassing the country than the others, resolved to march thither and lay siege to it. They therefore issued a summons from the city of Poitiers in the name of lord Thomas Percy, sénéschal of Poitou, which was obeyed by all knights and squires. They amounted to five hundred spears and full two thousand footmen, with large shields, among the archers who accompanied them. There were sir Guiscard

card d'Angle, ſir Louis d'Harcourt, the lords de Partenay, de Pinane, de Tannaybouton, du Cupegnac, ſir Percival de Coulongne*, ſir Geoffry d'Argenton, ſir Hugh de Vinoye, the lord de Coyes, the loid de Puiſſances, ſir James de Surgeres, ſir Maubrun de Linieres and ſeveral more. There were alſo ſome Engliſh, who at the time were reſident in Poitou, either from the offices they held there, or to aſſiſt in guarding the country; ſuch as ſir Baldwin de Franville, the earl of Angus, ſir Walter Hewett, ſir Richard de Pontchardon and others.

When they had been muſtered at Poitiers, and had completed their preparations, they marched from thence, taking the road for Montcontour, in full array, with every thing neceſſary for the ſiege of that place.

The caſtle of Montcontour is ſituated in the country of Anjou, is very ſtrong and handſome, and four leagues diſtant from Thouars. The Poitevins, to the amount of three thouſand combatants, continued their march until they arrived there, when they laid ſiege to it, and inveſted it on all ſides. There had been brought from Thouars and Poitiers large engines, which they pointed againſt the caſtle, and flung from them ſtones night and day. They made daily aſſaults, and the lords frequently had ſkirmiſhes with the garriſon, in which ſeveral gallant actions were per-

* Sir Percival de Coulongne Barnes calls him ſir Percival Collins.

formed;

formed: there were with the Poitevins ſeveral of the free companies, who were unwilling to remain during the ſiege, ſuch as John Creſwell and David Hollegrave: theſe two, with ſir Walter Hewett, were their leaders.

Sir Peter de Guerfille * and Jourdain de Coulongne, who were in the caſtle, defended it valiantly, and advanced every day to the combat with the Engliſh at their barriers. On the tenth day after their arrival, in the midſt of theſe attacks, the Engliſh and Poitevins aſſaulted it ſo briſkly, and in ſuch good order and ſtrength, that they broke down the walls of the caſtle, through which they paſſed, and conquered the French. All within were ſlain, except ſir Peter and Jourdain, and five or ſix men at arms, to whom the companions granted quarter.

After the capture of Montcontour, lord Thomas Percy †, ſir Louis de Harcourt and ſir Guiſcard d'Angle, by the advice and conſent of the other barons and knights, gave the caſtle to ſir Walter

---

* In the hiſt. de Bretagne, he is called Pierre de la Greſille.

† Lord Thomas Percy—was knight of the Garter —*Anſtis MS. Collections.*

'He was brother to the firſt earl of Northumberland, and uncle to Hotſpur who was created earl of Worceſter by Richard II. His barony was that of Haverfordweſt, and he had a conſiderable eſtate in South Wales, now in the poſſeſſion of the duke of Rutland.' Note in the above Collections, by Dr. Percy, biſhop of Dromore.

This eſtate is, I believe, ſold. at leaſt a rent reſolute was ſold by the duke (lieutenant of Ireland) to Mr. John Manners.

Hewett, John Cresswell and David Hollegrave and their companies, who were full five hundred combatants, for them to guard the frontiers against Anjou and Maine The lords then marched away, and dismissed their army. Thus was this castle made a guard for the borders by those to whom it had been given, who collected a numerous garrison, and had it completely repaired. They maintained possession of it for a very long time, and much harassed all the country about it; for there was not a day but they made some excursions into Anjou or Maine.

CHAP. XXIX.

SIR BERTRAND DU GUESCLIN, CONSTABLE OF FRANCE, BESIEGES THE TOWN OF UZES,* WHICH SURRENDERS TO HIM UPON CAPITULATION.

WE will now return to sir Bertrand du Guesclin, constable of France, who had remained at Paris, near the king, since the defeat of Pontvalin, where he and sir Oliver de Clisson had so

* Uzes. I am inclined to believe it must be Usson, a town in Auvergne, instead of Uzes, which is in Lower Languedoc, eight leagues from Avignon. See Hist. de Bretagne, vol. i. p. 336.

dreadfully

dreadfully beaten the English, as has been before related. It was told him that the English still kept the field in Poitou and Guienne: upon which he declared his intentions, that soon after Candlemas, at the commencement of spring, he should collect a very large force of men at arms and noblemen, and would make an incursion to another part of the country, since the English were thus employed in Quercy, Poitou and Rouergue.

Some of the English had very honourably remained in these countries, and had maintained themselves there since the renewal of the war. Sir John Devereux and his men had again got possession of Limousin, and had taken in Auvergne a castle with its dependencies, called Uzes, which the constable said was not to be suffered, and that he was determined to march thither. With the king's permission, he assembled a large body of men at arms, and, quitting Paris, his army increased daily until he arrived in Auvergne.

There came with him, under his command, the duke of Berry, the duke of Bourbon, the count d'Alençon, the count du Perche his brother, the count de St. Pol, the dauphin of Auvergne, the counts de Vendôme and de Porcien, the lords de Sully and de Montagu, sir Hugh Dauphin, the lord de Beaujeu, the lords de Rochefort and de Talençon, and a great many more barons and knights of France.

This army continued its march until it came before the city of Uzes, when they encamped, and, after remaining there fifteen days, during

 which

which time many fierce assaults were made, but without impression on the fortress, for it had an English garrison who very valiantly defended it, they broke up the siege and departed, the constable continuing his march into Rouergue. Some of the principal lords took this opportunity of going to Avignon to visit pope Gregory and the duke of Anjou, who at that time was with him. Soon after this visit, and having had a conference with the duke, they left the city of Avignon and followed the constable, who was advancing through Rouergue, taking towns and castles from the English. They came before the town of Milhaud *, which was held by Sir Thomas Wake †, and had been so for some time: they laid siege to it, as well as to the rock of Vauclerc; but the English knight surrendered upon terms, to sir Bertrand, this as well as some other castles on the borders of Limousin.

When sir Bertrand had refreshed his army, he marched away, taking the road on his return to the city of Uzes, to which he again laid siege. The constable and the dukes of Berry and Bourbon had ordered large machines to be brought from Rioms and Clermont, which they had pointed, as well as other warlike engines, against the walls of the castle.

---

* Milhaud,—a town in Rouergue, on the Tarne.

† Sir Thomas Wake. In all the editions, printed and MSS. which I have seen, this name is strangely disfigured. I have followed Barnes, for I could not make any thing of *Veulquefaire* or *Bueilcafaire*.

The Engliſh, who had before ſo gallantly defended the place, ſeeing the great preparations which were making againſt them, as well as the numerous army of the beſiegers, and having heard the manner in which ſir Thomas Wake had given up the ſtrong places in Rouergue, at the ſame time not expecting any ſuccours to come to their aſſiſtance, held a council, and reſolved to ſurrender upon capitulation, but not upon any other terms. They entered into a treaty with the conſtable, which was ſo well conducted on all ſides, that they were to march out without danger or blame, carrying off whatever they could take with them, and beſides were to be eſcorted as far as St. Severe in Limouſin. This treaty was ſtrictly obſerved, and the Engliſh marched out, having ſurrendered whatever they had held in the town and caſtle of Uzes, and were conducted without peril to the garriſon they had fixed upon. Sir Bertrand gained by this expedition a very large extent of country, of which the Engliſh had had poſſeſſion, and then returned to France.

CHAP.

CHAP. XXX.

THE KING OF ENGLAND'S ANGER AGAINST SIR ROBERT KNOLLES IS APPEASED.—PEACE IS MADE BETWEEN THE ENGLISH AND FLEMINGS.

YOU have before heard of the expedition which sir Robert Knolles* commanded in France, and how afterwards he retired to his castle of Derval in Brittany. In truth, some of the English, on

* Sir Robert Knolles—' was but of mean parentage in the county of Chester, but by his valour advanced from a common soldier, in the French wars under Edward III. to a great commander. Being sent general of an army into France, in despite of their power, he drove the people before him like sheep, destroying towns, castles and cities in such a manner and number that long after, in memory of this act, the sharp points and gable ends of overthrown houses and minsters were called Knolles' Mitres. After which, to make himself as well beloved of his country, he built a goodly fair bridge at Rochester, over the Medway, with a chapel and chauntry at the east end thereof He built much at the Grayfriars, London, and an hospital at Rome for English travellers and pilgrims. He deceased at his manor of Scone Thorpe in Norfolk,—was buried by the lady Constance, his wife, in the church of Grayfriars, London, 15th August 1407.'—*Weever's Fun. Mon.* p 436.

In 1365, John de Montfort, duke of Brittany, gave him, at the assembly of the states at Vannes, the lands, castle, &c. of Derval and Rougé, which had been excepted at the treaty of peace.—*Hist. de Bretagne.*

He

on their return home, ſpoke much againſt him, ſo that the king and his council had information of it, and were highly diſpleaſed with him. When ſir Robert heard of this, he ſent over his two principal ſquires to explain every thing, and to clear him of whatever might be ſaid againſt him; inſomuch that the king and his council were ſatisfied they had been wrongly informed, and thought as favourably of him as before. Sir Aleyne Boxhull, and other knights who were favourites with the king, aſſiſted in his diſculpation, and made ſir John Menſtreworth pay dearly for what he had done: he was taken, and publicly executed in the city of

---

He was created a knight of the Garter, Richard II and is the 74th knight.

Knolles, earl of Banbury, took his deſcent from ſir Robert Knolles.—*Dugdale's Baronage.*

Lobineau ſays, Derval, &c. was given to him and his deſcendants. In 1373, the duke, going into England, left his government to ſir Robert Knolles, but few lords obeyed him. The French beſieged his caſtle of Derval, which he had left in the cuſtody of Hugh Broc his kinſman, who capitulated to ſurrender if not relieved in two months. during which time no perſon was to be received there. But Knolles diſavowed the act of his nephew, alledging he could not treat without his conſent; ſo that the duke of Anjou ſent his herald to ſay, that having done contrary to his capitulation in admitting Knolles, in caſe he did not ſurrender, he would put to death the two knights and a ſquire who were the hoſtages; which being done, Knolles immediately executed three French knights and a ſquire, and threw their bodies into the ditch, whereupon the ſiege was raiſed.—*Lobineau*, p. 409.

London

London*. By this act of justice sir Robert Knolles was cleared of all the charges which had been laid against him, and remained in the good graces of the king and prince.

The king of England, who found himself hard pressed by this war with France, gained as many friends as he could on the other side of the sea. He had for allies the duke of Gueldeis, his nephew, and the duke of Juliers, who had engaged to raise a large force, as they were well able to do, and to make an incursion into France. At this time, the king sent the earl of Hereford † and some other knights of his household, handsomely equipped, to Brittany, to consult with the duke on the arrangements which it was necessary should be made between them.

The English and Flemings were not at this time on good terms, but attacked each other whenever the met on the seas; and so much had the Flemings lost that they were exceedingly angry. By accident, a fleet of each nation met off the island of

* His head was affixed to a pole on London Bridge, which, on the rebellion of Jack Straw, &c. was taken down to make room for the head of the bishop of London.—*Leland's Collectanea*, vol iii.

† Earl of Hereford,—Humphry Bohun, constable of England, 32d knight of the Garter. See Dugdale.

It appears however, from Rymer, that sir Robert de Neville and Raulyn de Barey, ecuyer de sa chambre, were the ambassadors from Edward.

Bas

Bas in Brittany*. The commander of the Flemings was John Peterſon, and of the Engliſh ſir Guy Brian†. As ſoon as they ſaw each other, they prepared for action, which was immediately begun; and very ſharp it was. The king's knights who accompanied the earl of Hereford, ſir Richard Sturey‡, ſir Thomas Vuiſque and the others were in this engagement.

Theſe knights and their men fought very valiantly againſt the Flemings, and exerted themſelves the more becauſe the enemy were in greater numbers, and were better prepared for action, as, during the whole ſummer, they had been wiſhing to meet the Engliſh. However, this time they did not gain much by the meeting. This ſea-

---

* The iſland of Bas is on the coaſt of Brittany, near Morlais. In the original, it is, the two fleets met in a harbour of Brittany, 'qu' on dit à la Baye.' and Carte ſays in 'the bay.' but I ſhould rather ſuppoſe it was meant as I have tranſlated it. This ſignal victory is very little noticed by our hiſtorians.

† Sir Guy Brian—was 57th knight of the Garter, in the ſtall of ſir John Chandos. He was third huſband to Elizabeth, dowager of William earl of Saliſbury—died 14th Richard II. He was brother to the biſhop of Ely.

Pat. 35. Ed. III. p. I. Guidoni de Bryan 200 marcos in pro vita quod prudenter deferebat vexillum regis, in quodam conflictu apud Cales.—*Anſtis MS. Collect.*

He is buried at Tewkſbury. In Gough's Sepulchral Monuments is a plate of his tomb.

‡ Sir Richard Sturey. I cannot find any thing of him but in the firſt volume of Leland's Collectanea, p. 183, date 1375. Ricardus Sturey revocatus in familiaritatem, et gratiam ab Edwardo rege.

fight

fight lasted full three hours: many gallant acts were performed, and many were killed and wounded by the arrows. The ships were grappled together with chains and hooks, so that they could not escape. In the end, the victory remained with the English; for the Flemings were discomfited, and John Peterson, their captain, made prisoner: the rest were either taken or slain, for none escaped.

The English made sail for England with their prizes and prisoners, which prevented them from continuing their voyage to Brittany.

The king was much rejoiced at the success of this engagement, and defeat of the Flemings, especially when he learnt that they were the aggressors.

John Peterson and his captains were put into close confinement, and the others dispersed in various parts of England.

After this defeat off the isle of Bas, the king of England ordered a large armament to be prepared against the Flemings, to engage the enemy where-ever they should meet with them, and to blockade their ports, so that no vessel could sail from them without risk of being taken.

When the citizens of Bruges, Ypres, and Ghent, heard of these orders, they summoned a council, and, after mature deliberation, resolved that it was not for their advantage to be at war or to have any ill-will with the English, who were their neighbours and connected with them by commerce, on account of any quarrel of their earl, nor would it be expedient for them to aid and support him. The principal towns, therefore, dissembled, but

sent

ſent able and good men to negociate with the king of England and his council, who managed the affair ſo well that on their return they brought peace to the country of Flanders and to the Flemings, conformable to certain articles in the treaty which was ſealed by each party. Thus was this buſineſs ſettled on a good and ſolid foundation.

We will now ſay ſomething of the king of Majorca.

CHAP XXXI.

THE KING OF MAJORCA IS RANSOMED FROM KING HENRY OF SPAIN.—HE MAKES WAR ON THE KING OF ARRAGON.

YOU have before heard how James, king of Majorca, was taken at Valadolid, when king Henry re-conquered Spain, and that he continued priſoner to king Henry. When the queen of Naples, his wife, and the marchioneſs of Montferrat, his ſiſter, heard this, they were much diſtreſſed, and immediately began to think of remedying it in the manner I ſhall mention. They ſent truſty men to king Henry to treat for his ranſom, who brought the matter about on conſideration of the ſum of one hundred thouſand francs, which thoſe ladies ſo graciouſly paid that king Henry was obliged to them.

The

The moment the king of Majorca gained his liberty, he ſet out for Naples, but remained there only ſufficient time to collect large ſums of money and a body of troops, with which he again ſet off to make war on the king of Arragon his adverſary, whom he could never love, as he had ſlain his father and detained his inheritance. The king continued his journey until he came to Avignon, to viſit pope Gregory XI. where he ſtaid upwards of a month. He made ſuch able remonſtrances with the holy father that he liſtened to his entreaties, and conſented to the war which he was deſirous of making on the king of Arragon, as the cauſe which urged him to it was the recovery of his heritage.

The king of Majorca engaged men at arms at a very high price wherever he could meet with them; Engliſh, Gaſcons, Germans, Bretons, and ſome of the free companions, under the command of ſir Gracien du Châtel, John de Maleſtroit, Sylveſtre Budes, and James Bray. They might amount to about twelve hundred fighting men, who marched with him, and entered Navarre, and there remained with the conſent of that king. From thence they advanced into Arragon, where the knights and men at arms made war on the king, over-ran his country, taking and deſtroying ſmall forts and ranſoming its inhabitants.

The king of Arragon, expecting this war, ſent ſome men at arms towards the frontiers of his kingdom, under the command of the count de Roquebertin and the count de Rodais.

Whilſt

Whilſt this war was carried on, which was done with much inveteracy and cruelty, the king of Majorca fell ſick again at Val di Soria, and the diſorder increaſed ſo much that he there died. By this means, the Arragonians had peace for a long time from that quarter. The free companions who had been engaged in this war returned to France, to that party from whom they thought they ſhould gain moſt.

We will now ſpeak of the duke of Lancaſter.

CHAP. XXXII.

THE DUKE OF LANCASTER ESPOUSES THE ELDEST DAUGHTER OF THE LATE DON PEDRO, KING OF SPAIN.—TREATIES OF ALLIANCE ARE ENTERED INTO BETWEEN THE KINGS OF FRANCE AND SPAIN.

DUKE John of Lancaſter remained in the city of Bourdeaux, and with him many knights, barons, and ſquires of Aquitaine; for, notwithſtanding ſome barons of Poitou and Limouſin had turned to the French party, that of the Engliſh was in a tolerably good ſtate, and made frequent inroads upon the French, on which occaſions they loſt nothing, but well ſcoured the country of thoſe who were defending the frontiers for the duke of Anjou.

The duke of Lancaſter was a widower ſince the death of the lady Blanche, ducheſs of Lancaſter and Derby: upon which the barons of Gaſcony, in concert with ſir Guiſcard d'Angle, conſidered that don Pedro, king of Spain, had left two daughters by his marriage with the ſiſter of the king of Portugal, who were then in the city of Bayonne, whither they had been conducted, under the ſafeguard of ſome knights, by ſea, from the neighbourhood of Seville, for fear of king Henry. As ſoon as they were informed of the death of don Pedro, theſe ladies were almoſt diſtracted with grief. Every one compaſſionated them, for they were the true heireſſes of Caſtille, which was their juſt right, by ſucceſſion to their father.

This matter was thus opened to the duke: 'My lord, it is time you ſhould think of re-marrying: we know of a very noble match for you, one from which you or your heirs will be kings of Caſtille. It will be a charitable deed to comfort and adviſe damſels who are daughters of a king, eſpecially when in ſuch a pitiable ſtate as thoſe ladies are. Take, therefore, the eldeſt for your bride. We adviſe you to do ſo; for at this moment we know not where you can more nobly ally yourſelf, nor from whence greater profit can accrue to you.'

Theſe and ſuch like words made an impreſſion on the duke, and were ſo agreeable to him that he conſented to what they had propoſed with much good will. He immediately ordered four knights to ſeek theſe ladies without delay, whoſe names were

were Conſtance and Iſabella. The duke himſelf ſet out from Bourdeaux, when he knew they were coming, to meet them in grand array. He married the eldeſt, the lady Conſtance, at a village on the road called Rochefort, on the other ſide of the city of Bourdeaux, and gave there, on the day of his marriage, a ſplendid feaſt, to which were invited a great number of lords and ladies to add to its magnificence. Soon after the wedding, the duke conducted his lady to Bourdeaux, where there were again grand entertainments. The ducheſs and her ſiſter were much feaſted by the ladies and damſels of Bourdeaux, who preſented them with magnificent gifts and preſents for the love they bore the duke.

News was brought to king Henry in Caſtille, and to all the barons of the realms who were allied to him by fealty and homage, that his niece had married the duke of Lancaſter, and that it was ſuppoſed the younger ſiſter would eſpouſe the earl of Cambridge upon the duke's return to England. The king was very melancholy on hearing this, and ſummoned his council. He was then adviſed to ſend able ambaſſadors to the king of France, to explain his ſituation. The king agreed to their opinions, and choſe the wiſeſt men in his kingdom to go to France. They ſet out with a grand retinue, and continued their road without interruption until they came to Paris, where they found the king, who received them with every politeneſs. The king of France had many interviews with theſe ambaſſadors, who had full powers, properly ſealed and authenticated, to enter into any treaties, and to act in every thing for their lord, ſo that many ſecret councils were held. At laſt, every thing was concluded; and a treaty was entered into between the two kings, of perpetual amity, love and alliance, which was moſt ſolemnly ſworn to be maintained, and that neither party would diſſolve or weaken without the other's conſent. The king of France ſwore, on the word of a king, that he would aid and aſſiſt the king of Caſtille in every matter which might concern him, and that he would never make peace with the king of England without his being a party.

Sir Bertrand du Gueſclin, who much loved the king of Spain, took great pains to bring this treaty about. After this buſineſs had been completely finiſhed, the ambaſſadors took their leave and returned to Spain. They found their king at Léon, who was much pleaſed at having ſo well concluded the matters they were ſent on. King Henry, from this alliance, felt himſelf ever after much more aſſured and comforted.

CHAP. XXXIII.

THE DUKE OF LANCASTER APPOINTS GOVERNORS IN GUIENNE: HE RETURNS TO ENGLAND, AND CARRIES HIS LADY WITH HIM.—SIR WALTER MANNY DIES IN LONDON.

WE now return to the duke of Lancaſter, who ſtill reſided in the city of Bourdeaux. He had determined that about Michaelmas he would embark for England, in order to make the king his father better acquainted with the affairs of Aquitaine. To this end he made every preparation; and, a little before his departure, he aſſembled in Bourdeaux all thoſe barons and knights of Gaſcony who were of the Engliſh party. When they were all collected, he addreſſed them by ſaying, he had a great deſire to return to England on particular buſineſs, as well for the advantage of all preſent as for the principality of Aquitaine; but that he would come back in the enſuing ſummer, if the king his father wonld permit it. Theſe words were very agreeable to all who heard them. He then appointed the captal de Buch, the lords de Mucident and de l'Eſparre, governors of all thoſe parts of Gaſcony which were attached to England. In Poitou, he nominated ſir Louis de Harcourt and the lord de Partenay. In Saintonge, ſir Louis d'Argenton and ſir William de Montendre.

He left all the ſénéſchals and other officers as they were before.

The council of the Gaſcons, Poitevins and Saintongers ordered ſir Guiſcard d'Angle, the lord de Pinane and ſir Aimery de Tarbe to accompany the duke to England, in order more fully to explain the affairs of Aquitaine; and the duke, by waiting for them, delayed ſome little his voyage.

When all was ready, they embarked on board of veſſels in the harbour of Bourdeaux, which is large and ſpacious. The duke was attended by a large body of men at arms and archers, having ſixty veſſels in the fleet, including thoſe with proviſions: he carried with him his lady and her ſiſter. They ſailed with favourable winds, which brought them ſafe to Southampton, where they diſembarked, and entered the town. They repoſed themſelves there for two days, when they ſet out, taking the road to Windſor, where the king reſided. He received his ſon the duke, the ladies, damſels, and the foreign knights with great joy and feaſts, but eſpecially ſir Guiſcard d'Angle, whom he was delighted to ſee.

About this time that gallant knight ſir Walter Manny* departed this life in the city of London; for which all the barons and knights of England were much afflicted, on account of the loyalty and prudence they had always found in him. He was

* Sir Walter Manny. See Dugdale. He came to England with queen Philippa—was knight of the Garter.

buried

buried with great pomp in the monaſtery of the Carthuſians*, which he had built, at his own expenſe, without the walls of London. His funeral was attended by the king, his children, and the barons and prelates of England.

All his landed property on each ſide of the ſea fell to John earl of Pembroke, who had married his daughter Anne. The earl ſent two knights to take poſſeſſion of the lands which had fallen to him in Hainault, and they performed their duty well towards duke Albert, who at that time governed the country in the name of his deranged brother William.

CHAP. XXXIV.

THE KING OF ENGLAND APPOINTS THE EARL OF PEMBROKE GOVERNOR OF AQUITAINE.—THE SPANIARDS, BEING ALLIES OF FRANCE, ATTACK HIM AT SEA, OFF LA ROCHELLE.

DURING this winter (1372), many councils were held in England on the ſtate of affairs, and upon the beſt methods of conducting them. The Engliſh had planned two expeditions; one to Guienne, another into France through Calais; and were gaining allies, as well in Germany as in

* Now the Charter Houſe.

other parts of the empire, where ſeveral knights and ſquires had joined them. They were buſily employed in making great preparations for the largeſt army which had been ſeen for a long time.

The king of France was regularly informed by ſome Engliſhmen of theſe tranſactions, the ſtate of them, and what was the end propoſed. Upon which, having duly conſidered his intelligence, he acted accordingly and laid in a ſufficiency of proviſion in all the cities, towns and caſtles of Picardy; having ſtrongly reinforced the garriſons with men at arms, that the country might not be ſurpriſed.

When ſummer was arrived, king Edward kept the feaſt and ſolemnity of St. George in Windſor caſtle, as he was yearly accuſtomed to do, when ſir Guiſcard d'Angle was elected a brother-knight with the king, the princes and barons, who were called, in this confraternity, The Knights of the Blue Garter. The king, after this went to London, to his palace of Weſtminſter, where he held a grand council on public affairs. The duke of Lancaſter was ordered to invade France by entering Picardy. He was to be accompanied by his brother the earl of Cambridge. The king, at the entreaty of ſir Guiſcard d'Angle and the Poitevins, appointed the earl of Pembroke governor of Aquitaine, in room of the duke of Lancaſter, with orders to haſten to thoſe countries, and to conduct the war againſt the French.

The Gaſcons and Poitevins had requeſted of the king by letters, as well as by ſir Guiſcard d'Angle, that

that if he ſhould be adviſed not to ſend any of his own children, he would nominate the earl of Pembroke, whom as they loved much they deſired to have, for they knew him to be a good and hardy knight. The king, therefore, ſpoke to the earl of Pembroke, who, with ſeveral other barons and knights, was preſent at this council, ſaying; 'John, my fair ſon, I ordain and inſtitute you governor and captain of all the men at arms in Poitou, who according to the accounts I have had, are very numerous; and alſo of thoſe you will conduct from hence thither. You will, therefore, accompany ſir Guiſcard d'Angle into Poitou.' The earl of Pembroke, falling on his knees, replied: 'My lord, I return you my warmeſt thanks for the high honour you have conferred upon me. I will act for your majeſty beyond ſeas as one of your ſmalleſt marſhals.' After this, the council broke up, when the king returned to Windſor, taking ſir Guiſcard d'Angle with him. They frequently converſed on the affairs of Poitou and Guienne. In one of theſe converſations, he ſaid; 'My lord, when our governor and captain ſhall arrive in that country, we ſhall carry on a good war; for we ſhall there find between four and five hundred lances, who will all cheerfully obey you, but they muſt be regularly paid.' The king anſwered; 'Sir Guiſcard, ſir Guiſcard, do not be uneaſy on account of wanting money to continue the war, for I have enough, and will eagerly employ it for ſuch an occaſion, as it very ſenſibly affects us and our kingdom.' In theſe and ſuch like diſcourſes did the king of England

amuſe

amuſe himſelf with ſir Guiſcard d'Angle, for he had great confidence in him, not indeed without reaſon.

The ſeaſon was now arrived for the departure of the earl of Pembroke, who took his leave of the king, as did all thoſe who accompanied him. It ſeems to me that ſir Otho de Grantſon *, *d'outre la Somme*, was appointed to go with him.

The earl of Pembroke had not a very large force with him, but only the knights of his houſehold, on account of the information which ſir Guiſcard d'Angle had given the king; but he carried a ſufficient ſum in nobles and florins to pay three thouſand fighting men. After taking leave of the king, they ſet out for Southampton, where they remained fifteen days waiting for a wind. On the ſixteenth, they had a wind to their wiſh; and, embarking, they ſailed out of the harbour for the coaſts of Poitou, recommending themſelves to the care of God and St. George.

King Charles of France was perfectly well acquainted with the greater part of the king of England's councils, (I do not know by whom or how they were revealed to him) and that ſir

* Sir Otho de Grantſon. Barnes calls him ſir Thomas Grantſon; but ſir Thomas Grantſon was made priſoner by Bertrand du Gueſclin, and, I ſuppoſe, was then at Paris. Froiſſart, I ſhould imagine, by mentioning *outre la Somme*, muſt mean a different perſon, one who had an eſtate beyond the Somme. In the MS. collections of mr. Anſtis, a ſir Otho Grantſon is ſpoken of; but, by a reference to Dugdale, it appears he muſt have lived in a much earlier period.

Guiſcard

Guiſcard d'Angle and his companions were gone to England to requeſt from the king an able leader. He already knew that the earl of Pembroke had the appointment, and that he was on his way thither. Upon which, the king of France had ſecretly raiſed a large naval armament; that is to ſay, it had been done at his requeſt, for it belonged to king Henry of Caſtille, who had ſent this armament in conformity to the treaty which had been lately concluded between them. This Spaniſh fleet conſiſted of forty large veſſels and thirteen barks, well provided with towers and ramparts, as the Spaniſh ſhips uſually are. Four valiant men were the commanders of this fleet: Ambroſio de Balequer, Cabeſſo de Vaccadent, Hernando de Léon, Rodrigo de Roſas*.

Theſe Spaniards had remained a conſiderable time at anchor, waiting for the return of the Poitevins, and the coming of the earl of Pembroke; for they were well informed that he was to land on the coaſt of Poitou, and had therefore placed themſelves at anchor before the town of la Rochelle.

It happened, therefore, that on the day preceding the vigil of St. John the Baptiſt, in the

* I have copied the names of theſe Spaniſh captains from Barnes, but am doubtful if they are right; for in Choiſi's hiſt. of Charles V. *Rodrique de Roux* is mentioned as admiral. In Villaret's hiſt. of France, *Boccanera* is called the admiral. Indeed, this is nearer to Froiſſart, who calls the firſt captain Ambroiſe de *Boucquenegre*. Barnes gives not any authority for his alterations.

year of grace 1372, when the earl of Pembroke and his fleet expected to enter the port of la Rochelle, they found that the Spaniards had blocked up the entrance by lying before its mouth, and were ready prepared to receive them. When the English and Poitevins saw the Spaniards thus posted, and that an engagement must happen, they encouraged each other, though they were not near an equal match, either in regard to the number of vessels or men, and made preparations for an immediate combat, posting their archers on the bows of the ships.

The Spaniards were well equipped with men at arms and foot soldiers, who had cross-bows and cannons: many had also large bars of iron, and staves loaded with lead, to make their attacks with. They advanced with shoutings and a great noise. These large ships of Spain made sail to gain the wind, so that they might bring their towers to bear on the English, who little suspected their intent, and less feared them. Thus did they bear down on them full sail. At this commencement, great were the shouts and cries on both sides. The English behaved gallantly, and the earl of Pembroke, his knights and squires acted worthy of their honour.

The engagement was very severe, and the English had enough to do; for the Spaniards who were in large vessels had great bars of iron and huge stones, which they launched and flung from their ships in order to sink those of the English, by which they wounded desperately both sailors and men at arms.

The

The knights of England and Poitou that day ſhewed excellent proofs of chivalry and prowefs. The earl fought gallantly, ſeeking his enemies every where, and did extraordinary feats of arms: Sir Otho de Grantſon, ſir Guiſcard d'Angle, the lord de Pinane and all the other knights behaved equally well.

CHAP. XXXV.

THE INHABITANTS OF LA ROCHELLE REFUSE TO ASSIST THE EARL OF PEMBRORE.—THE SENESCHAL AND THE LORD DE TANNAY-BOUTON, WITH OTHERS, COME TO HIS AID.

BY what I have heard from thoſe who were preſent at this engagement, the Engliſh and Poitevins ſhewed plainly they wiſhed for victory, and obtained great praiſe for their valour; for never people exerted more courage, nor fought more bravely, conſidering what a handful of men they were in compariſon with the Spaniards, and in ſuch ſmall veſſels that one cannot but marvel how it laſted ſo long: but their great prowefs and chivalry raiſed a mutual ſpirit of emulation, and, had their veſſels been of the ſame ſize with their enemy's, the Spaniards would not have had the advantage; for they handled their ſpears, which were well ſteeled, ſo briſkly, and gave ſuch terrible ſtrokes,

ſtrokes, that none dared to come near unleſs he were well armed and ſhielded; but the ſhowers of ſtones, lead and iron bars annoyed them exceedingly, and in this firſt engagement ſeveral knights and ſquires were ſeverely wounded.

The Rochellers ſaw plainly the whole of this engagement, but never offered to advance to the aſſiſtance of their countrymen, leaving them to ſhift for themſelves. This battle laſted until night, when each party ſeparated and caſt their anchors: but the Engliſh loſt two barges of proviſion, and all thoſe in them were ſlain.

Sir John Harpedon, who at that time was ſénéſchal of la Rochelle, employed himſelf all the night in entreating the inhabitants, the mayor, John Chauderon, and the others to arm themſelves, and to draw out the commonalty, and embark in the veſſels and barges which were lying on the ſhore, in order to aſſiſt and aid their fellow-ſubjects whom they had ſeen ſo valorouſly defend themſelves. The inhabitants, however, who had no inclination ſo to do, excuſed themſelves by ſaying they had their town to guard; that they were not ſeamen, nor accuſtomed to fight at ſea, nor with the Spaniards; but that, if the battle had been on ſhore, they would very willingly have complied with his requeſt. The buſineſs remained in this ſtate, and nothing could bring them to change their reſolution.

At this moment there were in la Rochelle the lord de Tannaybouton, ſir James de Surgeres and ſir Maubrun de Linieres, who handſomely acquitted

quitted themſelves in joining their entreaties with thoſe of the ſénéſchal. When theſe four knights ſaw they could not gain any thing, they armed themſelves, ordering their people, who were not in any great numbers, to do the ſame; and, on the return of the tide, they embarked in four boats which they took from the ſhore, at break of day, and made for the veſſels of their friends, who were right glad to ſee them. They told the earl of Pembroke and ſir Guiſcard d'Angle, that they muſt not expect any aſſiſtance from la Rochelle, as the townſmen had poſitively refuſed it; to which, as they could not better themſelves, they replied that they truſted in the mercy of God, and would wait the event; that a time might come when the Rochellers ſhould repent of their refuſal.

CHAP. XXXVI.

THE EARL OF PEMBROKE IS DEFEATED, AND MADE PRISONER BY THE SPANIARDS.—THEY SAIL FROM LA ROCHELLE WITH THEIR PRISONERS.—THE CAPTAL DE BUCH ARRIVES THERE, BUT TOO LATE.

WHEN it was day, and the tide had flowed full, the Spaniards weighed their anchors, and, with a great noiſe of trumpets and drums, formed

formed a line of battle, like to that of the preceding day, with their large veſſels, which were well manned and armed; and having gained the wind in hopes of inloſing the Engliſh veſſels, which were but few in compariſon, the before mentioned four captains led the van in handſome order.

The Engliſh and Poitevins, obſerving their line of battle, formed theirs accordingly, and, having collected themſelves together, placed their archers in front. The Spaniards, under the command of theſe captains, bore down on them full ſail, and began the engagement, which was dreadfully deadly. When they came to cloſe quarters, the Spaniards flung out grappling hooks with chains of iron, which laſhed the Engliſh to their veſſels, ſo that they could not ſeparate, and thus, as it were held them cloſe*.

With the earl of Pembroke there were twenty-two knights, who united good inclinations to tried valour, and who vigorouſly defended themſelves with ſpears, ſwords and other weapons. They remained there cloſely engaged, fighting deſperately, for a conſiderable time; but the Spaniards had too much the advantage, as their veſſels were larger and higher above the water than thoſe of the Engliſh, from which they flung down ſtones, bars of iron and lead, that much annoyed their ad-

---

* The Memoires de du Gueſclin ſay, that fire ſhips were firſt uſed in this engagement by the Spaniards, and that by their means thirteen of the largeſt Engliſh ſhips were deſtroyed. *Coll Memoires Hiſtoriques*, vol. i. p. 432.

verſaries.

verſaries. The engagement continued with great fury between them until near nine o'clock; and no people ever laboured harder than the Engliſh and Poitevins, but the greater part of their men were now wounded by the ſtones and other things which were thrown on them, and that gallant knight of Gaſcony ſir Aimery de Tarbe was ſlain, as well as ſir John Lauton, who was knight of the body to the earl of Pembroke.

Four large Spaniſh ſhips had grappled with that in which was the earl: they were commanded by Cabeſſo de Vaccadent and Hernando de Léon, and full of men at arms for the combat and to work the veſſels. After an obſtinate reſiſtance, they boarded the earl's ſhip, when he was made priſoner, and all on board ſlain or taken. Among the laſt were, ſir Robert Beaufort, ſir John Curzon, ſir John Grimſtone: ſir Simon Whitaker, ſir John Morton and ſir John Touchet ſhared the fate of the firſt.

At ſome diſtance, the Poitevins, under the command of ſir Guiſcard d'Angle, the lord de Pinane, the lord de Tannaybouton and other knights, with their followers, continued the fight; and in another ſhip ſir Otho de Grantſon was engaged againſt Ambroiſe de Boccanera and Roderigo de Roſas, who were too many for him; ſo that all theſe knights were taken by the Spaniards, not one eſcaped being killed or made priſoner. Their men were alſo in great danger, but their lords, when taken, deſired they would ceaſe the ſlaughter, as they would pay a proper ranſom for them.

Whoever may find himſelf in ſuch a ſtrait of arms as the earl of Pembroke or ſir Guiſcard d'Angle were in, before la Rochelle, muſt cheerfully ſubmit to whatever God or fortune may pleaſe to order. But know, that in the loſs of this day, of knights or ſquires, the king of England in compariſon was by far the greateſt ſufferer; for, in conſequence of this defeat, he loſt afterwards all Guienne, as you will have related in this hiſtory.

I was informed that the Engliſh veſſel which had on board the money for ſir Guiſcard d'Angle to pay the ſoldiers of Guienne was loſt, and every thing on board with it; ſo that it was not of profit to any one.

All this day, which was the vigil of St. John the Baptiſt, the enſuing night, and the morrow until noon, did the Spaniards remain at anchor before la Rochelle, ſhouting and rioting with joy.

It happened fortunately that a knight of Poitou, called ſir James de Surgeres, addreſſed the perſon who had taken him with ſo much eloquence that he agreed to give him his liberty for three hundred francs, which he paid down. He dined in la Rochelle on St. John's day; and by him it was known how the affair had ended, who were ſlain or made priſoners. Many citizens of the town pretended to be much concerned at this event, though in their hearts they rejoiced, for they never were well inclined towards the Engliſh.

In the afternoon of St. John's day, at high flood, the Spaniards weighed anchor, ſet their

ſails,

ſails, and departed with a great noiſe of drums and trumpets. They had on their maſt-heads ſtandards like to pennons, with the arms of Caſtille diſplayed on them, and of ſuch a length that their ends frequently touched the ſea. It was a fine ſight to ſee them thus ſail off, as they ſteered for the coaſt of Galicia.

In this ſame day, towards the evening, there came into la Rochelle a large body of men at arms, Gaſcons and Engliſh, who had not heard what had paſſed, but they knew that the Spaniards were lying before the town, and had done ſo for ſome time: they came, therefore, to reinforce it. The leaders of the Gaſcons were, the captal de Buch, ſir Beras de la Lande, ſir Peter de Landura, the ſouldich, ſir Bertrand du Trane: of the Engliſh, lord Thomas Percy, ſir Richard de Pontchardon, ſir William Farrington, the earl of Angus, ſir Baldwin Freville*, ſir Walter Hewet and ſir John Devereux†.

When theſe lords and their troops, which were full ſix hundred men, were arrived in la Rochelle, the inhabitants made appearance of being very glad to ſee them, for they dared not do otherwiſe. They learnt from ſir James de Surgeres the event of the

* Sir Baldwin Freville—had ſummons to parliament the 1ſt Edward III. See Dugdale. He was competitor for the office of champion at the coronation of Richard II. but the earl-marſhal decided on the ſuperior claim of the Dymocks.—See Dugdale's Warwickſhire, where the pedigree is.

† Sir John Devereux. See Dugdale. From him are deſcended the viſcounts Hereford, &c.

battle with the Spaniards, and the names of thoſe killed and taken. The barons and knights were ſorely afflicted at this news, and thought themſelves more unfortunate than they had ever yet been for not arriving ſooner. They regretted much the loſs of the earl of Pembroke and ſir Guiſcard d'Angle. I know not how many days they remained in la Rochelle, to conſider what would be the beſt manner for them to conduct themſelves, and whither they ſhould march. We will leave them for a while, and ſpeak of Evan of Wales, and of his exploits this ſeaſon:

CHAP. XXXVII.

EVAN OF WALES * DEFEATS THE ENGLISH OFF THE ISLAND OF GUERNSEY.—THE KING OF FRANCE SENDS HIM TO SPAIN TO SEEK FOR MEN AT ARMS, TO LAY SIEGE TO LA ROCHELLE.

EVAN of Wales was the ſon of a prince of Wales, whom king Edward, for ſome reaſon I am ignorant of, had put to death, and ſeized his territories

* Among the members of the council of war whom du Gueſclin called, before he attacked St. Maure ſur Loire, are Carenlouet capitaine de la Roche-poſay, Ivain de Galles, and another knight called the Pourſuivant d'Amours.—Note 83d in the ſame

territories and principality, which he had given to his ſon the prince of Wales. Evan went to France, to lay his complaints before king Charles of the injuries he had ſuffered from the king of England, by the death of his father and the ſeizure of his inheritance.

The king of France had retained him in his ſervice, and much advanced him, by giving him the command of a large body of men at arms. In this ſummer, he ſent him to ſea with four thouſand fighting men, with whom he acquitted himſelf much to his honour, as you ſhall now hear.

When he took command of theſe men at arms, and veſſels which the king of France had equipped and provided for him, he embarked in the port of Harfleur, and ſet full ſail for England, making the iſland of Guernſey, which lies oppoſite to Normandy. Edmund Roſs, ſquire of honour to the king of England, was then governor of that iſland.

On hearing of the arrival of the French under the command of Evan, he was much angered, and advanced out to meet him. He iſſued his ſummons throughout the iſland, which is not large, and collected, as well of his own men as of the iſlanders, about eight hundred, with whom he

---

ſame vol. ſays, ' This famous Pourſuivant d'Amours was alſo called le chevalier Bauwen.' Moſt probably a Welſhman of the name of Bowen : but how is this to be reconciled with the preceding quotations ?—See Memoires du Gueſclin, vol. iv. of the Hiſtorical Collection of French Memoirs, p. 397.

gave battle. It was ſharp and long; but the Engliſh, at laſt, were defeated, leaving upwards of four hundred dead on the field. Edmund was forced to fly, otherwiſe he muſt have been ſlain or taken. He eſcaped with great difficulty and ſaved himſelf in a handſome caſtle, called Cornet, ſituated at the diſtance of two leagues from the place where the battle had been fought, and which he had beforehand provided with every thing neceſſary for ſuch a fortreſs.

After this defeat, Evan, having collected his army, and hearing that Edmund had retreated into Cornet caſtle, advanced thither, and inveſted it cloſely, giving frequent aſſaults; but the caſtle was ſtrong and well provided with artillery, ſo that the French could not gain it.

It was during the time of this ſiege the unfortunate defeat and capture of the earl of Pembroke and ſir Guiſcard d'Angle happened before la Rochelle, which has been juſt related.

The king of France, when he heard of the ſucceſs of the Spaniards, was exceedingly rejoiced, and paid more attention than ever to the affairs of Poitou; for he thought, perhaps lightly enough, that if the Engliſh ſhould have a few more ſuch defeats, the cities and principal towns would willingly ſurrender to him. He therefore determined, with the advice of his council, to ſend the conſtable and all his men at arms into Poitou, Saintonge and the Rochellois, in order to carry on the war more briſkly by ſea and land, whilſt the

Engliſh

English party ſhould be without a leader, for the whole country was wavering in its allegiance.

He therefore ſent meſſengers to Evan of Wales, who was lying before Cornet caſtle, as he was perfectly acquainted with the ſtate of it, and knew it to be impregnable, ordering him inſtantly to break up the ſiege, and put to ſea in a veſſel equipped for him, and to make ſail for Spain to prevail on king Henry to grant him boats and galleys, with his admirals and men at arms, to blockade la Rochelle.

Evan, on receiving the meſſengers with the king's orders, promptly obeyed them, as was right; broke up the ſiege, and diſbanded his men, lending them veſſels to carry them to Harfleur. He himſelf immediately embarked on board a large ſhip, and made ſail for Spain. Thus was the ſiege of Cornet caſtle raiſed.

CHAP. XXXVIII.

THE KING OF ENGLAND IS MUCH CAST DOWN AT THE CAPTURE OF THE EARL OF PEMBROKE.—EVAN OF WALES MEETS THE EARL A PRISONER IN SPAIN.

YOU muſt know, that when the king of England heard of the defeat of the armament he had ſent to Poitou, and that it had been overcome by the Spaniards, he was greatly afflicted; ſo were all thoſe who were attached to him; but for the moment he could not amend it. The wiſeſt in the kingdom imagined that this unfortunate buſineſs would cauſe the loſs of the countries of Poitou and Saintonge; and they ſtated this as their opinion to the king and duke of Lancaſter. They held many councils upon it. The earl of Salisbury was ordered thither with five hundred men at arms. However, notwithſtanding this order, he never went, for other affairs came into agitation reſpecting Brittany, which prevented it from taking place. The king repented of this afterwards, when it was too late.

The Spaniards who had taken the earl of Pembroke and his companions were detained ſome little time at ſea by contrary winds. They arrived at the port of St. Andero in Biſcay, and entered the town about mid-day, when they conducted their priſoners to a ſtrong caſtle, and faſtened them

with

with iron chains according to their usual custom; for the Spaniards know not how to shew courtesy to their prisoners, but act like the Germans.

Evan * of Wales had the same day arrived with his ship at St. Andero, and had entered the hôtel where don Fernando de Rosas and Cabesso de Vaccadent had conducted the earl of Pembroke and his knights. This was told to Evan in his apartment, saying; 'Sir, come and see the English knights whom our people have made prisoners, they will enter this hôtel, for it is not long since they arrived.' Evan being very desirous of seeing them, to know who they were, went out. He met, on quitting his chamber, in the apartment of the landlord, the earl of Pembroke, whom he directly recognized, though he had scarcely ever seen him before. He addressed him in a reproachful manner: 'Earl Pembroke, are you come into this country to do me homage for the lands you hold of me in the principality of Wales, of which I am the heir, and which your king has deprived me of, through the advice of evil counsellors?'

The earl of Pembroke was much displeased and ashamed, feeling himself a prisoner in a strange country, to be thus apostrophised in his own language by one whom he did not know, and replied, 'Who are you that you address me in such words?'

* By every thing I can find, this Evan was an impostor.—Llewelyn, the last prince of Wales, was treacherously slain, near Builth, in Edward I.'s reign. Probably the king of France knew this, but employed him in hopes of his assistance against England.—See Barnes and others.

Evan

Evan anſwered, ‘I am Evan, ſon and heir of prince Edmund of Wales, whom your king wickedly and wrongfully put to death, and diſinherited me afterwards. But I may perhaps be able, through the aſſiſtance of my very dear lord the king of France, to apply a remedy to this, and I will certainly then do ſo. I wiſh you to know, that if I can meet you in a proper place and time to offer you combat, I will ſhew you the wrongs you have done me, as well as the earl of Hereford and Edward Spencer; for by your father and other evil counſellors was my lord and father betrayed, which ought to anger me, and I will be revenged of it whenever I may have an opportunity.’

Sir Thomas St. Aubin, who was one of the earl's knights, ſtepped forward and eagerly ſaid; ‘Evan, if you mean to ſay and maintain, that my lord has now, or at any other time, committed a diſhonourable act, or that my lord his father has done ſo, or that he owes you any homage or any thing elſe, throw down you glove, and you will find one ready enough to take it up.’ Evan replied; ‘You are a priſoner: I ſhall gain no honour in calling you out, for you are not your own maſter, but belong to thoſe who have taken you: but when you have gained your liberty, I ſhall ſpeak out more boldly, for things ſhall not remain as they now are.’

As he finiſhed theſe words, ſome knights and Spaniſh men of valour got between them, and ſeparated them. The four admirals did not, after this, make any long ſtay, but led their priſoners

to

to Burgos, to deliver them up to the king of Spain, who at that time resided there.

When the king heard of their coming, and that they were near to Burgos, he sent his eldest son, John, who was called the Infanta of Castille, attended by a large company of knights and squires, to meet and to do them honour; for king Henry knew well that it became him so to act; and he himself paid them much attention, as soon as they were come into his presence. Shortly after, the king issued out his orders, when they were sent to different places in the kingdom of Castille.

CHAP. XXXIX.

THE CONSTABLE DU GUESCLIN TAKES THE CASTLE OF MONMORILLON *, AND OTHER PLACES IN POITOU.

WE will return to the affairs of Poitou, which at that time were not trifling matters, and say how those knights from England and Gascony acted who had come into la Rochelle at the feast of St. John the Baptist, as has been before related. They were exceedingly vexed they had not arrived there the preceding day, and been in time

---

* Monmorillon,—a town in Poitou, eleven leagues from Poitiers.

for

for the Spaniards. They held long councils how they ſhould act, and which way they ſhould advance, for they already had their ſuſpicions of the loyalty of the Rochellers. They appointed ſir John Devereux ſénéſchal of la Rochelle, with three hundred men at arms for the defence of the caſtle, for as long as they ſhould be maſters of that, the town dared not to rebel. This buſineſs done, the captal de Buch, who commanded the expedition, lord Thomas Percy, the earl of Angus, ſir Richard de Pontchardon, the ſouldich, ſir Beras de la Lande, and the others, with their men, marched from la Rochelle. About four hundred lances took the road for Soubiſe *; for there were ſome Bretons near that place, who having taken poſſeſſion of ſeveral churches and ſmall forts, had fortified them: but as ſoon as theſe lords approached they fled, and the country was freed of ſuch viſitors.

At this time, the conſtable of France, the dukes of Berry and Bourbon, the count d'Alençon, the dauphin d'Auvergne, the lord Louis de Sancerre, the lords de Cliſſon and de Laval, the viſcount de Rohan, the lord de Beaumanoir, and numbers of the barons of France, had taken the field, and were with the army in the countries of Anjou, Auvergne and Berry: in all, upwards of three thouſand ſpears.

Thoſe lords who were under the immediate command of the conſtable advanced into Poitou,

* Soubiſe,—a town in Saintonge, ſix leagues from la Rochelle.

where they kept in a body, and then proceeded to lay ſiege to a caſtle called Monmorillon. On their arrival, they aſſaulted it briſkly, and gained it, putting all within to the ſword. They reinforced it with another garriſon.

They then marched to Chauvigny*, on the river Creuſe, and beſieged it. They remained there two days, but on the third it ſurrendered, and the garriſon were ſpared. They continued their march towards Luſſac †, where there is a town and caſtle, which ſurrendered immediately without waiting the aſſault. They advanced towards the city of Poitiers, and lay one night in the vineyards, which very much alarmed the city, as they were fearful of being beſieged, but for this time they were free, for they marched off the following day, advancing towards Moncontour. John Creſswell and David Hollegrave commanded in the place, and had under them about ſixty good companions, bold and hardy, who had very much haraſſed the ſurrounding countries of Anjou and Touraine, as well as all the French garriſons, ſo that the conſtable declared he would not undertake any thing before he had gained this town.

---

* Chauvigny,—ſix leagues from Poitiers.

† Luſſac,—near Monmorillon

CHAP. XL.

THE CONSTABLE OF FRANCE TAKES MONCONTOUR BY A CAPITULATION.—HE MARCHES FROM THENCE TO FORM A JUNCTION WITH THE DUKE OF BERRY IN THE LIMOUSIN, WHEN THEY LAY SIEGE TO ST. SEVERE.

THE conſtable of France, the duke of Bourbon, the count d'Alençon, the lord de Cliſſon, the viſcount de Rohan, the lords de Laval, de Beaumanoir and de Sully, with the others, advanced until they came before Moncontour, a handſome caſtle, ſix leagues from Poitiers. On their arrival, they began the ſiege, and made different aſſaults in good order, but, as the ditches were very deep round the walls, they could not eaſily approach. They ordered the peaſants to cut timber and ſaggots, which they cauſed to be drawn and thrown into them, and afterwards covered with ſtraw and earth. Four days were taken up in doing this. When they had completed it, they began their attacks in earneſt, and in a regular way. Thoſe within defended themſelves well, for they were maſters of their profeſſion; and they ſuſtained the aſſault one whole day, when they had hard fighting, and were in great danger of being taken. On the ſixth, the conſtable advanced himſelf with his Bretons in regular order, to make a fiercer aſſault than any of of the former ones. Being covered with large ſhields, and armed with pick-axes and mattocks, they came up cloſe to the walls, which they immediately battered, pulling out ſtones in various places, inſomuch that the garriſon began to be alarmed: they, however, defended themſelves as well as ever garriſon did.

John Creſswell and David Hollegrave, the governors, ſaw the peril they were in, and gueſſed that ſir Bertrand, from this manner of proceeding, would not quit the place before he had conquered it; ſo that, ſhould they be taken by aſſault, they would certainly be put to death; and, not ſeeing nor hearing of any ſuccour coming to them, they opened a treaty to ſurrender the place, on their lives being ſpared.

The conſtable, who did not wiſh to harraſs his own people, nor to puſh too far the garriſon, whom he knew to be reſolute men at arms, accepted the terms, and agreed they ſhould leave the caſtle, taking nothing with them but gold or ſilver, and that they ſhould be eſcorted to Poitiers.

In this manner did the conſtable get the caſtle of Moncontour, of which he took poſſeſſion, and had it well repaired. He remained in it to refreſh himſelf and men, for he was not determined whither he ſhould march next, to Poitiers or elſewhere.

When the news was known in the city of Poitiers, that the conſtable and his Bretons had retaken the caſtle of Moncontour, they were more alarmed than before, and immediately ſent off meſ-

ſengers

ſengers to lord Thomas Percy, their ſénéſchal, who was on the expedition with the captal de Buch.

At the ſame time that lord Thomas Percy received this information, ſir John Devereux, who reſided in the caſtle of la Rochelle, was told that the conſtable of France, having encamped before Poitiers, had reconnoitred the place, and that the inhabitants were the more afraid he would beſiege it becauſe their ſénéſchal was abſent. Sir John did not hear this intelligence with indifference, but ſet about to aid and comfort the Poitevins: he marched from la Rochelle, with only fifty lances, having appointed, on his departure, one of his ſquires, named Philip Manſel, governor of the caſtle until his return. He took the road to Poitiers, which he entered, and the citizens teſtified their obligations to him for it.

The principal citizens who brought the news from Poitiers to lord Thomas Percy, ſerving in the captal's army, begged of him to haſten thither; and as they expected an immediate ſiege, to bring with him as ſtrong a force as he could, for the French army was very conſiderable. On hearing this, lord Thomas explained the buſineſs to the captal, to know what he would ſay to it. The captal, having conſidered it, was unwilling to break up his expedition, but gave lord Thomas Percy leave to go there: he ſet off, and on his arrival in Poitiers was received with great joy by the inhabitants, who were very deſirous of having him among them. He found ſir John Devereux there, and

great

great feastings and rejoicings were made on the occasion.

All this was known to the constable, who had continued in Moncontour, and also that Poitiers had been reinforced with a body of men at arms. At the same time he heard from the duke of Berry, who commanded a large army in Auvergne, Berry, and Burgundy upon the borders of Limousin, that he was desirous of laying siege to St. Severe*; which town belonged to sir John Devereux, but was garrisoned, under his orders, by sir William Percy, Richard Gill and Richard Orme, and a large body of men at arms, who had overrun the countries of Auvergne and Limousin, doing much mischief to both of them. The duke of Berry, on this account, wished to march thither, and therefore entreated the constable, if he had not any other views, that he would join him before St. Severe.

The constable, who was very wise, prudent and inventive in all his undertakings, considered that at that moment he could not expect success before Poitiers, even if he were to march his men thither, for the city had been greatly reinforced with men at arms: he therefore declared he would join the duke of Berry. He set out from Moncontour with his whole army after he had appointed a garrison to defend it, and joined the duke, who thanked him much for coming, as well as all his knights and

* St Severe,—a town in Saintonge, near Saintes.

ſquires. When this junction was formed, there was plenty of men at arms.

The duke of Berry, in company with the conſtable, reconnoitred St. Severe: their force was about four thouſand men at arms: they directly laid ſiege to the place, declaring they would not depart until they had poſſeſſion of it. They began the ſiege with great vigour, and ſir William Percy and his companions defended themſelves equally well.

News was brought to ſir John Devereux in the city of Poitiers, how the duke of Berry, the dauphin d'Auvergne, the conſtable of France, the lord de Cliſſon, the viſcount de Rohan, with four thouſand men at arms, were beſieging his caſtle of St. Severe.

He was very penſive on hearing this, and ſpoke to lord Thomas Percy, who was preſent when the intelligence came: 'Lord Thomas, you are ſénéſchal of this country, and have ſufficient influence and power to do what I am about to requeſt of you; which is, that you would adviſe and aſſiſt me in ſuccouring my people, for unleſs they are reinforced they muſt be taken by aſſault.'

'By my faith,' replied lord Thomas, 'I have every inclination and good wiſh to aſſiſt you; and, through love to you, I will ſet out, and ſpeak to my lord the captal de Buch, who is not far diſtant. I will do all in my power to induce him to accompany us, to raiſe the ſiege, and to offer battle to the French.'

They

They immediately ſet out from Poitiers, leaving the city under the guard of the mayor of the place, whoſe name was John Regnault, a good and loyal man. Theſe knights rode until they met the captal de Buch, in the plain, advancing towards St. Jean d'Angely. They remonſtrated with him in a courteous manner, how the French had taken Monmorillon, near Poitiers, as well as the ſtrong caſtle of Moncontour, and that they were now employed at the ſiege of St. Severe, which belonged to ſir John Devereux, to whom certainly ſome good ſervices were due. Beſides, there were ſhut up in the caſtle, ſir William Percy, Richard Gill and Richard Orme, who were too valiant men to be loſt.

The captal de Buch, having conſidered a moment, replied, 'Gentlemen, what is it you wiſh me to do?' Some knights who were near had been called to this council, and they replied; 'It is now a long time ſince we have heard you expreſs a ſtrong deſire for an opportunity of fighting with the French, you can never find a more favourable one than by haſtening to St. Severe; and, if you will iſſue your ſummons to Anjou and Poitou, we ſhall have a ſufficient number to combat the French with the good will we have to meet with them.' 'By my faith,' anſwered the captal, 'I wiſh nothing better; and we will ſoon meaſure our ſtrength with theirs, if it pleaſe God and my lord St. George.'

The captal immediately iſſued his ſummons to all barons, knights and ſquires of Poitou and

Saintonge attached to the English, entreating and enjoining them strictly to meet him, at a certain fixed place, armed and prepared in the best manner they could.

Every knight and squire who received these letters made all possible dispatch to make himself ready, and took the field to meet the captal as speedily as he could. Among the principal were, the lord de Partenay, sir Louis de Harcourt, sir Hugh de Vinoue, sir Thomas his brother, sir Percival de Coulonge, sir Aimery de la Rochechouart, sir James de Surgeres, sir Geoffry d'Argenton, the lords de Puissances, de Roussillon, de Crupenac, sir John d'Angle, sir William de Montendre, and many other barons and knights; so that they mustered full nine hundred lances and five hundred archers.

CHAP XLI.

THE GARRISON OF ST. SEVERE, AFTER A SHARP ASSAULT, SURRENDERS TO SIR BERTRAND DU GUESCLIN.—THE CITY OF POITIERS TURNS TO THE FRENCH PARTY.

INTELLIGENCE was brought to sir Bertrand du Guesclin and the army before St. Severe, that the English, Poitevins and their allies were fast approaching with a great force, in order to oblige them to raise the siege.

When the constable heard of this, he was no way alarmed, but ordered every one to arm and to to march directly to the assault. No one disobeyed this command, but French and Bretons advanced to the fort armed and well covered by their shields, when they began a vigorous attack, each lord under his own banner and surrounded by his people. It was a handsome sight to look at, for at this assault there were forty-nine banners, and numbers of pennons. The constable, and the marshal lord Louis de Sancerre were there at their proper posts, labouring hard to encourage the men to conduct their attack with greater valour. Knights and squires of all nations were eager to gain honour and advancement, and performed many gallant exploits. Several crossed the ditches, which were full of water, with their shields on their heads, and marched up to the walls. In doing this, they never retreated, notwithstanding the things which were thrown down on them, but advanced the nearer to the fort. The dukes of Berry and Bourbon, the count d'Alençon and the dauphin d'Auvergne, with several other great lords, were on the ditch encouraging their men, who, on account of such spectators, advanced boldly, fearless of death and danger.

Sir William Percy and the two squires of honour, who were governors of the castle, perceiving how briskly the attacks were made, and that they never cooled nor ceased, were sensible, that, if it thus continued, they could not long resist, and, according to their imagination, no aid was coming to them from any part; for, if they had suspected that a reinforcement was within ten leagues, they

 would

would have taken courage, and have held out until they ſhould have been relieved: but, being ignorant of this, they opened a treaty with the conſtable, to avoid further loſs. Sir Bertrand, who had had certain intelligence that before evening he ſhould ſee or hear of the Engliſh, eagerly concluded the negociation, granting them their lives: on which he made great rejoicings.

He then ordered the army to march into the plain, and draw up in order of battle, ſaying to the chief commanders; 'Gentlemen, look to yourſelves, for the enemy is advancing, and I hope that we may have a battle before night.' Each made ready, upon hearing this, as well for the attack as to defend himſelf.

The Engliſh, however, were in no hurry to march further, when they learnt for certain that St. Severe was taken. We will, therefore, ſpeak of what was paſſing in Poitiers.

At this time there were great diſſentions in Poitiers, for three parts of the town wiſhed to turn to the French; but John Regnault, the mayor, and a part of the commonalty, wanted to remain with the Engliſh. Notwithſtanding this, the richeſt citizens and the churchmen, of whom there were there plenty, would, whatever might be the conſequences, have the conſtable ſent for: indeed they ſecretly adviſed him to make haſte and take poſſeſſion of the city, for on his approach they would open to him the gates.

The conſtable was much rejoiced, and told it to the dukes of Berry and of Bourbon, who deter-

mined

mined that he ſhould leave the army with three hundred men at arms, mounted on the fleeteſt courſers they had. They rode that day and the following night, with ſcarcely any repoſe, upwards of thirty leagues by another road than that the Engliſh had taken, and by day-break arrived at Poitiers. They found the gates ready opened, and their party prepared to receive them. Had they but delayed one half hour, they would have loſt the opportunity; for John Regnault and his friends, having learnt the intention of the others, had ſent off in great haſte to ſir John Devereux and lord Thomas Percy, who, with a hundred ſpears and as many archers, were within one ſhort league of the city.

The barons and knights of Poitou were thunderſtruck at the capture of Poitiers, as well as thoſe from Gaſcony and England, who were collected in Poitou, to the amount of eight hundred lances and four hundred archers.

They called a council to conſider in what manner they ſhould act, for they ſaw themſelves in great difficulties, and were doubtful in whom they could put confidence. The barons and knights of Poitou therefore, the better to re-aſſure the Engliſh, thus addreſſed them: ‘ Certainly, gentlemen, it is exceedingly diſagreeable for us to ſee the affairs of this country in ſuch a ſtate that we cannot bring any remedy to them; but depend upon it, that as long as we exiſt, and there ſhall remain any houſe or fort in Poitou to receive us, we will always remain ſteadily and loyally attached to our natural lord the king of England and to you.'

The Engliſh knights replied, 'We place our entire confidence in you, and you will find in us companions and friends to death.' There were very long debates, when it was at laſt reſolved, that the Poitevins ſhould march off one way, and the Engliſh to a different quarter. They parted from each other in the moſt amicable manner, that is to ſay, the lord de Partenay, the lords de Thouars and de Rouſſillon, ſir Aimery de la Rochechouart, ſir John d'Angle, ſir Louis de Harcourt, ſir Percival de Coulogne governor of Thouars, Hugh de Brionne, Reginald de Thouars, William de Crupenac, James de Surgeres, and other knights and ſquires of Poitou, who took the road to Thouars. The Engliſh, ſuch as ſir John Devereux, lord Thomas Percy, ſir Richard de Pontchardon, the earl of Angus, ſir Geoffry d'Argenton, ſir Matthew Foulkes, ſir Thomas Gournay, ſir Walter Hewett, ſir John Creſwell and others, took the road to Niort, which they intended to enter without halting; but, when they arrived there, they found the gates ſhut and the draw-bridge raiſed, and were told by the inhabitants they ſhould not have admittance.

The Engliſh lords immediately called a council, and declared ſuch an inſult was not to be ſuffered: they drew up in good array, and attacked the town with great courage, which was defended by the inhabitants: but there was not any gentleman or knight within it to order or lead them, only mechanics,

chanics, who knew not what it was to make war; ſo they were conquered by the Engliſh. Could they have held out until veſpers, they would have been aſſiſted, for the conſtable had ordered Thibaut du Pons, with two hundred combatants, to reinforce the garriſon. They did not, however, arrive in time, for the town was taken by aſſault, and pillaged, while men and women were promiſcuouſly put to the ſword.

The Engliſh took up their quarters in Niort, waiting for intelligence.

CHAP. XLII.

THE FRENCH MAKE THE CAPTAL DE BUCH PRISONER.—LA ROCHELLE TURNS TO THE FRENCH.

DURING the time the Engliſh were in Niort, from whence, in truth, they were afraid of departing, Evan of Wales, in company with the Spaniſh admiral don Roderigo di Roſas, arrived at la Rochelle with fourteen large ſhips and eight galleys, laden with men at arms and proviſion. They anchored before the town, ſo that nothing could enter or come out without danger of being taken. Upon which the Rochellers, who were wavering, had a ſecret interview with Evan and the

the Spaniſh admiral; and it was agreed mutually not to hurt each other.

The Spaniards and French remained at anchor before la Rochelle; but they had ſpies in the countries of Poitou and Saintonge, to inform them what was going forwards. The governor of la Rochelle was at that time Philip Manſel.

The conſtable of France ſtill continued in Poitiers, but he ſent the lord du Pons and Thibaut du Pons, with three hundred ſpears, including every one, to the caſtle of Soubiſe.

Soubiſe is a very ſtrong caſtle ſituated on the ſea-ſhore, directly at the mouth of the river Charente, where it diſembogues itſelf into the ſea. The lady of Soubiſe was in the caſtle, but had not many men at arms to garriſon it: ſhe therefore directly ſent off a ſquire to John de Grailly, captal de Buch, conſtable of Aquitaine, to aſk for ſuccour, who was at the time in St. Jean d'Angely. He ſent orders for ſir Henry Haye, ſéneſchal of Angoulême, ſir William de Marneil, nephew to the lord Raymond de Marneil, lord Thomas Percy and ſir John Creſswell, to come immediately to St. Jean d'Angely.

Evan of Wales was informed of all the particulars of this ſiege, as well as the aſſembly of St. Jean d'Angely. He therefore picked out four hundred lances of thoſe moſt to be depended upon from his whole army, and, embarking them on board thirteen barges, ſet ſail with ſir James de Montmoy and Morellet his brother. He left the Spaniſh admiral, with the remainder of the armament before

before la Rochelle, and arrived undiſcovered on the oppoſite ſhore to the caſtle of Soubiſe where the lord de Pons was, who knew nothing of this embarkation.

The captal was alſo ignorant of it, as he was collecting his forces in St. Jean d'Angely; for, had he ſuſpected any thing of the ſort, he would have had a larger body of men: but he ſent back a conſiderable number, having alſo left many in St. Jean d'Angely.

He marched with only two hundred lances at the utmoſt, and about night arrived near to the French army and to the caſtle of Soubiſe. They diſmounted on the outſide of a ſmall coppice, to tighten their gloves of mail and regirth their horſes. Having remounted, they diſplayed their banners, daſhing among the French with their ſhouts of war. Many were ſlain and wounded at this onſet, for the French were not on their guard. The lord du Pons and Thibaut du Pons, with ſixty of their principal men, were made priſoners, and the reſt put to flight.

At this moment, Evan of Wales with his forces advanced, having haſtily croſſed the Charente, with torches and other lights, for it was exceedingly dark. Theſe four hundred lances, who were determined men and quite freſh, fell upon the Engliſh and Gaſcons, who thought they had accompliſhed their buſineſs. Many were ſcattered about pillaging, and the knights were attending to their priſoners. They were treated by theſe

new

new comers very roughly, and in a ſhort time completely defeated.

An able ſquire of Vermandois, called Peter Danvilliers *, advanced and came ſo near the captal de Buch that he made him his priſoner by a gallant deed of arms. The captal was, at this period, the knight of Gaſcony attached to England whom the king of France and the Frenchmen wiſhed moſt to gain, for he was a hardy and enterpriſing captain.

Lord Thomas Percy was alſo that day made priſoner by a Welſh prieſt, called David Howel †. Sir Maubrun de Linieres, ſir Henry Haye, and ſeveral other knights and ſquires were taken likewiſe. Sir Walter Hewett, ſir Petiton de Courton, ſir William Farrington and Carmille ‡ eſcaped with great difficulty: they made for the town of Soubiſe, but would have failed of help if the lady had not been on the walls, who had the gate inſtantly opened. They entered the place with ſeveral others.

On the next morning, Evan of Wales ordered all his barges and boats to be drawn up before Soubiſe, on which he made a briſk attack. The

* Danvilliers. Froiſſart calls him Pierre Danielles; but I copy from Villaret's hiſt. de France, tom v. who ſays that Charles V. gave the ſquire twelve hundred livres for the ranſom of the captal, and cites le Treſor de Chartres for the receipt.

† David Howel. Villaret calls him David Honnel. I ſuppoſe it ſhould be David Howel In thoſe days, it was common for prieſts to engage in war, nothwithſtanding their prieſthood.

‡ Carmille. Q.

lord

lord du Pons and ſir Thibaut du Pons, who had been reſcued, aſſaulted it on the oppoſite ſide. The garriſon and town defended themſelves valiantly; but the lady called a council of the knights and barons, as the place was not ſtrong, and could not hold out for any time; for ſhe did not, in the preſent ſtate of affairs, expect any ſuccuur; and ſent them to negociate with the French.

A treaty was made on ſuch terms that the knights who were in the town might retire in ſafety to Niort, Saintes, Luſignan or whitherſoever they pleaſed; but the lady of Soubiſe was to place herſelf under the obedience of the king of France.

The Engliſh departed from Soubiſe, and were ſafely eſcorted wherever they choſe to go. The French took poſſeſſion of the town and received the fealty of the lady, who ſwore allegiance to the king of France for herſelf and for her dependencies.

Evan of Wales, ſir James de Montmoy, and their men, returned to their boats, carrying with them the captal de Buch, and their other priſoners, to the large fleet, which was lying before la Rochelle.

The lord du Pons and the Bretons haſtened their march toward St. Jean d'Angely, to join the other men at arms whom the cōnſtable had ſent thither. There were the viſcount de Rohan, the lords de Cliſſon, de Tournemine, de Beaumanoir and de Rochfort, ſir William des Bourdes, ſir Oliver de Mauny, ſir Reginald de Limouſin, ſir Geoffry Ricon, Yvon de Laconnet, Alain de St. Pol, Carſuelle and ſeveral more, who came before the

town

town of St. Jean d'Angely, and made a great ſhow as if they meant to aſſault it. The inhabitants, ſeeing the country was loſt, and their captain taken, at the ſame time not expecting ſuccour from any part, ſurrendered themſelves to the French.

The Bretons then marched towards Angoulême, which turned to the French, as did Taillebourg. They next advanced to Saintes, where they remained two days and two nights; for the governor, ſir William Farrington, ſaid he would not ſurrender ſo eaſily, and made preparations for its defence; but the biſhop of the town, who was a Frenchman, worked upon the citizens ſo far as to induce them to ſeize the governor, and declare they would put him to death if he would not permit them to ſurrender.

Sir William conſented, provided when they treated for themſelves they did ſo for him, and that he ſhould be permitted to march out free. This treaty was accepted, and the French took poſſeſſion of Saintes and its caſtle. Sir William Farrington marched out, and was eſcorted to Bourdeaux.

Evan of Wales ſtill lay before la Rochelle in company with the Spaniſh admiral, don Roderigo de Roſas, with forty large ſhips, thirteen barges and eight galleys. There were many negotiations between them and the citizens; but theſe laſt could not do any thing ſo long as the caſtle was in the hands of the Engliſh. They waited therefore, diſſembling their intentions, until the Engliſh

ſhould

ſhould have drawn off the greater part of the garriſon, as they were doing by little and little, and until ſir John Devereux had left it under the command of Phillip Manſel, who had but a hundred companions one with the other.

At this time, a citizen called John Candorier*, mayor of the town, aſſembled a meeting of thoſe that were more inclined to the French than to the Engliſh, and addreſſed them: 'Gentle ſirs, we ſee our neighbours taking part with the French on all ſides of us, and we ſhall ſoon be ſo incloſed that we ſhall not know which way to turn ourſelves, nor even to go out of our town. It would therefore be expedient, as the moment ſeems favourable, to conſider in what manner we may be able to gain poſſeſſion of the caſtle, which has ſo much annoyed and vexed us, for the garriſon is now much weakened. Phillip Manſel is not very crafty. I will therefore tell him I have received orders from the king of England, which command me to arm and muſter all the inhabitants of the town in a place which I will name, but that I muſt know the number of the garriſon as well as the townſmen, ſo that I may be enabled to ſend him an exact account. I will deſire him to march out of the caſtle and make his muſter before me, which I am perſuaded he will do. We will then have provided an ambuſcade among the old ruins, on the outſide of the caſtle, of two hundred companions, who, when the garriſon have

* Candorier. He was called Chaudron before.

marched out, ſhall poſt themſelves between them and the draw-bridge, which will have been let down. We will alſo have a ſufficient force elſewhere, who muſt advance in their front and make them priſoners; by which we ſhall take both caſtle and garriſon, if you, gentlemen, approve of my plan.'

They all replied in the affirmative, and adopted it, appointing the mayor captain of the enterprize.

The mayor, ſhortly afterward, ſent to invite the governor to a grand entertainment, where he met moſt of the principal inhabitants that were in the plot. The converſation ran chiefly on the king of England and his affairs: during which a large packet was brought to the mayor, ſealed with the great ſeal of England, the better to impoſe on Phillip Manſel, who could not read, but knew well the ſeal. The mayor read aloud this letter, putting ſuch words in it as ſuited his purpoſe, but which were not written. He then addreſſed his gueſt: 'Governor, you ſee and hear what the king our lord's commands are to you and me. You muſt make your muſter to-morrow, as we will do ours.' The governor, who but too well believed all he had heard, ſaid he would willingly obey, and with this he took his leave.

During the courſe of the night, the mayor choſe two hundred men, whom he well armed, and before day placed them in ambuſh among the old walls on the outſide of the caſtle. After nine o'clock, the mayor ordered the bells to ring and the

the townſmen to arm themſelves. Soon after, Phillip Manſel armed his garriſon, of ſixty able men, and fit to defend the place. They marched out of the caſtle; but when they had paſſed the draw-bridge, the men who formed the ambuſcade ſallied forth, and poſted themſelves between the Engliſh and the gate.

The garriſon now ſaw they were betrayed, and marched towards the ambuſcade in hopes of regaining the entrance of the caſtle; but at this moment the mayor advanced, with upwards of two thouſand of the inhabitants, ſo that the Engliſh, being attacked in front and rear, were all made priſoners: they ſurrendered, on having their lives ſaved. The caſtle was not yet taken; for the Engliſh had left twelve of their men within, who had ſtrongly cloſed the gate.

The mayor then came up to the governor and his men, and ſaid; 'Gentlemen, attend to what I ſay: if you do not immediately give orders for the caſtle to ſurrender, you may be aſſured we will have you all beheaded at the foot of this bridge.' The Engliſh replied, they would willingly do all in their power, and held ſeveral parleys with thoſe of the caſtle. It was agreed on all ſides, that thoſe who had been made priſoners and the remainder in the caſtle ſhould be embarked on board a ſhip, and conducted by the mayor and burgeſſes to Bourdeaux.

Thus did the Rochellers win their caſtle. When the dukes of Berry, Burgundy, Bourbon, the marſhal de Sancerre, the viſcount de Rohan, the lords de Sully, du Pons, de Cliſſon, de Beaumanoir, and the other barons and knights of France were informed of it, they quitted Berry, Anjou and Limouſin, where they had made their quarters, and took the direct road for Poitiers, where the conſtable reſided. In their march, theſe lords took a town in Poitou called St. Maixant*, which ſurrendered as ſoon as they came before it. The caſtle was taken by aſſault, and all in it put to the ſword. They afterward took the caſtle of Merle, the caſtle of Aunay, and ſeveral other forts in their road.

When they were arrived at Poitiers, they ſent meſſengers to treat witht he Rochellers, but they would not open their gates to them. They told the meſſengers, that the inhabitants would not ſurrender themſelves in ſo eaſy a manner; but that if the duke of Berry and the before-mentioned lords were willing to agree, within ſix days to ſend them paſsports to come to Poitiers, they would then declare to them their intentions, and fully explain what they meant to do.

The meſſengers returned, and told what the inhabitants had ſaid.

Paſſports were granted, and ſome of the burgeſſes came to Poitiers, when they declared to the lords that it was their intention to place themſelves under the obedience of the king of France; but that they would not allow of any caſtle, and

* St. Maixant,—in the road between Saintes and Poitiers, 15 leagues from the latter.

the

the preſent one muſt be razed to the ground: that it ſhould be declared, under the king's ſeal, that no other ſhould be erected: that the town of la Rochelle, and country dependant on it, ſhould remain for ever as the particular domain, and under the juriſdiction, of the kings of France, and that it ſhould never be ſevered from it by marriage, peace, or by any other means, whatever fortune may befal the kingdom of France: that the town ſhould be allowed a mint, with liberty to coin florins, and black and white money, with the ſame alloy and form as thoſe of Paris.

The French lords would not agree to theſe terms until the king had conſidered them, and they gave the Rochellers paſſports to wait on him at Paris.

Twelve burgeſſes went to the king, who granted them every thing they had aſked. He entertained them handſomely, and gave them ſeveral rich jewels. When they returned to la Rochelle, they diſplayed their charters, which were ſealed with the king's ſeal, and had been confirmed in the parliament of the king and his peers.

They immediately began to demoliſh and raze to the ground the large and ſtrong caſtle of la Rochelle. They then ſent to inform the lords who were at Poitiers, that if they would come thither the gates would be open to them.

The conſtable of France went with only two hundred men at arms. They received him with great joy, and did to him their homage and fealty as to the king of France; for he ſhewed them a lawful commiſſion from the king, which conſtituted him his repreſentative in all thoſe parts of the realm.

CHAP XLIII.

SIR BERTRAND DU GUESCLIN TAKES SEVERAL CASTLES IN THE ROCHELLOIS.—THE KING OF ENGLAND EMBARKS TO COME TO THE ASSISTANCE OF THOUARS, BUT IS PREVENTED BY CONTRARY WINDS: UPON WHICH THOSE OF THOUARS, AND MANY OTHERS IN POITOU, SURRENDER TO THE FRENCH.

WHEN ſir Bertrand du Gueſclin had reſided four days in la Rochelle, and had pointed out to the inhabitants in what manner they ſhould ſupport and demean themſelves henceforward, he ſet out on his return to the lords he had left at Poitiers, whom he inſtantly marched off to conquer other ſtrong places in Poitou. They were full three thouſand lances.

On their departure from Poitiers, they laid ſiege to the caſtle of Benon*, and declared they would not leave it until it had changed maſters. A

* Benon,—a ſmall town in Aunis, dioceſe of la Rochelle.

ſquire

ſquire from the county of Foix, named William de Pau, was governor of the place, under the captal de Buch: he had with him a Neapolitan knight, called ſir James, but without any ſurname. Many violent aſſaults were made, which were well repulſed by the garriſon.

Not far diſtant was the town of Surgeres*, which was garriſoned with Engliſh, by orders of the captal, then a priſoner, who ſaid one evening they would beat up the French quarters. They therefore marched out, according to an agreement with thoſe of Marans†, and muſtered in the whole about forty lances: they fell upon the quarters of of the conſtable of France, wounded many, and particularly ſlew one of his own ſquires. The army were rouſed, and the French collected together as faſt as they could; but the Engliſh, who had performed all they intended, re-entered their fortreſſes unhurt.

The conſtable was ſo enraged at this, that he ſwore he would never quit the ſpot where he was without conquering the caſtle of Benon, and putting to death all within it. He gave orders that very morning for every one to be ready for the aſſault, and had large machines brought, ſo that for a long time ſuch an attack had not been ſeen. The men at arms and the Bretons did not ſpare themſelves: they entered the ditches with ſhields on their heads, and advanced to the foot of the

* Surgeres,—a town in Aunis, ſix leagues from la Rochelle.

† Marans,—a town in Aunis, ſix leagues from la Rochelle.

walls with pick-axes and iron crows, with which they worked ſo effectually that a large breach was made, through which they might eaſily enter. The caſtle was taken, and all within put to the ſword.

The conſtable had it repaired and new garriſoned. He then advanced towards Marans, the garriſon of which ſurrendered on having their lives and properties ſaved. He next came to Surgeres, which alſo put itſelf under the obedience of the king of France; for the Engliſh garriſon had gone away, being afraid to wait the arrival of the conſtable. He marched after this to the caſtle of Fontenay le Comte*, where the lady of ſir John Harpedon reſided. He aſſaulted both town and caſtle frequently: at laſt, the garriſon left it on capitulation, and retreated to Thouars with the lady, under paſſports from the conſtable. The French therefore took poſſeſſion of the caſtle and town, and halted there to reſt themſelves.

Sir Bertrand and the lords of France marched to beſiege Thouars, whither the greater part of the knights of Poitou had retired, namely the viſcount de Thouars, the lords de Partenay, de Pouſanges, de Cors, de Crupignac, ſir Louis de Harcourt, ſir Geoffry d'Argenton, ſir James de Surgeres, ſir Percival de Coulogne. They had cauſed to be made at Poitiers and at la Rochelle large machines and cannons, with which they much

* Fontenay le Comte,—a city in la Vendée, biſhoprick of la Rochelle.

haraſſed

haraſſed theſe lords of Poitou in Thouars; who, having mutually conſidered their ſituation, propoſed a treaty, the terms of which were, that there ſhould be a truce for them and all that belonged to them until Michaelmas enſuing, 1372: during which time, they ſhould let the king of England, their lord, know the ſtate of the town and country: and if, within that period, they were not ſuccoured by the king of England or ſome of his children, they were, for themſelves and their territories, to ſwear obedience to the king of France.

When the treaty was agreed to, ſome of the knights returned to Paris. The captal de Buch was conducted thither, and impriſoned, under a good guard, in one of the towers of the Temple. The king was ſo much pleaſed with this prize that he gave to the ſquire that had taken him twelve hundred francs.

The meſſengers from the lords of Poitou arrived in England, to acquaint the king, the prince of Wales (who at that time had pretty well recovered his health) and the council with the ſituation of Poitou and Saintonge.

The king, learning that he was thus loſing all the territories which had coſt him ſo much to conquer, remained penſive and ſilent: at laſt he ſaid, that in a very ſhort time he would go to that country with ſuch a powerful force as would enable him to wait for the army of the king of France. and never return to England before he had regained all that had been conquered from him, or lose what remained.

At this period, the army under the command of the duke of Lancaster was completed. It was very numerous, and had been ordered to Calais; but the king and council changed its destination, having determined it should go to Poitou, Saintonge and la Rochelle, as being the places where the business was the most pressing. The king of England issued a special summons throughout the realm, ordering all persons capable of bearing arms to come properly equipped to Southampton and its neighbourhood by a certain day, when they were to embark.

None either wished or dared to disobey the command, so that numbers of men at arms and archers of all sorts marched towards the sea-coast, where there were about four hundred vessels of different sizes ready to receive them. The principal nobility waited on the king and his family, who resided at Westminster.

It had been settled between the king and prince, that if either of them should die in this expedition, the son of the prince, named Richard, born at Bourdeaux, should succeed to the crown. When therefore all the nobles were assembled about the king before his departure, the prince caused them to acknowledge, that in case he should die before his father, he son should succeed as king of England after the decease of his grandfather. The earls, barons, knights, and commonalty of the country

country were ſo much attached to the prince for his gallantry at home and abroad, that they cheerfully aſſented to his requeſt; the king firſt, then his children, and afterward the lords of England. The prince put them upon their oath, and made them ſign and ſeal to obſerve this arrangement before they ſeparated.

Matters being thus ſettled, the king, the prince, the duke of Lancaſter, the earls of Cambridge, Saliſbury, Warwick, Arundel, Suffolk, and Stafford, the lord Deſpenſer (who was but lately returned from Lombardy), the lords Percy, Neville, Roos, de la Warre, and all the principal barons of England, with about three thouſand lances and ten thouſand archers *, arrived at Southampton, when they embarked on board the fleet, which was the largeſt that ever a king of England ſailed with on any expedition whatever.

They ſteered for la Rochelle, coaſting Normandy and Brittany, and had various winds. The king of France, in the mean time, was collecting a great army in Poitou, to maintain his pretenſions to Thouars; ſo that the whole country was full of ſoldiers. The Gaſcons, on the other hand, were as actively employed in raiſing men under the command of the lord Archibald de Grailly, uncle to the captal de Buch, who had come forward at the entreaties of ſir Thomas Felton, ſeneſchal of Bourdeaux: they amounted to full

* My MS. ſays, ' four thouſand men at arms and twenty thouſand archers'

three

three hundred spears. In this number were, the lords de Duras, de Courton, de Mucident, de Rosen, de Langoren, and de Landuras, sir Peter de Landuras, sir Peter de Courton, and sir William Farrington, an Englishman.

This body of men left Bourdeaux, and advanced to Niort, where they found sir Walter Hewett, sir John Devereux, sir Thomas Gournay, sir John Cresswell, and several others. When they were all assembled, they amounted to about twelve hundred combatants. Sir Richard de Pontchardon arrived there also, and brought with him twelve hundred more.

The king of England and his children, with his large army, were beaten about on the sea, and could not land at la Rochelle, nor any where near it, for wind and weather were against them. They remained in this situation for nine weeks, and Michaelmas was so near at hand that he found it was not possible for him to keep his engagement with the Poitevin lords in Thouars. He was severely disappointed at this, and disbanded his troops to go whither they wished. The king, on his return, said of the king of France, 'that there never was a king who had armed himself so little, nor one who had given him so much embarrassment.'

Thus did this large fleet steer to England, when it had as favourable a gale as could be wished. After they were disbanded, there arrived at Bourdeaux upwards of two hundred merchant ships for wines.

When

When Michaelmas was nearly arrived, the barons of England and Gascony, who had advanced to Niort in order to attend the king of England at Thouars, were very much surprised that they heard not any tidings of him. In order, therefore, to acquit themselves, they sent messengers to the Poitevin lords in Thouars, who said to them; 'Very dear lords, we are sent hither by the lords of Gascony in the dependence of the king of England, and by those English lords now in company with them, who have desired us to inform you, that they have collected all their forces, which may amount to about twelve hundred fighting men*, ready and willing to serve you. They entreat you to inform them, if, in the absence of the king of England and his children, they can assist you, and if the relief may now be accepted; for they are eager to adventure their lives and fortunes in your company.'

The barons of Poitou replied; 'We will call a council on what you have said; and we return our kind thanks to the barons of Gascony and

* All the printed copies and MSS. except the one I have lately quoted, have 1200. In the preceding page, Froissart says 1200 men came to Niort with sir John Devereux, &c. and that sir Richard de Pontchardon brought 1200 *more.* They ought, therefore, to have been 2400. My MS nearly reconciles this by saying, that, 'the herald Chandos, who carried the message to the knights in Thouars, informed them his lords were assembled in Niort with 1200 lances, English and Gascons, and about 2000 archers and lusty varlets.'

England for sending to us, and for being so well prepared and willing to assist us.'

The knights of Poitou assembled; but at the first meeting they could not agree on any determination, for the lord de Partenay, who was one of the principal barons, was desirous they should defend themselves, as if the king of England had been present: but others maintained, that they had given under their seals a declaration, that if neither the king of England nor any of his children were present they would surrender themselves to the obedience of the king of France. The lord de Partenay returned to his hôtel in a very ill humour, but he was afterwards so much talked to that he consented to agree with the others. They therefore sent word, that according to their treaty, it was absolutely necessary for the king of England or one of his sons to be present. The English and Gascons at Niort were much vexed on hearing this, but they could not prevent it.

The dukes of Berry, Burgundy, Bourbon, the constable of France, the lord de Clisson, the viscount de Rohan, the dauphin of Auvergne, the lord Louis de Sancerre, the lord de Sully, and the barons of France: in all, about ten thousand lances, without reckoning the others, advanced from Poitiers, and drew up in battle-array before Thouars the eve of Michaelmas-day, and also on the feast day until evening, when they retired to their quarters. On the morrow, the two brothers of the king of France and the constable sent to the knights of Poitou in Thouars, to remind them of of what they had ſworn and ſealed. They returned for anſwer, that they ſhould very ſoon retire to Poitiers, when they would put themſelves and their dependencies under the obedience of the king of France.

The lords of France, ſatisfied with this anſwer, departed from before Thouars; and the dukes diſbanded the greater part of their men.

On this ſeparation, the lord de Cliſſon, with a large body of men at arms, of whom the conſtable had given him the command, came before Mortaigne ſur mer, which at that time was attached to the Engliſh. An Engliſh ſquire, called James Clerk, was governor of the place, and might have had with him about ſixty companions.

When the lord de Cliſſon came before Mortaigne, he aſſaulted it very vigorouſly: but, though he did not ſpare himſelf on the occaſion, he gained nothing; upon which he retreated to his quarters.

The governor, who found he ſhould be hard puſhed, ſent off ſecretly to thoſe knights of Gaſcony and England who were at Niort, to deſire they would come that night to Mortaigne; that he would lodge them in his hôtel, and that they might eaſily paſs through the quarters of the French forces, who were but two hundred fighting men.

Theſe lords ſet out from Niort, with five hundred lances, and rode all night to arrive at Mortaigne, for they had a great deſire to catch the lord de Cliſſon. But a ſpy, who had left Niort with them, having overheard ſome part of their

intentions,

intentions, made as much haste as possible to the lord de Clisson, whom he found sitting at his supper. He informed him that the enemy had marched from Niort with five hundred combatants, and were advancing fast towards him.

Upon hearing this, the lord de Clisson pushed the table from before him, and hastily armed himself. He mounted his steed, and set off suddenly, with all his men, leaving the greater part of what belonged to them on the field. He never stopped until he arrived at Poitiers. The English were much vexed at their disappointment. They returned to Niort, where they left in garrison sir John Devereux, the earl of Angus and Cresswell. Sir Walter Hewett went to England. All the others went back to Bourdeaux, burning in their way the whole of the territories of the lord de Partenay.

Thus was all Poitou conquered, except the fortresses of Niort*, Elifeth, Mortemer, Mortaigne, Lusignan, Chastel-Accart†, la Roche sur Yon, Gauzar, la Tour de l'Arbre, Merxis and others. These castles, however, held out, and made frequent inroads and attacks on their neighbours; sometimes invading, at other times chaced back again.

---

* Niort,—a city in Poitou, fifteen leagues from Poitiers.

† Châtel l'Archer,—a village in Poitou.

CHAP. XLIV.

THE DUKE OF BRITTANY DARES NOT OPENLY DECLARE FOR THE KING OF ENGLAND.—SIR BERTRAND DU GUESCLIN LAYS SIEGE TO CIVRAY*.—THE ENGLISH ARE DEFEATED, AND THE WHOLE OF THE COUNTRIES OF POITOU, SAINTONGE, AND LA ROCHELLE, ARE GIVEN UP TO THE FRENCH.

THE duke of Brittany, who remained peaceably in his duchy, was much hurt at the losses of the English; for he said, such as he was the king of England and his power had made him, as he never should have been any thing of himself: that he owed all to the English king, who had made war in his behalf, had lent him large sums of money, and had given to him his daughter in marriage, he would therefore have been happy to have added Brittany as an ally of England: but all the barons, knights, and squires of that country were too much attached to the French, particularly the lords de Clisson, de Laval, and the viscount de Rohan, who at that time were the greatest lords in Brittany. They addressed the duke in these words: ' Dear lord, as soon as we shall clearly perceive that you take any part with

* Civray,—a town in Poitou, on the Charente, ten leagues from Poitiers.

the

the king of England againſt the king of France, our ſovereign lord, we will all quit you and the country of Brittany.'

The duke could but ill diſguiſe his anger: however, he only ſaid, 'they did great wrong to the king of England.' He now began to open himſelf more, and to diſcover his ſentiments to others of the lords of Brittany.

The king of France, who had gained over to him all the principal perſons in that country except ſir Robert Knolles, had beſought them to inform him whenever they found the duke acting contrary to their wiſhes, aſſuring them he would provide a remedy.

The duke ſaw that he was not only ſuſpected, but narrowly watched; which alarmed him leſt they ſhould ſeize his perſon, and ſend him to Paris. He therefore ſignified to the king of England his ſituation, and entreated him to ſend men at arms to aſſiſt him if there ſhould be any occaſion. The king ordered thither four hundred men at arms and as many archers, under the command of lord Neville, who arrived at St. Mathieu Fin de Terre*, where they remained all the winter, without doing any damage to the country, paying for every thing they had, for the duke, on account of the ſuſpicions of his nobles, did not chuſe to put them into any of his caſtles. When

* St Mathieu Fin de Terre, or St. Mahé, is a village in Brittany, dioceſe of St Pol de Léon. Froiſſart calls it St. Mathieu de Fine Pôterne.

the

the knights of Brittany ſaw the Engliſh thus come to the aſſiſtance of the duke, they were very indignant, and ſhut up their own caſtles, ſhewing much ill will againſt the duke. Things remained in this doubtful manner all the winter.

As ſoon as the ſeaſon permitted, ſir Bertrand du Gueſclin marched from Poitiers with full fourteen hundred combatants, and laid ſiege to the town and caſtle of Civray. There were with him, of Breton knights, ſir Alain de Beaumanoir, John de Beaumanoir, Arnoul Limouſin, Geoffry Ricon, Yvon de Laconet, Geoffry de Kerimel, with many other knights and ſquires. They fixed their quarters before Civray, and ſurrounded them with paliſadoes to prevent being ſurpriſed in the night. Frequently the moſt expert of them advanced to make trials of ſkill with thoſe of the caſtle, who defended themſelves valiantly.

During the ſiege, ſir Robert Micon, and Nicotin l'Eſcot*, the governors of Civray, ſent intelligence of their ſituation to ſir John Devereux and the earl of Angus, who were in garriſon at Niort. They inſtantly ordered the garriſons from Luſignan and Gouzar to march to Niort, when they amounted all together to ſix or ſeven hundred good men at arms, well equipped, without counting the pillagers. They advanced until they came near to Civray, which is but four leagues from Niort; when they halted ſome time to ar-

* Sir Robert Micon and Nicotin l'Eſcot. My MSS. have ſir Robert Miton and ſir Martin Scott.

range themselves, but it had been better for them had they proceeded to the quarters of the constable*.

News was brought to him of the arrival of the English, whilst they were forming themselves in the plain. He was not any way alarmed at it, but ordered his men to arm without making any delay, and to march out in a body. When he saw them all assembled, he said to them; 'My good gentlemen, what hearts have you for a battle? I fancy we must engage our enemies.' They replied; 'My lord, we are very willing to do so, thanks to God.'

The constable then ordered an ambuscade to be formed, of two hundred combatants, near to the castle; for he judged the garrison would of course make a sally. He then commanded the greater part of the palisadoes to be levelled to the ground, that there might not be any hindrance when he should march out, and drew up his forces in two battalions. Sir Alain de Beaumont commanded one, and sir Geoffry de Marneil† the other. It was strictly forbidden for any one to advance before his banner until ordered, and he was to remain till then quietly in his rank.

---

* The historian of Brittany says, they there intoxicated themselves.

† Marneil. The different editions have a variety of names for this person. I have followed the oldest MS. I have, which, from its writing, seems to be of the age with Froissart. but I should rather suppose it ought to be sir Geoffry de Kerimel, as he is particularly mentioned before.

We

We will now return to ſir Robert Miton and ſir Martin Scott, who, from the heights of the caſtle, ſaw the Engliſh in the plain drawn up in battle-array. They ſaid, ‘ Let us make ready to quit the caſtle, for we can eaſily paſs through theſe Bretons; and when our friends ſhall ſee we are engaged, they will come to our help, and we may do much miſchief before they will be prepared to defend themſelves or ſuſpect our intent.’

About ſixty combatants that were to make this ſally armed themſelves, who, when ready, ſallied forth on horſeback to ſkirmiſh with the enemy; but they were attacked by the ambuſcade which had been laid for them. Hard indeed was the fight, but the Engliſh were ſo ſurrounded that they could neither advance nor retreat: they were all ſlain or made priſoners, not one eſcaping: the two governors were alſo taken.

The Engliſh remained in battle-array in the plain, and the conſtable of France in his quarters; for he imagined the Engliſh had placed a large ambuſcade in a coppice on his rear. The Engliſh had brought with them a rout of pillaging Poitevins and Bretons, amounting to about two hundred, whom they ſent forward to ſkirmiſh with the French.

As ſoon as theſe pillagers came oppoſite to the battalion of the lord conſtable, they declared themſelves loyal Frenchmen, and, if he pleaſed, would ſerve under him. The conſtable immediately aſſented, commanding them to wheel on one ſide, when he learnt from them the arrangement

of

of the English force, and that there was not any ambuscade. On hearing this, the constable was more easy than before; and, having ordered his men to form, he advanced with his banner, marching on the wing of the two battalions. They had dismounted, and pushed towards the palisadoes which they had allowed to remain standing, every one shouting, 'Nôtre Dame Guesclin!'

The English, on seeing them issue out of their fort, drew up also on foot, and advanced with great alacrity. Their first onset was against the battalion of the constable, which was fierce and desperate. The English drove quite through this battalion, and overthrew many. But the Bretons had wisely drawn up their army: there were two battalions on the wing, who, being quite fresh, followed the constable, and, falling upon the English who were tired, beat them most dreadfully. They, however, like men of courage, turned about, without shrinking from their ill-fortune, and combated most valiantly with the arms they had, such as battle-axes and swords of Bourdeaux, with which they dealt many hard blows. Several excellent knights of each side adventured boldly, to exalt their renown. This battle was as well fought, as many gallant deeds performed, and as many captures and rescues took place as had been seen for a long time in all that country; for both armies were on foot, on a plain, without advantage to either. Each laboured to perform his duty well, and many were slain outright or desperately wounded. In short, all the English who had

marched

marched thither were so completely discomfited that not one escaped death or captivity

Two good squires were there slain, Richard Neville and William Worsley. James Willoughby was very badly wounded. Sir John Devereux, sir Aimery de Rochechouart, David Holgrave, Richard Oliver, John Creswell, and many others from England and Poitou, were made prisoners.

This battle of Civray happened on the 20th day of March, 1373.

The constable and his army returned to their quarters, where they cleaned and refreshed themselves, and attended to the wounded and prisoners, of whom they had great numbers. The constable then sent sir Alain de Beaumont to hold a parley with the garrison, who told them, that if they suffered themselves to be taken by assault, they would all be put to the sword without mercy. Upon this, the garrison surrendered to the constable, who allowed them to leave the place and march to Bourdeaux, with a passport from him. The French gained this castle and territory, which submitted to the obedience of the king of France.

The Bretons advanced eagerly towards Niort, which is a handsome town in Poitou, and had always supported the interest of the English, who had kept there a very large garrison. As soon as the inhabitants of Niort heard the constable was marching thither, they went out to meet him, and, presenting him the keys of the town, conducted him and all his men into it with great rejoicings *.

The Bretons remained there four days to recover themselves, when they departed in great array, with about fourteen hundred lances, for Lusignan †, which surrendered upon condition the garrison should march out unhurt, carrying away all they were able, and with a passport for the constable to conduct them to Bourdeaux. The French gained this castle, which was very grand and handsome, and all the lordship dependant on it, whose vassals became liege men to the king of France.

After this, the Bretons marched to Châtel l'Archer, when the constable sent immediately to the lady de Plainmartin, who was the wife of sir Guiscard d'Angle, and resided in it. She entreated he would grant her an escort, that she might speak with the duke of Berry at Poitiers. The constable complied with her request, and ordered one of his knights to conduct her. When she came before the duke she prostrated herself to the ground. The duke caused her to rise, and demanded what she wished to say: 'My lord,' replied

* Niort is said to have been gained by a stratagem. After the defeat at Civray the constable ordered his knights to dress themselves in the emblazoned surcoats of his prisoners, which caused the garrison at Niort to open their gates, believing them the English knights returning victorious from Civray —*Hist. de Bretagne.*

† Lusignan,—a town in Poitou, twelve leagues from Niort.

ſhe, 'I am ſummoned by the conſtable to put myſelf and my lands under the obedience of the king of France. You know well, my lord, that my huſband is now lying a priſoner in Spain: his lands, therefore, are under my direction. I am but a weak woman, and cannot diſpoſe of my huſband's property as I pleaſe; for, if by accident I ſhould do any thing contrary to what he would have wiſhed, he will be angered and blame me for it. However, to ſatisfy you, and to keep my lands in peace, I offer you a compoſition for me and mine, on theſe terms: that no war ſhall be made on us, nor will we engage in any offenſive or defenſive war. When my lord ſhall have gained his liberty and be returned to England, whither I ſuppoſe he will retire, I will inform him of the terms of this compoſition, and whatever anſwer he ſhall ſend to me, the ſame I will forward to you.'

'Lady,' anſwered the duke, 'I grant it on condition that neither for yourſelf, nor caſtles, nor fortreſſes, you lay in a greater ſtore of proviſion, artillery, or men at arms than are now within them.'

The lady returned to Châtel l'Archer, when the ſiege was raiſed; for ſhe ſhewed the agreement made with the duke of Berry.

This army of Bretons, of which the conſtable was the leader, departed, and came before Mortemer. The lady de Mortemer ſurrendered herſelf and lands to the obedience of the king of

 France.

France. She gave up alſo the caſtle of Didonne *, which belonged to her. Thus was all Poitou, Saintonge and la Rochelle freed and delivered from the Engliſh.

When the conſtable had placed ſufficient garriſons every where, and found nothing rebellious, as far as the river Gironde, he returned to Paris. The dukes of Berry, Burgundy and Bourbon, with the greater part of the barons of France who had been concerned in theſe conqueſts, had already arrived there. The king had entertained them moſt handſomely on their return; but this was nothing to the honours that were ſhewn ſir Bertrand du Gueſclin when he came to Paris: the king did not think he could ſufficiently teſtify his regard and eſteem for him, and detained him conſtantly about his perſon at Paris and elſewhere.

* Didonne,—or St. Georges de Didonne,—a ſmall town in Saintonge.

I believe it was a dependance of the ſandich de Trane.—See Aſhmole.

CHAP.

CHAP. XLV.

THE SIEGE OF BECHEREL*.—PEACE BETWEEN THE KINGS OF FRANCE AND NAVARRE.—THE DEATH OF THE KING OF SCOTLAND.

ABOUT this time, the lords de Cliſſon, de Laval, d'Avaugour, de Tournernine, de Rieux, de Rochefort, the viſcount de Rohan, ſir Charles de Dinan banneret of Brittany, the marſhal de Blainville, the lords de Hambie, de Ruille, de Fonteville, de Granville, de Farmille, de Denneval, and de Cleres, bannerets of Normandy, with many others from Normandy and Brittanny, laid ſiege to the ſtrong caſtle of Becherel, and preſſed it hard by their aſſaults. There were in this caſtle two able captains from England, ſir John Appleyard and ſir John Cornewall, who, with their companions, bravely defended themſelves: and at this time there were various gallant deeds, ſallies, ſkirmiſhes, and reſcues, performed before Becherel.

Not far diſtant was the town of St. Sauveur le Vicomte, in which were, ſir Thomas Trivet, ſir Aleyne Boxhull, ſir Philip Pechard, and the three brothers Maulevrier; ſo that, before the ſiege of Becherel, theſe two garriſons over-ran all Lower Normandy, and nothing could eſcape, but what

* Becherel,—a town in Brittany, two leagues from St. Malo.

was

was inclosed in forts, from being taken and carried to one or other of these towns. They ransomed the bishopricks of Bayeux and Evreux, in which the king of Navarre had connived, and reinforced them with men and provision from the garrisons he held in the county of Evreux.

He was not in good humour with the king of France; insomuch that the garrisons of Cherbourg, Cocherel Conches, Breteuil, Evreux, and several others dependant on the king of Navarre, had much impoverished and ruined the country of Normandy. However, about this period, the differences were accommodated between the two kings, and treaties entered into, through the mediations of the count de Saltzbourg, who had made many visits to each party, and the bishop of Evreux. The two kings met in an amicable manner in the castle of Vernon, when they swore, in the presence of several of the great lords of France, peace, love, amity and alliance henceforward for ever.

The king of Navarre accompanied the king of France to Paris, who shewed him and his companions all manner of respect. The king of Navarre put his territories in Normandy under the government of his brother-in-law the king of France, and left his two sons, Charles and Peter, with the king their uncle. He then affectionately took his leave, and returned to Navarre.

This peace continued for four years; but then great dissentions arose between them, as you will hear in the course of this history, if I should live

to

to finiſh it: I do not think, however, that it will be concluded in this book.

The 7th day of May 1373, king David of Scotland departed this life in the city of Edinburgh, and was buried in the abbey of Dunfermline, beſide Robert the Bruce his father. He left behind him neither male nor female offspring, and was ſucceeded by his own nephew, Robert the Stewart of Scotland, who was a fine knight, and had eleven ſons*.

CHAP. XLVI.

THE EARL OF SALISBURY, SIR WILLIAM NEVILLE, SIR PHILIP COURTENAY, WITH MANY OTHER MEN AT ARMS, LAND IN BRITTANY.—THE CONSTABLE OF FRANCE MARCHES THITHER; ON WHICH THE DUKE OF BRITTANY GOES TO ENGLAND.

ORDERS were given in England for the earl of Saliſbury, ſir William Neville and ſir Philip Courtenay, to put to ſea with a large body of men at arms, to guard the coaſts; for it was reported that the Spaniards and Evan of Wales

* Lord Hailes, in his Annals, ſays; 'David II. died 22d February, 1370-1, in the caſtle of Edinburgh, in the 47th year of his age and the 42d of his reign. He was buried in the church of the abbey of Holyrood, before the great altar.'

were

were on the ſeas, with ſix thouſand men, to invade and burn the country.

Theſe lords had under their command forty large ſhips, without counting ſloops, and two thouſand men at arms, not including archers. They ſet ſail from Cornwall, where they had embarked for the coaſts of Brittany, and, arriving at St. Malo, burnt in the harbour ſeven large Spaniſh ſhips that were lying there. The country was much ſurpriſed at this, and ſaid the duke had ſent them orders to come thither: they began to ſuſpect his intentions more than ever, and ſtrengthened all their towns, caſtles and cities.

The duke had placed his confidence in ſome of the knights of Brittany, who had betrayed his ſecret, ſo that the king of France ordered his conſtable to invade Brittany with a large body of men at arms, and to take poſſeſſion for him of all cities, towns, caſtles and fortreſſes, as well as ſuch perſons whom he ſhould find in rebellion, and confiſcate their property.

The conſtable marched from Paris to Angers, and from thence iſſued his ſummons. He was there joined by the duke de Bourbon, the count d'Alençon, the count du Perche, the count de Porcien, the dauphin d'Auvergne, the viſcounts de Meaux and d'Auſnay, ſir Raoul de Coucy, Robert de St. Pol, Raoual de Raineval, Louis de Sancerre marſhal of France, with numbers of barons and knights from the countries of Vermandois, Artois and Picardy, without counting thoſe from Anjou, Poitou and Touraine.

The

The earl of Salisbury, who was at St. Malo with his army, was informed of this assembly of men at arms, and also that the whole of Brittany was in opposition to the duke. He set sail with his fleet, and bore away until he came to Brest, which has one of the strongest castles in the world.

When the duke of Brittany heard of the march of the constable, he was afraid of trusting himself to the inhabitants of Vannes or Dinan, or indeed to any of his principal towns: he thought if he should shut himself up in any one of them, he would run great risks. He went, therefore, to the castle of Auray, which is situated between Vannes and Rennes, and was attached to him; for he had given the command of it to an English knight, called sir John Austin. The duke left his lady under the care of this knight, entreating him to guard her well, which he promised to do. After this, he rode to St. Mahé; but they shut the gates against him: from thence he went to Concarneau*, where he embarked for England.

The constable of France entered Brittany, attended by those barons and knights of the country who had been at the siege of Becherel, they having left the continuance of it to the knights and lords of Normandy.

On the arrival of the constable before Rennes, the inhabitants knew that his visit was to take possession of the whole country; for the king and his

* Concarneau,—a sea-port in Brittany, about four leagues from Quimper.

council

council had publiſhed a declaration that the duke had forfeited it, becauſe he had ſurrendered to the Engliſh different towns, caſtles and forts, and had even wiſhed to take part with the king of England againſt the crown of France, from which he held his duchy by faith and homage. They were unwilling to incur the horrors of war, and received the conſtable in a peaceful manner, acknowledging the king of France for their lord.

After the conſtable had gained poſſeſſion of Rennes, he haſtened to Dinan, which ſurrendered to the obedience of the king of France. He next advanced to Vannes, which did the ſame. Luzumont*, however, held out for the duke; it was roughly aſſaulted and taken by ſtorm, ſo that all within were put to death. The conſtable marched to Jugon, which accepted the terms of the king of France; as did the caſtle of Goy la Forêt; la Roche-derrien, the towns of Guincamp, St. Mahé, and St. Malo. In like manner, did Quimpercorentin, Quimperlé, Credo, Galande, as well as ſeveral other fortreſſes in the neighbourhood, turn to the French. The conſtable marched firſt through Lower Brittany, becauſe it was more attached to duke John de Montfort than the upper parts.

When the duke of Brittany embarked for England, he nominated ſir Robert Knolles, governor of the duchy, but very few lords obeyed him. He,

* Probably Sucinio,—a caſtle near Vannes, which was taken by aſſault, and the garriſon ſlain. *Hiſt. de Bretagne.*

however,

however, ſufficiently reinforced his caſtle of Derval with men, and, having provided it with every neceſſary, gave the command of it to his couſin Hugh Brock. Sir Robert ſhut himſelf up in Breſt.

The conſtable came before Hennebon: the governor was an Engliſh ſquire, called Thomelin Ubich*, nominated by the duke. There was alſo with him in the caſtle a knight named ſir Thomas Prior, who had been ſent thither by ſir Robert Knolles; and their garriſon might conſiſt of about fourſcore men, without counting the inhabitants of the town.

The French, on their arrival, began to make a violent attack on the caſtle: they always carried with them many large engines and cannons, by means of which they had taken ſeveral towns, caſtles and forts in Brittany: in particular, they had ſtormed the town of Quimperlé, of which James Roſs, a valiant ſquire of England, was governor. He could obtain no quarter, for he fell into the hands of ſir Oliver de Cliſſon, who ſlew him and ſeveral others with his own hand: he had no mercy nor pity on any Engliſhman.

Let us return to the ſiege of Hennebon. The conſtable of France, after he had pointed his engines and cannon againſt the walls of the town and caſtle, which the lord Charles de Blois could never conquer, ordered all the men at arms to

* Thomelin Ubich. Q. Wich, or Holbeck. Barnes calls him Thomas Wich.

make

make a brisk assault, for he had resolved to sup in the place that evening.

They made a most fierce attack, without sparing themselves; and the inhabitants, assisted by the English, made as gallant a defence. Upon this, the constable called out to them, saying, 'Attend to me, you men of Hennebon: it is quite certain we must conquer you, and that we will sup in your town this evening: if, therefore, any of you be bold enough to throw a stone, arrow, or by any means hurt the smallest of our boys so that he be wounded, I vow to God I will have you all put to death.'

These words so much frightened the inhabitants that they retired to their houses, leaving the English to defend the place as well as they could: but the town was too large for them to guard every part of it, so that the army of the constable entered, and put all the English to death except the two captains, whom they made prisoners. Because the townsmen had obeyed the orders of the constable, he commanded that no one, when they stormed the place, should dare any way to injure them.

When sir Bertrand du Guesclin had thus won the town and strong castle of Hennebon in Brittany, he remained there for fifteen days, and then marched towards Concarneau.

In the mean while, the earl of Salisbury, sir William Neville, sir Brian Stapleton, and sir William Lucy, having reinforced and re-victualled the fort of Brest with men at arms, archers and provisions,

provisions, had embarked on board their ships in order the better to defend it against the French, whom the English knew to be in Brittany, but were uncertain to what quarter the constable would lead them.

The constable on coming before Concarneau, which is a sea-port, took it by storm, and slew all the English, except their captain, sir John Langley, who received quarter. The French repaired the town, and strengthened it with men at arms and all sorts of provision. They then advanced to Brest, in which were sir William Neville and sir Robert Knolles, with two hundred men at arms, and as many archers.

The lords of France and of Brittany laid siege to Brest: they had with them about six thousand combatants. Shortly after they had commenced this siege, the duke of Anjou sent for sir Oliver de Clisson, who had under his command some of his men, to come and lay siege to la Roche sur Yon, which the English still held. Sir Oliver surrounded the place, and pointed against it large engines, which he had brought from Angers and Poitiers.

In company with these Bretons came several nobles and gentlemen of Poitou and Anjou: they kept up a sharp attack, and pressed hard the garrison of la Roche sur Yon, saying they would never leave the place before they had conquered it.

The duke of Anjou returned to his own country, but frequently sent provision and other articles to those who were carrying on the siege.

The constable, the duke of Bourbon, the counts d'Alençon and de Perigord, the dauphin d'Auvergne and the great barons of France still maintained the siege of Brest; but too little did they gain, for it is one of the strongest castles in the world. As sir Robert Knolles was the governor, the lords of France resolved to send a body of men to invest his castle of Derval. Many noblemen of Brittany and of Touraine went on this expedition: they were, in the whole, about four hundred fighting men.

CHAP. XLVII.

THE FRENCH BESIEGE FOUR DIFFERENT PLACES. —LA ROCHE SUR YON SURRENDERS TO THE FRENCH.—THE SIEGE OF BREST IS RAISED BY A CAPITULATION, WHICH IS NOT KEPT.

THE lords of France were at this time besieging four towns at once; namely, Becherel, Brest, la Roche sur Yon, and the one just formed before, Derval. The besiegers had many an assault to make, and many gallant feats of arms to perform, in order to obtain success.

The

The inhabitants of la Roche ſur Yon, being the fartheſt off from any aſſiſtance, and ſurrounded on all ſides, entered into a capitulation, that if they were not ſuccoured within one month, the garriſon would march out, and deliver up the caſtle to the king of France.

The lord de Cliſſon and the other lords returned at the appointed day; and, when no reinforcements appeared to raiſe the ſiege, the caſtle ſurrendered, and the Engliſh, under the paſſports of the lord de Pons, marched away for Bourdeaux *.

After this, ſir Oliver de Cliſſon and the others who had been at this conqueſt, marched to Derval, whither they had cauſed large machines and engines to be brought. To this ſiege of Derval came the conſtable of France, the duke of Bourbon, the counts d'Alençon and du Perche, with numbers of the knights and barons of France, for they. found they were only loſing their time before Breſt. Two thouſand, however, remained behind, who built a block-houſe in ſuch a ſituation that no one could enter Breſt to reinforce or re-victual it.

Sir Hugh Brock and the garriſon in Derval, ſeeing themſelves attacked by ſuch a force, were alarmed leſt they ſhould be taken by ſtorm, and propoſed a treaty for a truce of two months; and if within that time they were not relieved by the duke of Brittany, or others in ſufficient force to keep the field, to raiſe the ſiege and to combat the

---

* My MS. mentions ſir Robert Grenacres as governor of la Roche ſur Yon.

French, they would ſurrender themſelves and the caſtle to the duke of Anjou or to the conſtable: but if a body of men at arms ſhould arrive, and offer battle to the French, the garriſon ſhould remain in peace.

This treaty was concluded, and information ſent to the duke of Anjou, who was on the borders: he approved of it, on condition that the garriſon of Derval ſhould not during the truce receive any one into the caſtle.

Sir Hugh Brock ſent ſeveral knights and ſquires as his hoſtages for the due execution of the treaty.

After this capitulation, the conſtable of France made an excurſion to the city of Nantes. The citizens ſhut their gates, becauſe he had with him a large army, and went forth to know his intentions. The conſtable told them he had been nominated and ſent by the king of France, their lord, to take ſeiſin and poſſeſſion of the duchy of Brittany, which ſir John de Montfort, who called himſelf duke, had forfeited.

The citizens requeſted time to hold a council, to deliberate on what he had ſaid before they gave an anſwer. After a long time debating the buſineſs, they returned and ſaid to the conſtable; 'Dear lord, it ſeems quite marvellous to us how the king of France can thus ſeize the inheritance of our lord the duke; for the king, not long ſince, commanded us to receive him as our duke. We have therefore ſworn fealty and homage to him, and he has in return promiſed and ſworn to govern us as ſubjects, which he has hitherto punctually done. We

have

have never had any grounds for suspecting him of fraud or guile. If you enter this town by virtue of the procuration you say you have, we will allow you so to do; but on condition, that if it should happen that the duke of Brittany return to this country, and be desirous of becoming a good Frenchman, so that all prelates, barons, gentlemen and good towns in Brittany, shall acknowledge him for their lord, we shall be acquitted without loss for what we now do, or may have before done; and that you will not consent to any violence being offered to us, nor will you receive the rents or revenues of Brittany, but they shall remain as a deposit with us until we have other information, or hear news more agreeable to us than what you have brought.'

The constable swore to keep every thing as procurator for the king of France in this case. He and all those who were with him then entered the city of Nantes, which is the principal town in Britanny.

When sir Robert Knolles heard that his cousin, sir Hugh Brock, had concluded a capitulation for the castle of Derval with the French, and found that unless he also entered into a negociation he could not by any means leave his post to succour it, sir Robert made offers of treating with the French and Bretons, who had remained before Brest: they replied, that they could do nothing without the constable. An English knight and two squires, having had passports, came to a mansion near Nantes, where the constable resided, on the banks of the Loire, with other knights from France and Brittany.

A treaty was entered into, on these terms; that the garrison of Brest should have a truce for forty days, during which time, unless there should arrive a sufficient force to fight with the constable, the fort was to be surrendered. The garrison was to remain on the same footing it then was, without receiving any reinforcements of men or provision.

The negociators returned to sir Robert Knolles, who sent, as pledges to the constable, able and sufficient knights and squires. These hostages, on their arrival, were ordered to the prison of the constable; and all those who had been at the siege of Brest departed. The constable gave also leave for several others to go away, whom the king of France sent to garrison his cities, castles, towns, and forts in Picardy, for the duke of Lancaster had landed at Calais with a large army.

When the earl of Salisbury (who had all that season cruised on the coasts of Brittany and Normandy, having for that purpose been reinforced by the king of England, so that he might have on board with him a thousand men at arms and two thousand archers,) heard of the capitulation of Brest, he said, that if it pleased God, he would offer combat to the French. He made sail, and arrived at Brest, which is situated on the sea shore. when he disembarked, and drew up his men in order of battle before Brest: at night, they all retreated to their vessels. This he daily performed, in order to be ready to fight the enemy ſhould they advance to that quarter.

The conſtable had diſmiſſed the greater part of his men: he had alſo on his hands, the ſieges of Becherel and of Derval, and did not imagine the earl of Saliſbury would have arrived on the coaſt ſo ſoon. He ſet out fiom near Nantes when the day approached for the ſurrender of Breſt, but did not march quite ſo far; for he had had intelligence that the Engliſh were in ſufficient force to fight with him. On hearing this, he halted where he was, and remained there quiet for about ſeven days, being deſirous of having the advice of a full council of war which he had ſummoned.

The earl of Saliſbury had poſted himſelf very advantageouſly before Breſt; and, finding that the conſtable and Bretons did not advance, he ſent a herald to ſir Bertrand du Gueſclin, who, on his arrival, reſpectfully ſaluted him, and ſaid; 'My lord, the earl of Saliſbury and the lords of England ſignify by me, who am a herald at arms and their ſervant, that as you had for a long time beſieged the town and caſtle of Breſt, and certain treaties and capitulations had been enteied into for its ſurrender unleſs it ſhould be ſuccoured before a certain day, which is not far diſtant, they wiſh to inform you that they have encamped themſelves before Breſt to fulfil this engagement and to defend the caſtle: they beg and entreat of you, therefore, to advance, when you ſhall be fought with without fail; and ſuppoſing you refuſe your conſent to this, that you will ſend back the hoſtages.'

 The

The conftable replied; 'Herald, you bring us agreeable news, and you are welcome. You will tell your mafters, that we are more defirous to combat them than they are to meet us; but that they muft march to the place where the treaty was firft entered into and agreed upon. You will inform them, that if they will advance to that place, they fhall infallibly have a battle.'

The herald returned to his mafters before Breft, and delivered his meffage: they fent him back to the conftable, to whom he faid; 'My lord, I come again from my lords and mafters, to whom I repeated the words you charged me with: they fay, that as they are only attached to the fea-fervice they have not brought any horfes with them, and are not accuftomed to march on foot; for which reafon they inform you, that if you will fend them your horfes, they will come without delay to any place you fhall pleafe to appoint, and fight with you.'

'My good friend,' anfwered the conftable, 'we will not, pleafe God, give fuch advantage to our enemies as we fhould do were we to fend them our horfes. It would alfo be confidered as an infult; and, fhould we think of fuch a thing, it would be right we fhould have good and fufficient fecurity to anfwer for our horfes.'

'In truth,' replied the herald, 'they have not charged me to add any thing on this head, only, that if you do not accept their propofition, they fay you have not any caufe to detain their hoftages, and that in returning them you will act but juftly.'

The

The conſtable ſaid, he was not of that opinion.

Thus did the buſineſs remain; and the herald returned to the earl of Saliſbury and the knights before Breſt, who, when they found they could not gain any thing, and that the hoſtages were not ſent back, were exceedingly vexed: they, however, remained ſteadily before the place, without moving, until the appointed day was paſſed, and then perceiving the conſtable would not advance to fight with them, they entered Breſt, which they greatly reinforced and re-victualled.

The conſtable, finding the Engliſh were not likely to come to offer him battle, marched off, carrying with him the Engliſh hoſtages as priſoners, and ſaid, the Engliſh had not kept what they had bound themſelves to perform*.

After

---

* My MS. has the following additions:

'The herald, on receiving his laſt meſſage, returned to his lords before Breſt, who held a council on it.

'Shortly after this, the conſtable, the duke of Bourbon, the count d'Alençon, the lords de Cliſſon and de Laval, with the other barons and knights, amounting to four thouſand lances and twenty thouſand other men, marched to within one day's journey of Breſt, where having ſtrongly encamped themſelves, they ſent to let the Engliſh know they were now on the ſpot where the treaty had been concluded, and if they would march thither they would be combated; otherwiſe they would loſe their hoſtages. The earl of Saliſbury, on learning this, found the French were trickiſh and had not any real intention of fighting, ſo that he returned for anſwer by his own herald, who accompanied the French herald, that if the conſtable would advance two-thirds of the way, they would on foot perform the other third;

After the relief of Breſt, the earl of Saliſbury put to ſea to guard the coaſts according to the orders he had received. Sir Robert Knolles ſet out alſo from Breſt, and arrived at his caſtle of Derval. As ſoon as this was known, information of it was ſent to the duke of Anjou, who was with the conſtable near Nantes. They gueſſed what would be the conſequence of this; for ſir Robert broke all the treaties which his couſin had entered into, and ſent to tell the duke of Anjou and the conſtable, that he ſhould not keep one article of them, as his people had not the power to enter into any treaty without his knowledge and conſent. The duke, on hearing this, came in perſon to the ſiege of Derval.

---

third; or, if the French would not do this, the Engliſh would advance half of the way on foot, if the French would there meet them on foot: or, if the French would not accept either of theſe propoſitions, they were bound in juſtice to return the hoſtages, for the Engliſh had cheerfully and honourably performed their engagement.'

CHAP.

CHAP XLVIII.

THE DUKE OF LANCASTER LANDS AT CALAIS, AND INVADES PICARDY.—A PART OF HIS ARMY DEFEATED BY THE LORD DE BOURSIERS* BEFORE RIBEMONT †.—ANOTHER PART OF HIS ARMY IS DEFEATED NEAR SOISSONS BY AN AMBUSCADE OF BURGUNDIANS AND FRENCH.

UPWARDS of three thousand men at arms and ten thousand English archers had landed at Calais. Three years before, this expedition had been planned and provided for: of course, it was well furnished with all things. The following knights passed over with the dukes of Lancaster and Brittanny: the earls of Warwick, Stafford and Suffolk, Edward lord Despencer, first baron of the realm, and at that time constable of the army, the lords Willoughby, de la Pole, Basset, Roos, Latimer, lord Henry Percy, lord Lewis Clifford, lord William Beauchamp, the canon de Robesart, sir Walter Hewett, sir Hugh Calverley, sir Stephen Cossington, sir Richard de Pontchardon, and many other knights and squires from England; but I cannot name them all.

The king of France, who knew well that the English would cross the sea, had reinforced his ci-

* Denys Sauvage calls him the lord de Soubise, but gives no reason for it. My MSS. have Boursiers.

† Ribemont is a town in Picardy, four leagues from St. Quentin.

ties

ties, towns, caſtles and forts in Picardy, Artois, and alſo in Vermandois, and had every where poſted men at arms in ſufficient numbers; ſuch as Bretons, Burgundians, Picards, Normans, and many whom he had ſubſidized from the empire.

The Engliſh left Calais as ſoon as they had mounted and arranged their carriages, of which they had great numbers. They marched in three battalions, and in ſuch good order as it was not eaſy to improve: that of the marſhals marched firſt, of which the earls of Warwick and Suffolk were the leaders; then the dukes of Lancaſter and Brittanny, who had many gallant knights to accompany them: the conſtable, the lord Deſpencer, brought up the rear. They marched in cloſe order, without any one being ſuffered to quit his rank; and the van was always armed ready for combat. They were quartered together at night, keeping a ſtrong and ſtrict guard to prevent a ſurpriſe. They advanced three leagues a-day, and no one dared to march before the banners of the marſhals unleſs he had been ordered forward as a ſcout.

They paſſed by Montrieul, of which the lord Handebourg* was governor, St. Omer, and afterwards Terouenne, but without attacking them. The light troops burnt all the lands of the count de St. Pol, and the army advanced very near to Arras, when the two dukes took up their quarters in the monaſtery of St. Eloy, and remained there two days.

---

* Handebourg. Q.

They

They then marched off by the walls of Arras, but made no aſſault, for they knew it would be loſt time. They came to Bray ſur Somme*, where the two marſhals had a ſharp engagement before the gates; for there was a good garriſon within of able knights and ſquires of Picardy, under the command of the viſcount de Meaux and ſir Raoul de Rayneval. The canon de Robeſart ſtruck down three with his ſpear before the gate, and the ſkirmiſh was ſevere; but the French ſo well defended the gates, that they loſt nothing. The Engliſh continued their march, following the courſe of the river Somme, which they thought to croſs between Ham, in Vermandois, and St. Quentin. Thus did this army advance under the command of the duke of Lancaſter, according to orders from the king his father.

The lord de Bourſiers was at this time returning from Hainault into France, and arrived ſo opportunely at Ham that the inhabitants moſt earneſtly entreated of him to remain there to aſſiſt them in defending their town againſt the Engliſh. He complied with their requeſt, ſtaying with them two days, during the time the Engliſh paſſed by, following the courſe of the river Somme, to enter the Vermandois and to croſs the river at the narroweſt part.

When the lord de Bourſiers heard that the Engliſh had almoſt all paſſed, and that they were ad-

* Bray ſur Somme,—a village of Picardy, election of Peronne.

vancing towards St. Quentin and Ribemont, where the lord du Chin, whose daughter he had married, possessed a large estate, and where he also had lands in right of his wife, he took leave of the citizens of Ham, who thanked him much for his services, as he knew the castle of Ribemont was quite unprovided with men at arms. He was attended by as many companions as he could muster, but they were few in number, and rode on until he came to St. Quentin, where he did not arrive without great danger, for the whole country was overspread with English. He got into the town just in time, for the English light troops came to the gates as he entered them.

The lord de Boursiers found there sir William des Bourdes, who was governor of it for the king: he was received by him joyfully, and much pressed to stay there, to help him in the defence of the town.

The lord de Boursiers excused himself by saying, that he had undertaken to go to Ribemont, to defend that town and castle, which was without any garrison; and he entreated sir William so much for assistance that he gave him twelve cross-bows. He had not advanced far before he saw a company of English; but, as he knew the country well, he took a more circuitous road to avoid them: the English never quitted their line of march.

He was this whole day in much peril on his road towards Ribemont. He met a knight from Burgundy, called sir John de Bueil, who was going to St. Quentin; but, after some conversation with the

lord

lord de Bourſiers, he returned with him towards Ribemont. His force might now conſiſt of about forty ſpears and thirty croſs-bows.

As they were approaching Ribemont, having ſent forward one of their ſcouts to inform the inhabitants that they were coming to their aid, they perceived a body of Engliſh advancing, who appeared to conſiſt of at leaſt fourſcore men on horſeback. The French ſaid, ‘ Here are our enemies returning from pillage : let us meet them.’ Upon which they ſtruck ſpurs into their horſes, and galloped off as faſt as they could, crying out, ‘ Nôtre Dame Ribemont :’ they fell upon the Engliſh, whom they defeated and ſlew. Happy were they who could eſcape.

When the French had thus conquered theſe Engliſh, they came to Ribemont, where they found the lord du Chin, who a little before had entered the town with forty spears and twenty croſs-bows. Whilſt theſe three noble knights were on the ſquare of the town before the caſtle, and many of their men had gone to their quarters to diſarm themſelves, they heard the ſentinel on the caſtle-wall cry out, ‘ Here are men at arms advancing to the town.’ On which they went nearer the caſtle, and aſked how many he thought there might be : he anſwered, ‘ About fourſcore.’ Upon which, the lord de Bourſiers ſaid ; ‘ It behoves us to go and fight with them, for otherwiſe we ſhall have much blame in having ſuffered them thus to come up to our very walls unnoticed.’

The

The lord du Chin replied; 'Fair ſon, you ſay well: order out our horſes, and diſplay my banner.' Sir John de Bueil rejoined; 'Gentlemen, you ſhall not go without my company: but I would adviſe you to act more deliberately in this buſineſs; for peradventure they may be men at arms lightly mounted, whom the marſhals or conſtable may have ſent hither to draw us out of our fortreſs, and our ſally may turn out to our loſs.'

The lord de Bourſiers ſaid; 'If you will adopt my plan, we will go and fight them, and that as ſpeedily as may be; for, whatever may happen, I am determined to do ſo.' On ſaying this, he fixed on his helmet and tightened his armour, and then ſallied forth with about one hundred and twenty combatants. The Engliſh were about fourſcore, part of the troop of ſir Hugh Calverley, though ſir Hugh himſelf had remained with the duke of Lancaſter: there were as many as ſix knights and other ſquires, who had advanced to revenge the deaths of their companions.

On the French coming out at the gate, they met the Engliſh, who lowering their ſpears, vigorouſly attacked them: they opened their ranks, when the Engliſh galloped quite through: this cauſed ſo great a duſt that they could ſcarcely diſtinguiſh each other. The French ſoon formed again, and ſhouted their cry of 'Nôtre Dame Ribemont!' Many a man was unhorſed on both ſides. The lord du Chin fought with a leaden mace, with which he ſmaſhed every helmet that came

within

within reach of it; for he was a ſtrong and luſty knight, well made in all his limbs: but he himſelf received ſuch a blow on his caſque that he reeled, and would have fallen to the ground had he not been ſupported by his ſquire. He ſuffered from this blow as long as he lived.

Several knights and ſquires of the Engliſh were greatly ſurpriſed that the arms on the lord du Chin's banners were preciſely the ſame as thoſe of the lord de Coucy, and ſaid, 'How is this? has the lord de Coucy ſent any of his men hither? he ought to be one of our friends.' The battle was very mortal; for in the end almoſt all the Engliſh were killed or made priſoners, few eſcaping. The lord de Bourſiers took two brothers of the name of Pembroke; one a knight, the other a ſquire. Sir John de Beuil took two others, with whom they retreated into Ribemont.

The Engliſh army marched by, but made no aſſault, for they thought it would be loſing time. Orders were given to do no damage, by burning or otherwiſe, to the lands of the lord de Coucy, who was at the time in Lombardy, and interfered not with the wars in France.

The Engliſh fixed their quarters in the valleys below Laon and lower down than Bruyeres* and Crecy†, whence they did much miſchief to the Laonnois. But before this, the king of France

* Bruyeres,—a town in Picardy, dioceſe of Laon.

† Crecy ſur Serre,—a town in Picardy, three leagues from Laon.

had ordered every thing valuable to be carried into the towns and ſtrong places, which were ſo well garriſoned that the Engliſh could not gain any thing by attacking them, nor indeed had they any thoughts of ſo doing, but were only anxious that the French would meet them in battle in the plain. The king, however, had forbidden this very ſtrictly in his daily orders. He had them followed by the reſt of his cavalry ſo cloſe on their rear, as to intimidate them from quitting the main army. The French took up their quarters every evening in fortified towns, and in the day-time purſued the Engliſh, who kept themſelves in a compact body.

It happened that one morning a party of Engliſh to the number of ſix ſcore lances, who were over-running the country beyond Soiſſons, fell into an ambuſcade of Burgundians and French. It was commanded by ſir John de Vienne, ſir John de Bueil, ſir William des Bourdes, ſir Hugh de Porcien, ſir John de Coucy, the viſcount de Meaux, the lords de Rayneval and de la Boue, with ſeveral more knights and ſquires, amounting in the whole to full three hundred lances. They had followed the Engliſh, and this night they had encamped in the fields of the Soiſſonnois, where they had placed an ambuſcade in a ſmall coppice. The Engliſh came in the morning to plunder a village behind which their army was quartered. When they had paſſed the ambuſh, the French ſallied forth with banners and pennons diſplayed. The Engliſh, ſeeing ſuch a large body ſo near them,

them, halted, and would have ſent to their army, which was a good league off: but ſir Walter Huet, a great Engliſh captain, and near the ſpot where this ſurpriſe happened, mounting his horſe in great haſte, his lance in its reſt, but without helmet or vizor, and only his coat of mail on, galloped forward without further thought or conſideration: his men followed him as well as they could. In the confuſion, he had his neck quite pierced through with a ſpear, and fell dead on the field.

The Engliſh fought very valiantly, but at laſt were almoſt all taken or ſlain. The French made priſoners of the following knights: ſir Matthew Redmayne, ſir Thomas Fowkes, ſir Hugh Brudenel, ſir Thomas Spencer, ſir Thomas Emerton, ſir Nicholas Gaſcoign, ſir John Chandler, ſir Philip Cambray, ſir John Harpedon, ſir Matthew Gournay, ſir Robert Twyford, ſir Geoffry Say, ſir John Bourchier, ſir Geoffry Worſley, ſir Lionel Daultry; and, of eſquires, William Daultry, John Gaillard, Thomas Bradley, Henry Montford, Guy Hewett, John Meynil, William Goſtwick, John Flamſtead, Thomas Sollerant, William Quentin, Robert Boteler, Robert Audley, Ralph Stanley, aud Thomas Archer*.

News was carried to the main body, that their men were engaged: upon which, the marſhals, with the whole army, haſtened thither: though they could not make ſuch ſpeed but that the buſi-

* I have copied theſe names from Barnes.

ness was finished, and the Burgundians and French had left the field.

The English knew not where to seek the French.

Thus passed this action, according to the information I have received, near to Soucy in the Soissonnois, the 20th September, 1363.

After these two encounters at Ribemont and Soucy, nothing further befel the duke of Lancaster and his army that is worth mentioning. They marched through various narrow passes and defiles, but kept in close and good order. The council of the king of France therefore said to him; 'Let them go: by their smoke alone they cannot deprive you of your kingdom: they will be tired soon, and their force will dissolve away; for as storms and tempests appear sometimes in tremendous forms over a whole country, yet they dissipate of themselves, and no essential harm happens, thus will it befal these English.'

CHAP. XLIX.

THE HOSTAGES SENT FROM DERVAL ARE BEHEADED.—SIR ROBERT KNOLLES RETALIATES ON THOSE PRISONERS WHOM HE HAD TAKEN.—THE DUKE OF LANCASTER FINISHES HIS EXPEDITION.

SIR Robert Knolles, as I have before related, was returned to his castle of Derval, which he considered as his own inheritance, and had determined to break the treaty which had been entered into by his cousin and the duke of Anjou: on which account, the duke himself was come to the siege of Derval, attended by numbers from Brittany, Poitou and the lower countries.

The king of France was desirous that his constable, who was there, and the lord de Clisson, with several more, should return to France, to assist his brother the duke of Burgundy in the pursuit of the English. He frequently renewed these orders to the different lords, who were anxious to obey them, and also to gain possession of this castle of Derval.

When the day was passed on which the castle was to have been surrendered, the besiegers wondered what the garrison were thinking on: they imagined that sir Robert Knolles had thrown himself into it

 with

with reinforcements. The duke and conſtable ſent to ſir Robert, and to ſir Hugh Broc who had made the treaty.

The herald, on arriving in the ſquare of the caſtle, ſaid to the gentlemen preſent; 'My lords ſend me here to enquire from you the reaſons, which they would willingly learn, why you do not ranſom your hoſtages by ſurrendering the caſtle according to the terms of the treaty to which you, ſir Hugh, have ſworn.

Sir Robert Knolles then addreſſed the herald, ſaying; 'Herald, you will tell your maſters, that my couſin had no authority to enter into any capitulation or treaty without my conſent firſt had; and you will now return with this anſwer from me.'

The herald went back to his lords, and related to them the meſſage ſir Robert Knolles had charged him with: they ſent him again to tell the garriſon, that from the tenor of the treaty, they ought not to have received any one into the fort, and that they had received Sir Robert Knolles, which they ſhould not have done; and likewiſe to inform them for a truth, that if the caſtle was not ſurrendered, the hoſtages would be beheaded.

Sir Robert replied; 'By God, herald, I will not loſe my caſtle for fear of the menaces of your lords; and if it ſhould happen that the duke of Anjou, through arrogance, puts my friends to death, I will retaliate, for I have here in priſon ſeveral knights and ſquires of France, and if I were offered one hundred thouſand francs I would not ſhew mercy to any one of them.'

When

When the herald had delivered this anſwer, the duke of Anjou ſent for the headſman, and ordered the hoſtages, who were two knights and a ſquire, to be brought forth, and had them beheaded before the caſtle, ſo that thoſe within might ſee and know them.

Sir Robert Knolles inſtantly ordered a table to be fixed without ſide of the windows of the caſtle, and had led there four of his priſoners, three knights and a ſquire, for whom he might have had a great ranſom, but he had them beheaded and flung down into the ditch, the heads on one ſide and the bodies on the other.

The ſiege was raiſed after this, and all the men at arms returned to France; even the duke of Anjou went to Paris to viſit the king his brother: the conſtable, with the lord de Cliſſon and others, marched to the city of Troyes, for the Engliſh were already in that part of the country: they had croſſed the river Marne, and were taking the road towards Auxerre.

At this time, pope Gregory XI. had ſent the archbiſhop of Rouen and the biſhop of Carpentras in legation to France, to endeavour, if poſſible, to make peace between the kings of France and England: theſe two prelates had many difficulties in travelling towards the king of France and his brothers, and afterwards to the duke of Lancaſter: the Engliſh, however, kept advancing through the country of Fôrets, having paſſed Auvergne, Limouſin, and the rivers Loire, Allier, Dordonne, and Lot. Neither the Engliſh nor French were much at their eafe in this expedition: three knights of Hainault, fir Fateres de Berlammont, fir Bridol de Montagin, and le bègue de Warlan, as well as fome on the fide of the Englifh, died on their march.

The dukes of Lancafter and Brittany continued their route with the army until they were arrived at Bergerac, four leagues from Bourdeaux, continually purfued by the French.

The duke of Anjou and the conftable of France were in the upper countries near Rouergue, Rodais, and Touloufe, and had advanced as far as Perigueux, where they had fixed their quarters.

The two before-mentioned prelates journeyed from each party, preaching to them feveral reafons why they fhould come to an agreement. But each held fo obftinately to his own opinion that they would not make any conceffions, without having confiderable advantages given them.

The duke of Lancafter came to Bourdeaux about Chriftmas, and the two dukes remained there the whole winter and the following Lent. Several knights went away, on the expedition being finifhed: the lord Baffet and his company returned to England, for which king Edward reprimanded him.

CHAP.

CHAP L.

THE DUKE OF ANJOU'S CAMPAIGN INTO UPPER GASCONY*.

SOON after Eafter, in the year 1374, the duke of Anjou, who refided at Perigord, made a great mufter of his forces; at which the conftable of France and the greater part of the barons and knights of Brittany, Poitou, Anjou, Touraine, were prefent. There were alfo, from Gafcony, fir John d'Armagnac, the lords d'Albret and de Perigord, the counts de Comminges and de Narbonne, the vifcounts de Caraman, de Villemure and de Thalar, the count dauphin d'Auvergne: moft of the lords of Auvergne and of Limoufin: the vifcount de Minedon, the lords de la Barde and de Pincornet, and fir Bertrand de Charde. They amounted to fifteen thoufand men on foot, and a large body of Genoefe and crofsbows. They began their march towards upper Gafcony, and came before St. Silvier†, of which an abbot was lord. Notwithftanding it was talked of as a ftrong town, the abbot was afraid of lofing it by force; fo that he began to treat with the duke of Anjou, telling him that neither himfelf

* For a more chronological account of this campaign, fee the hift. de Languedoc, vol. iv. p. 580.

† St. Silvier. Probably St. Sever de Ruftan, in Bigorre.

nor

nor his territories wiſhed to wage war againſt him, or in any way incur his indignation, and that the ſtrength of his town and all he could bring to defend it were as nothing in compariſon with the towns and caſtles of upper Gaſcony, whither, it was ſuppoſed, he intended to march. He therefore entreated that he might remain in peace, upon the terms that he ſhould obſerve an exact neutrality; and that, whatever thoſe lords of Gaſcony who poſſeſſed meſne fiefs ſhould do, he would do the ſame. His requeſt was granted, on his giving hoſtages, who were ſent to priſon in Perigueux.

The whole army, of which the duke of Anjou was commander, marched away towards Montmarſen*, and the town of Lourde† in upper Gaſcony, of which ſir Arnold de Vire was governor. The French beſieged and ſurrounded it on all ſides, having firſt demanded if they were willing to ſurrender themſelves to the duke of Anjou. The inhabitants of Lourde ſoon agreed to it; but the knight ſaid, that the count de Foix had appointed him to that poſt, and he would not ſurrender it to any man except to him.

When the conſtable of France heard this, he ordered the army to advance and briſkly aſſault it, which they did with ſo much vigour that the town was taken and the governor ſlain, as well as ſeveral men and women: the town was pillaged and ruined,

* Montmarſen,—a town in Gaſcony.

† Lourde,—a town in Gaſcony,—the capital of the valley of Lavedan, dioceſe of Tarbes.

and

and left in that ſtate: however, on their departure they placed therein ſome of their men.

The French entered the lands * of Châtel-bon, which they deſpoiled, they then paſſed through the territories of Châtel-neuf, which they attacked, and continued their march upwards towards Bierne, and came to the entrance of the lands of the lord de l'Eſcut: they advanced until they came to a good town and ſtrong caſtle, called Sault †, which was dependant on the county of Foix.

The prince of Wales had frequently intended, before his expedition to Spain, to make war on the count de Foix for all theſe meſne fiefs, which he had in Gaſcony, becauſe the count would not acknowledge that he held them from him: the affair had remained in this ſituation in conſequence of the Spaniſh expedition. Now, however, the duke of Anjou, who was conquering all Aquitaine, ſeemed willing to take poſſeſſion of it, and had thus beſieged Sault in Gaſcony, which was not a trifle nor eaſy to gain: the governor of it was ſir William de Pau.

When the count heard they were conquering his lands and the meſne fiefs, for which it was but juſt he ſhould pay homage either to the kings of France or England, he ſent for the viſcount de

* Theſe lands are beyond the Pyrenées: therefore, it more probably alludes to the town of Mauvoiſin and the other lands the viſcount held under the king of England—See Hiſt. de Languedoc, vol. iv. p. 583.

† Sault de Navaille,—a ſmall town in Gaſcony, near Orthez.

Châtel-Bon, the lords de Marsen and de l'Escut, and the abbot de St. Silvier. He then demanded a passport from the duke of Anjou, who was occupied with the siege of Sault, that they might wait upon him in safety: the duke granted it. They therefore went and held a conference with him and his council, when it was agreed that the aforesaid lords and their territories should remain in peace until the middle of August, on condition that those who should then be the strongest before the town of Monsac * on the part of the kings of France or of England, and there keep the field, should have the enjoyment of these rights, and to that party these lords of mesne fiefs should ever after belong. The count de Foix and the other lords gave hostages for their due performance of this agreement. The duke of Anjou returned to Perigueux with his army, but did not dismiss any one.

* A town in Perigord, near Bergerac.

CHAP.

CHAP. LI.

THE EARL OF PEMBROKE AND HIS COMPANIONS ARE RANSOMED.—A SHORT TRUCE BETWEEN THE FRENCH AND ENGLISH.—BECHEREL SURRENDERS ON TERMS.—THE DEATH OF THE EARL OF PEMBROKE.

ABOUT this time there was an exchange made of the lands of the conſtable of France and ſir Oliver de Mauny, which the king of Spain had given to them for their gallant ſervices. The conſtable exchanged his eſtate of Soria in Caſtille for the earl of Pembroke, who had been made priſoner off la Rochelle. Sir Oliver de Mauny gave up his eſtate of Grette for ſir Guiſcard d'Angle and his nephew William, Otho de Grantſon, John de Grinieres and the lord de Tannaybouton.

Whilſt this treaty was going forward, another was opened between the dukes of Anjou and of Lancaſter, through the means of the two before mentioned prelates. The duke of Lancaſter ſent, under paſſports, to the duke of Anjou at Perigord, (where he reſided and governed as king or regent the lordſhips of England and France,) the canon de Robeſart, and the lords William Hellunay and Thomas Douville. A truce was agreed on, between theſe dukes and their allies, until the laſt day of Auguſt; and they engaged themſelves to be, in the month of September, in the country of

Picardy,

Picardy,—the duke of Anjou at St. Omer, and the duke of Lancaſter at Calais.

After this truce, the dukes of Lancaſter and of Brittany, the earls of Warwick, Suffolk and Stafford, the lords de Spencer and Willoughby, the canon de Robeſart, lord Henry Percy, the lord Manne *, with the other lords and knights, ſet out from Bourdeaux the 8th day of July, and returned to England.

Sir John Appleyard and ſir John Cornewall held their caſtle of Becherel for nearly a year againſt the French, who were cloſely beſieging it, and had much conſtrained them; but not receiving any intelligence of ſuccours coming to their aſſiſtance, and their proviſions beginning to fail, they held a council whether it would not be adviſable to offer terms for its ſurrender. They entered, therefore, into a treaty with the lords d'Hambuye, d'Eſtonville, de Blainville, de Frainville, and the barons of Normandy, who were quite tired with the ſiege having continued ſo long. But they would not conclude any thing without the knowledge of the king of France. He conſented, that if the duke of Brittany in perſon did not come in ſufficient force before Becherel, by All Saints-day next approaching, to raiſe the ſiege, the garriſon ſhould ſurrender on capitulation. Hoſtages were given to obſerve theſe terms.

The earl of Pembroke was ranſomed for 120,000 francs, which the Lombards of Bruges agreed to

* Q. Maine.

pay

pay when he ſhould be arrived in good health at Bruges. The earl journeyed, under the paſſport of the conſtable, through the kingdom of France: but a fever, or ſome other ſickneſs, overtook him on the road, ſo that he was obliged to travel in a litter unto the city of Arras, where his diſorder increaſed ſo much as to occaſion his death. The conſtable, by this event, loſt his ranſom*.

The earl of Pembroke left by his ſecond wife, the lady Anne, daughter of ſir Walter Manny, a fair ſon, who at that time was two years old.

Sir Guiſcard d'Angle obtained his ranſom, as you ſhall hear. You remember that the lord de Roye remained priſoner in England: he had an only daughter, a great heireſs. The friends of the lord de Roye entered into an agreement with ſir Oliver de Mauny, a Breton knight, and nephew to ſir Bertrand du Gueſclin, that if he could deliver the lord de Roye from his priſon by means of an exchange, he ſhould have the daughter of the baron de Roye for his wife, who was of very high birth.

Upon this, ſir Oliver de Mauny ſent to the king of England, to know which of the knights he would wiſh to have ſet at liberty for the lord de Roye. The king was moſt inclined for ſir Guiſcard d'Angle. The lord de Roye wts therefore

---

* The conſtable carried on, for three years, a fruitleſs lawſuit with the Flemiſh merchants for this ranſom, which they refuſed to pay, He at length gave up his claim to the king of France for 50,000 Francs —*Hiſt. de Bretagne.*

ſent

ſent home free, and the lord de Mauny eſpouſed his daughter.

Shortly afterwards, the lord de Roye himſelf married the daughter of the lord de Ville and de Floron in Hainault.

The other knights, that is to ſay, the lord de Tannaybouton, ſir Otho de Grantſon, and ſir John de Grinieres obtained their liberties, and compounded in a handſome manner for their ranſom with ſir Oliver de Mauny.

CHAP. LII.

SEVERAL TOWNS IN GASCONY SURRENDER TO THE KING OF FRANCE.—SIR HUGH DE CHASTILLON RETURNS FROM PRISON.—THE CASTLE OF BECHEREL SURRENDERS TO THE FRENCH.

WHEN the middle of August approached, which was the appointed time for the meeting before Monſac, the duke of Anjou arrived with a grand array of men at arms. He fixed his quarters in the plain before Monſac, where he was lodged for ſix days without any one coming to meet him. The Engliſh thought that the truce which had been entered into would have annulled this agreement. But the duke of Anjou and his council did not conſider it in this light. Sir Thomas Felton,

Felton, sénéschal of Bourdeaux, argued the matter for a long time; but he could not gain any thing.

The duke, therefore, sent to the count de Foix, the viscount de Châtel Bon, to the lords de Marsen, de Châteauneuf, de l'Escut, and to the abbot de St. Silvier, to summon them to keep their agreements, or he would put to death their hostages, and enter their lands in such a manner as would oblige them to throw themselves on his mercy.

These lords, therefore, placed themselves and their lands under the obedience of the king of France. The inhabitants of Monsac opened their gates, and presented the keys to the duke of Anjou, doing to him fealty and homage. The lords who attended the duke entered the town with him, where they remained for eighteen days; during which time they held councils as to what part they should next march.

Shortly after the middle of August, when the truces which had been entered into between the English and French in Gascony were expired, these lords recommenced the war. The duke of Anjou, came before la Réole *; and, after three days siege, the inhabitants submitted to the king of France. From thence he marched to Langon †, which also

* La Réole,—a town in Bazadois, eighteen leagues and a half from Bourdeaux.

† Langon,—a town in Bazadois, six leagues from Bourdeaux.

ſurrendered; as did St. Macaire*, Condom†, Baſille‡, la Tour de Prudenec, Meuléon§ and la Tour de Drou. Full forty towns and caſtles turned to the French in this expedition: the laſt was Auberoche¶. The duke of Anjou placed in all of them men at arms and garriſons; and, when he had arranged every thing according to his pleaſure, he and the conſtable returned to Paris, for the king had ſent for them.

He diſmiſſed, therefore, the greater part of his army: and the lords de Cliſſon, de Beaumanoir, d'Avaugour, de Ray, de Riom, the viſcounts de la Val, de Rohan, and the other barons, returned to the ſiege of Becherel, to be ready at the time appointed; for it was reported that the duke of Brittany, ſir Robert Knolles and the lord de Spencer would attempt to raiſe the ſiege.

You have before heard how ſir Hugh de Châtillon, maſter of the croſs bows, had been made priſoner near Abbeville, by ſir Nicholas Louvain, and carried into England: he was unable to obtain his liberty on account of the large ſum aſked for his ranſom: however, a flemiſh merchant ſtepped forward, and exerted himſelf ſo effectually that he

---

* St. Macaire,—nine leagues from Bourdeaux.

† Condom, a city of Gaſcony, four leagues from the Garonne.

‡ Baſille. Not in Gazetteer.

§ Mauléon, a town in Armagnac, dioceſe Aire.

¶ Auberoche,—a town in Perigord near Perigueux.

cunningly

cunningly got him out of England. It would take too much time to enter into the whole detail of this business: therefore, I shall pass it over.

When he was returned to France, the king gave him back his office of master of the cross-bows, and sent him to Abbeville, as he had before done, to guard that frontier, with two hundred lances under his command. All the captains of castles and towns were ordered to obey him; such as sir John de Berthouilliers governor of Boulogne, sir Henry des Isles governor of Dieppe, and those who commanded in the frontier towns of Terouenne, St. Omer, Liques, Fiennes and Montroye.

It happened that the lord de Gommegines, governor of Ardres, and sir John d'Ubrues, collected their forces in Ardres, to the amount of about eight hundred lances. They marched, one morning early, well mounted, towards Boulogne, to see if they should meet with any adventures.

That same morning, sir John de Berthouilliers, governor of Boulogne, had also mado an excursion, with about sixty lances, towards Calais, and with the same intent. On his return, he was met by the lord de Gommegines and his party, who immediately charged the French, aud overthrew them, so that their captain saved himself with great difficulty, but lost fourteen of his lancemen. The lord de Gommegines, after the pursuit, returned to Ardres.

The master of the cross-bows this day made a

muster of his forces: he had with him a great number of men at arms from Artois, Vermandois, and from that neighbourhood: in all, upwards of three hundred lances.

The count de St. Pol, who had lately come to Picardy from his estates in Lorraine, was on his road to fulfil a pilgrimage to our Lady of Boulogne: he was informed on his way, that the master of the cross-bows was about to undertake an excursion, which made him wish to be of the party: they therefore rode together, and advanced before Ardres, where they remained drawn up for some time; but they knew nothing of the English being abroad, nor the English of them.

After the French had continued some time before Ardres, and saw that none attempted to sally from the town, they began their retreat towards the abbey of Liques. No sooner had they marched away than an Englishman privately left the place, and rode through lanes and cross-roads (for he knew the country well) until he met the lord de Gommegines and his party returning to Ardres, who, when he learnt the expedition of the French, slowly advanced with his men in a compact body.

When the French had passed Tournehem, having also had intelligence of the English being abroad under the command of the governor of Ardres, they immediately marched towards them, and placed an ambuscade in a coppice, above Liques, of three hundred lances, of which sir Hugh de Châtillon

Châtillon was the captain. The young count de St. Pol was ordered forward on the look-out, and with him weɵt many knights and ſquires.

Not far diſtant, by the ſide of a large hedge, the lord de Gommegines and ſir Walter Ukeues * had halted, and drawn up their force on foot in a very handſome manner. Sir John Harleſtone ſet off on a gallop, with twenty lances, to entice the French into this ambuſcade, ſaying he would allow himſelf to be purſued to the place where they were: he therefore entered the plain.

The young count de St. Pol, who was arrived thither with a hundred lances, ſpying ſir John Harleſtone's troop, called out to his companions, 'Forward, forward! here are our enemies.' Upon which they ſtuck ſpurs into their horſes, and haſtened as faſt as they could to come up with the Engliſh. But ſir John Harleſtone began his retreat, allowing them to purſue him until he came to the hedge where the Engliſh were drawn up, with their archers in front.

On the arrival of the French, the Engliſh received them with battle-axes, ſwords and ſpears: the archers began ſo briſk an attack that men and horſes were overthrown. Many gallant deeds were done; but in the end the French were ſurrounded, and the greater part ſlain. The young count de St. Pol was made priſoner by a ſquire of Gueldres: the lords de Pons and de Clary, ſir William de

* He is before called ſir John d'Ubruues.

Nielle, ſir Charles de Châtillon, Leonnet d'Araînes, Guy de Vaiſnel, Henry des Iſles and John his brother, the châtelain de Beauvais and ſeveral other knights and ſquires were alſo captured.

Shortly after this defeat, the lord de Châtillon came, with his banner and three hundred lances, to the path of the hedge; but, when he ſaw that his men were defeated, he wheeled about with his troops, and returned without ſtriking a blow: upon this, the Engliſh and Hainaulters led their priſoners to the town of Ardres.

The lord de Gommegines, that evening, bought the count de St. Pol from the ſquire who had taken him: he ſoon after carried him to England, and preſented him to the king, who thanked him kindly for ſo doing, and made him great preſents.

When the duke of Anjou and the conſtable were returned to Paris from Gaſcony, they found the archbiſhop of Rouen and the biſhop of Carpentras had been ſome time with the king. Theſe prelates continued their journey, and arrived at St. Omer. The duke of Lancaſter and the lord Bacinier had croſſed the ſea to Calais, and from thence went to Bruges. The duke of Anjou ſoon after came to St. Omer in grand array, and ſent for his couſin ſir Guy de Blois to meet him, who left Hainault handſomely equipped to wait on the duke.

The conſtable of France, the lords de Cliſſon, de la Val, and ſir Oliver de Maunny, with upwards of ſix hundred lances, had poſted themſelves on the

the frontiers between France and Flanders, near to Aire, la Croix, Bailleul, Caſſel, and in that neighbourhood, to guard the country, and to prevent any injury being offered to the count of Flanders; for he had not any great confidence in the negotiators, nor would he go to Bruges notwithſtanding their earneſt ſolicitations.

You have before heard how the garriſon of Becherel had held out for upwards of a year, and had entered into a capitulation to ſurrender, if they were not relieved before All-ſaints-day. When the day was near approaching, the king of France ordered thither many men at arms; and all the knights of Brittanny and Normandy were entreated to be there, except ſuch as were with the conſtable. The two marſhals of France, the lord Louis de Sancerre and Lord Mouton de Blainville, the earl of Harcourt, ſir James de Vienne admiral of France, the dauphin of Auvergne, ſir John de Bueil and ſeveral more arrived before Becherel. Theſe lords kept the day with great ſolemnity; but as none appeared to relieve the caſtle, it was ſurrendered, and thoſe who were ſo inclined left it. Sir John Appleyard and ſir John Cornwall marched out with their men, embarked and croſſed over to England. The barons of France took poſſeſſion of the place, which they repaired, re-victualled and reinforced with men, proviſion and artillery.

By orders from the king of France, theſe men at arms ſhortly after laid ſiege to St. Sauveur le

Vicomte in Coutantin, which had belonged to ſir John Chandos; and after his death the king of England had given it to ſir Alcyne Boxhull, who at that time was in England: he had left there as governor a ſquire called Carenton *, with ſir Thomas Cornet, John de Burgh, and the three brothers Maulevriers: there might be with them about ſix ſcore companions, all armed and ready for defence. St. Sauveur was firſt beſieged on the ſide next the ſea by ſir John de Vienne admiral of France, with all the barons and knights of Brittany and Normandy. There was alſo a large army before it, with plenty of every thing. Theſe lords of France had pointed large engines againſt it, which much harraſſed the garriſon.

* Probably Carrington.

CHAP.

CHAP. LIII.

A TRUCE AGREED ON AT BRUGES BETWEEN THE KINGS OF FRANCE AND ENGLAND.—THE DUKE OF BRITTANY RETIRES TO HIS OWN COUNTRY, AND REGAINS SOME OF HIS TOWNS AND CASTLES.

WE will now return to the noble negotiators at Bruges, that is to ſay, the dukes of Anjou * and Burgundy, the count de Saltzbourg, the biſhop of Amiens, the elected biſhop of Bayeux, the duke of Lancaſter, the earl of Saliſbury and the biſhop of London †. In order that no harm might happen to theſe Lords, nor to their people, who were going from one to the other, it was agreed there ſhould be a truce, to laſt to the firſt of May 1375, in all the country between Calais and the river Somme; but that it ſhould not interfere with the other parts of the country now at war. Upon this being done, the lords de Cliſſon and de la

* The hiſtorian of Languedoc ſays, the duke of Anjou was not preſent at this meeting, but in Avignon; and that, when the treaty was concluded, the duke of Burgundy ſent from Bruges orders for the ſénéſchal of Beaucaire to publiſh it.—Vol. iv. p. 357.

Paſſports were, however, granted to the duke of Anjou, by Edward, to come to Bruges.—RYMER.

† In addition, there were, ſir John Cobham, ſir Frank van Hall, ſir Arnold Savage, and maſter John Shepeye and maſter [illegible] doctors of laws.—See their warrant in Rymer.

Val

Val were ſent back to Brittany with their forces, to aſſiſt in guarding that country and the neighbouring frontiers.

During the time theſe negotiations were going forward at Bruges, the duke of Brittany, as has been before ſaid, remained in England, where he felt much for the diſtreſs of his country, the greater part of which had turned againſt him: his ducheſs alſo was beſieged and ſhut up in the caſtle of Auray. The duke, while he reſided with the king of England, was very melancholy: upon which the king, who much loved him, ſaid; 'Fair ſon, I well know that through your affection to me, you have put into the balance, and riſked, a handſome and noble inheritance: but be aſſured that I will recover it for you again, for I will never make peace with the French without your being reinſtated. On hearing theſe fine promiſes, the duke bowed reſpectfully to the king and humbly thanked him.

Soon after this converſation, the duke of Brittany aſſembled at Southampton two thouſand men at arms and three thouſand archers, who all received their pay for half a year in advance, by orders from the king of England*.

---

* Edward nominated the earl of Cambridge conjointly with the duke of Brittany his lieutenants in France, with full powers to act as they pleaſed, without prejudice to the rights of the duke or to the patrimony of the church, dated 24th November 1374.—See Rymer.

Among

Among the commanders were the earls of Cambridge and March, the lord de Spencer, ſir Thomas Holland, ſir Nicholas Camoire, ſir Edward Twiford, ſir Richard de Pontchardon, ſir John Leſley, ſir Thomas Granrſon, ſir Hugh Haſtings, the lords de Manne * and de la Pole, with many other knights and ſquires.

The duke and all his men at arms arived at St. Matthieu de Fine Pôterne in Brittany, where, after they had diſembarked, they attacked the caſtle very ſharply. This caſtle was out of the town, and ill ſupplied with men and artillery, ſo that the Engliſh took it by ſtorm, and ſlew all who were in it. When the inhabitants of the town, were informed of this, they opened their gates, and received the duke as their lord.

The Engliſh next advanced to the town of St. Pol de Léon, which was ſtrong and well incloſed. The duke took his ſtation, and, during a marvellouſly well conducted attack, the archers, who were poſted on the banks of the ditches, ſhot ſo excellently, and ſo much together, that ſcarcely any dared appear to defend them: the town was therefore taken and pillaged.

After this, they came before St. Brieu, which at that time was well provided with men at arms and all other proviſions and ſtores; for the lords de Cliſſon, de Beaumanoir, the viſcount de Rohan, and many other barons of Brittany, whoſe quarters were at Lamballe, had lately been there and had

* Q. Maine.

reinforced

reinforced it with every thing neceſſary. The duke and the Engliſh beſieged this town.

When the garriſon of St. Sauveur le Vicomte heard that the duke of Brittany and the Engliſh lords were arrived in Brittany, they expected them to come and raiſe their ſiege; which they much deſired, for they were greatly ſtraitened by the engines, which day and night caſt ſtones into the caſtle, ſo that they knew not where to retire to avoid them. Having called a council, they reſolved to make overtures to the French lords, to obtain a truce for ſix weeks, until Eaſter 1375; and propoſed, that if within that time there ſhould not come any relief, which might be ſufficient to offer battle and raiſe the ſiege, they would ſurrender themſelves, their lives and fortunes being ſpared, and the fortreſs ſhould be given up to the king of France. This treaty went off, and the ſiege continued; but no harm was further done to thoſe of St. Sauveur, for the beſiegers and garriſon were both inactive.

CHAP. LIV.

SOME BRETON LORDS OF THE FRENCH PARTY ARE NEAR BEING TAKEN BY THE DUKE OF BRITTANY, BUT ARE DELIVERED BY THE TRUCES AT BRUGES.

THE viſcount de Rohan, the lords de Cliſſon and de Beaumanoir were guarding the frontiers againſt the duke of Brittany and the Engliſh, at that time before St. Brieu. Sir John Devereux was then quartered near to Quimperlé, and was deſtroying that part of the country: he had cauſed to be repaired and fortified by the peaſants a ſmall fort which he had made his garriſon, and called it the New Fort, in which he reſided, ſo that none could venture out of the town without riſk of being taken. This information the townſmen of Quimperlé ſent to the lord de Cliſſon and the other lords at Lamballe.

They marched immediately thither, leaving a ſufficiency of men to guard that town, and rode on until they came before this new fort, which they ſurrounded. News of this was carried to the Britiſh army before St. Brieu. The duke had ordered a mine to be ſprung, which they had worked at for fifteen days; but at that moment the miners had loſt their point, ſo that it was neceſſary for them to begin another: which when the duke and the lords of his army heard, they ſaid among them-

ſelves;

ſelves; ' Every thing conſidered, we are but loſing time here: let us go to the aſſiſtance of ſir John Devereux, and if we ſhall be able to fall in with thoſe who are beſieging him in the open field, we ſhall perform a good exploit. Upon this, they held a council, and marched off, taking the road for the new fort, which the lords of Brittany were then aſſaulting. They had done ſo much that they were already at the foot of the walls, and dreaded not what might be thrown down upon them; for they were well ſhielded, but thoſe within the fort had not wherewithal to annoy them in that manner.

Juſt at this inſtant, a ſcout came with ſpeed to the lords of Brittany who were buſy at the aſſault, ſaying, ' My lords, make off in haſte from hence; for the Engliſh are coming with the duke of Brittany, and they are not more than two leagues off.' The trumpet ſounded a retreat: they collected themſelves together, called for their horſes, ſet off, and entered Quimperlé which was hard by. They cloſed the gates; but ſcarcely had they raiſed the draw-bridges, and ſtrengthened the barriers, when the duke of Brittany with the barons of England were before it. They had paſſed by the new fort, and ſpoken with ſir John Devereux, who thanked them exceedingly for coming, otherwiſe he muſt have been very ſhortly made priſoner.

The duke and the Engliſh formed the ſiege of Quimperlé, and ordered their archers and foot ſoldiers, well ſhielded, to advance, when a ſharp attack commenced; for the Engliſh, as well as thoſe

thoſe in the town were very determined; ſo that there were many wounded on both ſides. Every day there were ſuch ſkirmiſhes and aſſaults that thoſe in the town ſaw they ſhould not be able to hold out much longer, and there did not ſeem any likelihood of their receiving aſſiſtance. They could not eſcape any way without being ſeen, ſo well was the town ſurrounded; and if they ſhould be taken by ſtorm, they doubted if they ſhould receive any quarter, more eſpecially the lord de Cliſſon, for he was much hated by the Engliſh.

Theſe lords of Brittany opened a treaty with the duke to ſurrender; but they wanted to depart on a moderate ranſom, and the duke would have them ſurrender unconditionally: they could only obtain a reſpite for eight days, and that with very great difficulty. This reſpite, however, turned out very fortunate to them; for during that time two Engliſh knights, ſir Nicholas Carſwell and ſir Walter Ourſwick *, ſent by the duke of Lancaſter from Bruges, where he had remained the whole winter, arrived at the army of the duke of Brittany. They brought with them deeds engroſſed and ſealed of the truces entered into between the kings of France and England. The duke of Lancaſter ſent orders, that in conſequence of the treaty of Bruges, the army ſhould be diſbanded without delay. The truce was immediately read and proclaimed through the army, and ſignified alſo to thoſe who were within Quimperlé.

* Sir Nicholas Charnels—ſir Walter Urſwick.—BARNES

The

The lords de Cliſſon, de Rohan and de Beaumanoir, and the others, were much rejoiced thereat, for it came very opportunely.

The ſiege of Quimperlé being raiſed, the duke of Brittany diſbanded all his troops, except thoſe of his houſehold, and went to Auray, where his ducheſs was. The earls of Cambridge and of March, ſir Thomas Holland earl of Kent, the lord de Spencer and the other Engliſh returned home.

When the duke of Brittanny had ſettled his affairs at his leiſure, and had reinforced the towns and caſtles of Breſt and Auray with artillery and proviſions, he ſet out from Brittany with his ducheſs, and went for England.

CHAP. LV.

ST. SAUVEUR LE VICOMTE SURRENDERS TO THE FRENCH.—THE LORD DE COUCY LEADS A LARGE ARMY INTO AUSTRIA, WHICH HE CLAIMS AS HIS INHERITANCE.

ON the day in which the truces were concluded at Bruges between the kings of France and of England, to laſt for one whole year, including their allies, the dukes of Lancaſter and Burgundy again ſwore they would return thither on All-ſaint day. Each party was to keep, during this truce, whatever

whatever he was then in possession of. The English thought that the capitulation respecting St. Sauveur le Vicomte would be voided by this treaty; but the French would not allow of this, and said the treaty did not affect the prior engagement concerning it: so that, when the day arrived for its surrender, the king of France sent troops thither from all quarters. There were assembled before it upwards of six thousand knights and squires, without counting the others: but no succour came to its relief, and when the day was expired, St. Sauveur was given up to the French, but most unwillingly, for the fortress was very convenient for the English.

The governor sir Thomas Cornet, John de Burgh, the three brothers Maulevriers, and the English, went to Carentan, where having embarked all which belonged to them, they sailed for England *.

The constable of France reinforced the town and castle of St. Sauveur le Vicomte with a new garrison, and appointed a Breton knight as governor. I heard at the time, that the king of France gave him the lordship of it.

* Froissart has forgotten to add sir Thomas Carington among the governors of St. Sauveur le Vicomte. Nothing was said against him until the reign of Richard II. when he was accused of having treacherously given up this place by sir John Annesley, who had married sir John Chandos' niece: he challenged him to single combat, fought and vanquished him in the lists, formed in Palace yard in the presence of the king. He was afterwards drawn to Tyburn, and there hanged for his treason.--See Dugdale, Fabian, &c.

The lord de Coucy at this period returned to France: he had been a long time in Lombardy with the count de Vertus *, son of the lord Galeas Visconti, and had made war on lord Bernabo Visconti and his allies, for the cause of the church and of Gregory XI. who at that time was pope, and for the holy college of Rome.

The lord de Coucy, in right of succession to the lady his mother, who was sister to the duke of Austria last deceased, was the true heir of that duchy. The last duke did not leave any child by legal marriage, and the inhabitants of Austria had disposed of the estate in favour of a relation, but farther removed than the lord de Coucy. This lord had frequently complained of such conduct to the emperor, the lord Charles of Bohemia.

The emperor readily acknowledged the lord de Coucy's right; but he could not compel the Austrians to do the same, who were in great force in their own country, and had plenty of men at arms. The lord de Coucy had gallantly carried on the war against them several times, through the aid of one of his aunts, sister to the aforesaid duke; but he had not gained much. On the lord de Coucy's return to France, the king entertained him handsomely. Having considered there were

* John Galeas Visconti, first duke of Milan, bore the title of count de Vertus, until Wenceslaus king of the Romans, invested him with the ducal dignity 1395. He gained, by treachery, possession of his uncle Bernabo, and put him to death by poison—For further particulars, see Muratori and Corio.

numbers

numbers of men at arms in France then idle, on account of the truce between the French and Engliſh, he entreated the king to aſſiſt him in obtaining the free companies of Bretons, who were overrunning and haraſſing the kingdom, for him to lead them into Auſtria. The king, who wiſhed theſe companies any where but in his kingdom, readily aſſented to his requeſt. He lent, or gave, I know not which, ſixty thouſand francs, in order to get rid of theſe companions. They began their march towards Auſtria about Michaelmas, commiting many ravages wherever they paſſed. Many barons, knights and ſquires of France, Artois, Vermandois, Hainault and Picardy, ſuch as the viſcounts de Meaux and d'Aunay, ſir Raoul de Coucy, the baron de Roye, Pierre de Bar, and ſeveral others offered their ſervices to the lord de Coucy. His army was increaſed by all thoſe who wiſhed to advance themſelves in honour.

CHAP. LVI.

THE TRUCE BETWEEN FRANCE AND ENGLAND IS PROLONGED.—THE DEATH OF THE BLACK PRINCE.—THE LORD DE COUCY RETURNS, HAVING HAD INDIFFERENT SUCCESS.

WHEN the feaſt of All-ſaints was drawing near, the duke of Burgundy, the count de Saltzbourg, the biſhops of Amiens and of Bayeux came to Bruges by orders of the king of France, to hold a conference. The duke of Anjou ſtaid at St. Omer, where he continued the whole time.

From the king of England there came, the dukes of Lancaſter and Brittany, the earl of Saliſbury and the biſhop of London: ſo that the town of Bruges was well filled by their retinues, more eſpecially by that of the duke of Burgundy, who kept a moſt noble and grand ſtate.

Sir Robert de Namur reſided with the duke of Lancaſter, and ſhewed him every attention as long as he remained in Flanders.

The ambaſſadors from the pope, the archbiſhop of Rouen and the biſhop of Carpentras, were alſo there, who went to and fro to each party, propoſing different terms for an accommodation, but without any effect; for theſe lords, in their firſt parley, were too much divided to come to any agreement. The king of France demanded re-payment of fourteen hundred thouſand francs which had been given for

for king John's ranfom, and that the town of Calais fhould be difmantled. This the king of England would never confent to. The truces were therefore prolonged until the feaft of St. John the Baptift in the year 1376. The lords remained all that winter in Bruges, and fome time longer. In the fummer, each returned to his own country, except the duke of Brittany: he continued in Flanders with his coufin the count Louis, who entertained him handfomely.

In this year, on Trinity-Sunday, that flower of Englifh knighthood the lord Edward of England, prince of Wales and of Aquitaine, departed this life in the palace of Weftminfter near London. His body was embalmed, placed in a leaden coffin, and kept until the enfuing Michaelmas, in order that he might be buried with greater pomp and magnificence when the parliament affembled in London*.

King Charles of France, on account of his lineage, had funeral fervice for the prince performed with great magnificence, in the holy chapel of the palace in Paris, which was attended, according to the king's orders, by many prelates and nobles of the realm of France.

The truces, through the mediation of the ambaffadors, were again prolonged until the firft day of April.

---

* The prince of Wales was buried in the cathedral at Canterbury.—For particulars, fee Mr. Gough's Sepulchral Monuments.

We will now say something of the lord de Coucy and the Germans. When those of Austria and Germany heard that he was advancing with so strong a force to carry on the war against them, they burnt and destroyed three days march of country by the river side, and then they retreated to their mountains and inaccessible places.

The men at arms, of whom the lord de Coucy was the leader, expected to find plenty of forage, but they met with nothing: they suffered all this winter very great distress, and knew not in what place to seek provision for themselves, or forage for their horses, who were dying of cold, hunger and disorders: for this reason, when spring came, they returned to France, and separated into different troops to recruit themselves. The king of France sent the greater part of the companies into Brittany and lower Normandy, as he imagined he should have occasion for their services.

The lord de Coucy, on his return into France, began to think of becoming a good and true Frenchman; for he had found the king of France very kind and attentive to his concerns. His relationship to the king made him consider it was not worth his while to risk the loss of his inheritance, for so slender a reason as the war with the king of England; for he was a Frenchman by name, arms, blood and extraction. He therefore sent the lady his wife to England, and kept with him only the eldest of his two daughters: the youngest had been left in England, where she had been educated.

The

The king of France ſent the lord de Coucy to attend the negotiations carrying on at Bruges, which continued all the winter. None of the great lords were there, except the duke of Brittany, who had ſtaid with his couſin the count of Flanders; but he entered very little into the buſineſs.

CHAP. LVII.

RICHARD, SON OF THE PRINCE OF WALES, IS ACKNOWLEDGED AS PRESUMPTIVE HEIR TO THE CROWN OF ENGLAND.—THE NEGOTIATIONS FOR PEACE HAVING FAILED, AND THE TRUCES EXPIRED, THE WAR IS RENEWED BETWEEN THE FRENCH AND ENGLISH.

AFTER the feaſt of Michaelmas, when the funeral of the prince had been performed in a manner ſuitable to his birth and merit, the king of England cauſed the young prince Richard to be acknowledged as his ſucceſſor to the crown after his deceaſe, by all his children, the duke of Lancaſter, the earl of Cambridge, the lord Thomas his youngeſt ſon, as well as by all the barons, earls, prelates and knights of England. He made them ſolemnly ſwear to obſerve this; and on Chriſtmas-day he had him ſeated next to himſelf, above all his children, in royal ſtate, that it might be ſeen and declared he was to be king of England after his death.

The lord John Cobham, the biſhop of Hereford and the dean of London were at this time ſent to Bruges on the part of the Engliſh. The French had ſent thither the count de Saltzbourg, the lord de Châtillon and maſter Philibert l'Eſpiote.' The prelates, ambaſſadors from the pope, had ſtill remained there, and continued the negotiations for peace.

They treated of a marriage between the young ſon of the prince and the lady Mary, daughter of the king of France: after which, the negotiators of each party ſeparated, and reported what they had done to their reſpective kings.

About Shrovetide, a ſecret treaty was formed between the two kings for their ambaſſadors to meet at Montrieul ſur mer; and the king of England ſent to Calais ſir Guiſcard d'Angle, ſir Richard Sturey and ſir Geoffry Chaucer. On the part of the French were, the lords de Coucy and de la Rivieres, ſir Nicholas Bragues and Nicholas Bracier. They for a long time diſcuſſed the ſubject of the above marriage; and the French, as I was informed, made ſome offers, but the others demanded different terms, or refuſed treating. Theſe lords returned therefore, with their treaties, to their ſovereigns; and the truces were prolonged to the firſt of May.

The earl of Saliſbury, the biſhop of St. David's, chancellor of England, and the biſhop of Hereford, returned

returned to Calais; and with them, by orders of the king of France, the lord de Coucy, and sir William de Dormans chancellor of France.

Notwithstanding all that the prelates could say or argue, they never could be brought to fix upon any place to discuss these treaties between Montrieul and Calais, nor between Montreuil and Boulogne, nor on any part of the frontiers; these treaties, therefore, remained in an unfinished state. When the war recommenced, sir Hugh Calverley was sent governor of Calais.

CHAP. LVIII.

POPE GREGORY XI. LEAVES AVIGNON, AND RETURNS TO ROME.—ON THE DEATH OF EDWARD III. RICHARD, SON OF THE LATE PRINCE OF WALES, IS CROWNED KING OF ENGLAND.

WHEN pope Gregory XI. who had for a long time resided at Avignon, was informed there was not any probability of a peace being concluded between the two kings, he was very melancholy, and, having arranged his affairs, set out for Rome, to hold there his seat of government.

The

The duke of Brittany, finding the war was to be renewed, took leave of his coufin the count of Flanders, with whom he had refided upwards of a year, and rode towards Gravelines, where the earl of Salifbury and fir Guifcard d'Angle, with a body of men at arms and archers, came to meet him, to efcort him to Calais, where the duke tarried a month: he then croffed over to England and went to Shene, a few miles from London, on the river Thames, where the king of England lay dangeroufly ill: he departed this life the vigil of St. John the Baptift, in the year 1377.

Upon this event, England was in deep mourning. Immediately all the paffes were fhut, fo that no one could go out of the country; for they did not wifh the death of the king fhould be known in France, until they had fettled the government of the kingdom. The earl of Salifbury and fir Guifcard d'Angle returned at this time to England.

The body of king Edward was carried in grand proceffion, followed by his children in tears, and by the nobles and prelates of England, through the city of London, with his face uncovered, to Weftminfter, where he was buried by the fide of his lady the queen.

Shortly afterward, in the month of July, the young king Richard, who was in his eleventh year, was crowned with great folemnity at the palace of Weftminfter: he was fupported by the dukes of Lancafter and Brittany. He created that

that day four earls and nine knights, namely, his uncle the lord Thomas of Woodſtock earl of Buckingham, the lord Percy earl of Northumberland, ſir Guiſcard d'Angle earl of Huntingdon, and the lord Mowbray earl of Nottingham.

The young king was placed under the tutorſhip of that accompliſhed knight ſir Guiſcard d'Angle, with the approbation of all, to inſtruct him in the paths of virtue and honour. The duke of Lancaſter had the government of the kingdom.

As ſoon as the king of France learnt the death of king Edward, he ſaid, that he had reigned moſt nobly and valiantly, and that his name ought to be remembered with honour among heroes. Many nobles and prelates of his realm were aſſembled, to perform his obſequies with due reſpect, in the holy chapel of the palace at Paris.

Shortly after, madame, the eldeſt daughter of the king of France, died. She had been betrothed to that gallant youth William of Hainault, eldeſt ſon of duke Albert.

CHAP. LIX.

THE KING OF FRANCE EQUIPS FOR SEA A LARGE FLEET, WHICH BURNS SEVERAL TOWNS IN ENGLAND.

DURING the negotiations for peace, the king of France had been very active in providing ships and galleys: the king of Spain had sent him his admiral, sir Fernando Sausse, who, with sir John de Vienne, admiral of France, had sailed for the port of Rye, which they burnt, five days after the decease of king Edward, the vigil of St. Peter, in June, and put to death the inhabitancs, without sparing man or woman.

Upon the news of this event coming to London, the earls of Cambridge and Buckingham were ordered to Dover with a large body of men at arms: The earl of Salisbury and sir John Mountague, on the other hand, were sent to the country near Southampton.

After this exploit, the French landed in the isle of Wight. They afterwards burnt the following towns: Portsmouth, Dartmouth, Plymouth, and several others. When they had pillaged and burnt all in the isle of Wight, they embarked and put to sea, coasting the shores until they came to a port called Poq *.

* Q. if not Pool.

The earl of Salisbury and sir John Mountague defended the passage, but they burnt a part of the town of Poq. They again embarked, and coasted towards Southampton, attempting every day to land; but the earl of Salisbury and his forces, who followed them along the shore, prevented them from so doing.

The fleet then came before Southampton; but sir John Arundel, with a large body of men at arms and archers, guarded well the town, otherwise it would have been taken. The French made sail from thence towards Dover, and landed near to the abbey of Lewes, where there were great numbers of the people of the country assembled. They appointed the abbot of Lewes, sir Thomas Cheney and sir John Fuselée their leaders, who drew up in good array to dispute their landing, and to defend the country. The French had not the advantage, but lost several of their men, as well might happen. However, the better to maintain the fight, they made the land, when a grand skirmish ensued, and the English, being forced to retreat, were finally put to flight. Two hundred at least were slain, and the two knights, with the abbot of Lewes made prisoners.

The French re-embarked, and remained at anchor before the abbey all that night. They then heard for the first time, from their prisoners, the death of king Edward and the coronation of king Richard, and also a part of the regulations of the kingdom, and that great numbers

bers of men at arms were under orders to march to the coaſt.

Sir John de Vienne diſpatched a ſloop to Havre, where there was a knight in waiting, who immediately rode to Paris to the king, and reported to him ſuch intelligence reſpecting the death of king Edward that he was convinced of its truth.

The French and Spaniards put to ſea, and, having the wind favourable, came with an eaſy ſail that ſame tide, about the hour of nine, before Dover. They amounted in all to about ſix ſcore galleys. At that time there were in Dover the earls of Cambridge and Buckingham, with immenſe numbers of men at arms and archers, who, with a hundred thouſand common men, were waiting for the arrival of the French, drawn up before the port with diſplayed banners, for they had ſeen them at a diſtance, and they were continually joined by people from the country who had noticed this large fleet.

The French came before the harbour, but did not enter it, making for deep water, as the tide began to ebb. Notwithſtanding this, the Engliſh continued ſtrict guard all that day and following night.

The French who were on the ſea came with the next tide before Calais, to the great ſurpriſe of the inhabitants, who cloſed their gates againſt them.

CHAP. LX.

THE TOWN OF ARDRES SURRENDERS TO THE FRENCH.—THE DEATHS OF THE CAPTAL DE BUCH AND OF THE QUEEN OF FRANCE.

WHILE these things were paſſing, ſir Hugh Calverley governor of Calais, ſir John Harleſtone governor of Guines, and the lord de Gommegines governor of Ardes, made very frequent excurſions into Picardy, three or four in every week. They advanced often before St. Omer, Arques, Mouton, Fiennes, and the towns in that neighbourhood, as well as to Boulogne and near to Terouenne, which were particularly moleſted by the garriſon of Ardres. Complaints of them had frequently been made to the king of France. On aſking how this was to be prevented, he was anſwered, ' Sire, the garriſon of Ardres is not ſo ſtrong but it may be won.' The king replied, ' Have it then we will, whatever it may coſt us.' He ſoon after iſſued a ſecret ſummons, and it was not gueſſed to what part he intended ſending this army, of which he made the duke of Burgundy general. There were in it twenty-five hundred lances of good and hardy men. They marched ſuddenly to the caſtle of Ardres, which they inveſted.

With the duke of Burgundy were the count de Guines, the marſhal de Blainville, the lords de Cliſſon and de la Val, de Rougemont, de la Riviere,

Riviere, de Bregide, de Frainville, d'Ainville, d'Ancoing, de Rayneval, and d'Angeſt, ſir James de Bourbon, the ſénéſchal of Hainault, with many other knights and barons. They had with them machines that caſt ſtones of two hundred weight, with which they made a moſt vigorous aſſault.

The lord de Gommegines, captain of the caſtle, was aſtoniſhed to ſee himſelf ſurrounded by ſuch numbers of gallant men at arms, who ſeemed determined, that if the place were taken by ſtorm, they would ſpare no one they ſhould find within it. As he was not provided with artillery for a long ſiege, through the mediation of his couſin-german, the lord de Rayneval, he offered to enter into a treaty for ſurrendering the place, on condition of their lives and fortunes being ſpared. This treaty was long debated; but at length the caſtle was ſurrendered, and all who choſe it departed, and were conducted by ſir Walter de Bailleul to the town of Calais.

Sir William des Bordes was appointed governor of Ardres: he was ſucceeded by the viſcount de Meaux, who remained there a long time: the third governor was the lord de Saimpy.

The ſame day that Ardres ſurrendered, the duke laid ſiege to the caſtle of Ardvick, which the three brothers Maulevriers held for England. During the three days he ſtaid there, many ſkirmiſhes paſſed, but they at laſt ſurrendered, and the garriſon was conducted to Calais by the marſhal of France.

After this, the duke beſieged Vauclignen, which alſo

alſo ſurrendered on the ſame terms as the others had done; and, when the duke had re-victualled and reinforced them with men at arms and croſs-bows, he diſbanded his army and returned to the king at Paris. The Breton lords went to Brittany, for they had heard that the duke of Brittany had arrived at Breſt with a large army. The barons of Burgundy and the others returned to their own homes.

You have before heard how the lord John captal de Buch, having been made priſoner before Soubiſe, was confined in the Temple at Paris. The king of England and his ſon greatly deſired his liberty, and it had been much debated at the negotiations at Bruges: they would willingly have given in exchange for him the young count de St. Pol and three or four other knights: but the king of France and his council would not conſent. The king had him informed through the grand prior, who had the guard of him, that if he would ſwear never to bear arms againſt the crown of France, he would liſten to terms for his liberty. The captal replied, that he would never make this oath, though he were to die in priſon. He remained therefore ſtrictly guarded for five years in confinement, to his great diſcomfort; for he bore it ſo impatiently that at laſt he died *.

* The prince of Wales gave to the captal de Buch, and his male heirs, the county of Bigorre, with all its towns, &c. the 7th June 1369. Confirmed by the king.—RYMER.

The king of France had him interred; and a solemn service was performed, which was attended by the barons, prelates and nobles of France.

England was thus losing her great captains; for, in this same year, the lord de Spencer, a great banneret of England, died. He left issue by his lady, the daughter of the late sir Bartholomew Burghersh, one son and four daughters.

Soon after the death of that gallant knight the captal de Buch, the queen of France was brought to bed of a daughter, who was named Catherine; and, whilst in childbed, the queen was seized with an illness that caused her death. This amiable queen was daughter of the valiant duke of Bourbon, killed at the battle of Poitiers. Her obsequies were performed in the abbey of St. Denis, where she was buried with great solemnity, to which were invited all the nobles and prelates of France in the neighbourhood of Paris.

CHAP. LXI.

THE WAR RECOMMECES BETWEEN THE KING OF FRANCE AND THE KING OF NAVARRE.—THE SIEGE OF CHERBOURG.—THE DUKE OF LANCASTER INVADES BRITTANY.—THE CASTLE OF AURAY SURRENDERS TO THE FRENCH.

SINCE the peace made at Vernon between the kings of France and Navarre, as has been before related, and since the king of Navarre had left

left his two children with their uncle the king of France, suspicions had fallen on a squire of the king's household. He had been placed there by the king of Navarre at the time he left his children: his name was James de la Rue. A lawyer, who was one of the king of Navarre's council, and his chancellor in the county of Evreux, was also implicated in this business: the name of this chancellor was master Peter du Tertre.

These two men were cruelly executed at Paris, and acknowledged, before all the people, that they had intended to have poisoned the king of France. The king immediately collected a large army, the command of which he gave to the constable: there were with him the lord de la Riviere and many other barons and knights. They marched into Normandy, to attack the castles of the king of Navarre, which were strong and well garrisoned, and laid siege to one of them called Pont au demer*. The French had with them many cannon, and various engines and machines, with which, in the course of different assaults, they pressed the garrison hard; but they defended themselves valiantly. Though there were many attacks and skirmishes, the siege lasted a long time: the castle was much ruined, and the garrison hard pushed. They were frequently required by the constable to surrender, or they would all be put to death, if the place were taken by storm: this

* Pont au demer,—a town in Normandy, on the Rille, 41 leagues from Paris

was the threat which the conſtable was accuſtomed to make.

The men of Navarre ſeeing their proviſions decreaſe, and finding themſelves much weakened, without any hopes of aſſiſtance from their king, who was at too great a diſtance, ſurrendered the caſtle, and were conducted to Cherbourg, carrying with them all their plunder.

This caſtle was razed to the ground, though it had coſt large ſums to erect; and the walls and towers of Pont au demer were levelled with the ground.

The French then advanced to beſiege the fortreſs of Mortain*, where they remained ſome time; but the garriſon, ſeeing no appearance of aſſiſtance from the king of Navarre, and that the other Navarre fortreſſes were too weak to reſiſt the French, ſurrendered themſelves on the ſame conditions with thoſe of Pont au demer.

You muſt know, that in this expedition, the conſtable put under the obedience of the king of France all the towns, caſtles, and forts in the county of Evreux: the caſtles and principal towns were diſmantled, that from henceforward no war ſhould be carried on againſt the kingdom of France from any town or caſtle which the king of Navarre held in the county of Evreux.

The king of France eſtabliſhed in them the gabelle and ſubſidies, in like manner as they were in the realm of France.

* Mortain,—a town in Normandy, 71 leagues from Paris.

On

On the other hand, the king of Spain had ordered his brother, the baſtard of Spain, to enter Navarre with a powerful army: he attacked towns and caſtles, and gained much country, in ſpite of the king of Navarre, who could do but little to defend himſelf. He ſent to inform king Richard of England how he was ſituated, in the hope that he would aid him in oppoſing the king of France in his county of Evreux; for that he himſelf would remain in Navarre, to guard his fortreſſes againſt the king of Spain.

King Richard, in conſequence of a council which had been called on this buſineſs, ſent ſir Robert le Roux* with a body of men at arms and archers, to Cherbourg. The garriſons of the different fortreſſes won by the conſtable in the county of Evreux were alſo collected at that town.

When all were aſſembled, they were a numerous and handſome body of picked men, who had provided the caſtle with ſtores, for they concluded it would be beſieged.

The conſtable and the lord de la Riviere, having viſited every place in the county of Evreux with their army, found that all the towns formerly belonging to the king of Navarre were now under the obedience of the king of France: they then came before Cherbourg, which is a ſtrong and noble place, founded by Julius Cæſar, when he conquered England, and likewiſe a ſea-port.

---

* Probably ſir Robert Rooſe, or Rouſe.

The French besieged it on all sides except that of the sea, and took up their quarters in such a manner before it as shewed they were determined not to quit until they had conquered it. Sir Robert le Roux and his forces made frequent sallies, for neither night nor day passed without skirmishing. The French could never form a wish for feats of arms but there were always some ready to gratify it. Many combats took place with lance and sword, and several were killed or taken prisoners on each side, during this siege, which lasted the whole summer.

Sir Oliver du Guesclin posted himself in an ambuscade near the castle: he then ordered his men to begin a skirmish, in which the French were repulsed by the English, and driven back as far as the ambuscade of sir Oliver, who immediately rushed out with his troop, sword in hand, and advanced boldly on the enemy, like men well practised in arms.

The encounter was sharp on both sides, and many a man was unhorsed, killed, wounded, or made prisoner: at last, sir Oliver du Guesclin was taken, and avowed himself a prisoner to a Navarrois squire, called John le Coq, an able man at arms: he was dragged into Cherbourg. The skirmish was now over, more to the loss of the French than of the English. Sir Oliver was sent to England, where he remained prisoner for a long time in London, and was at last ransomed.

The French remained before Cherbourg, at a heavy expense, the greater part of the winter, without

without having gained much. They thought they were losing time, and that Cherbourg was impregnable, as all sorts of reinforcements, men at arms, provision and stores, might be introduced into it by sea, for which reason the French broke up their camp, and placed strong garrisons in the places round Cherbourg, such as Montbourg, Pont Doue, Carentan, St. Lo, and in St. Sauveur le Vicomte. The constable then disbanded his army, and every one returned to the place whence he came. This was in the year 1378.

You have before heard how the duke of Brittany had left that country, and had carried his duchess with him to England. He resided at the estate he had there, which was called the honour of Richmond, and took great pains to obtain assistance from the young king, Richard, to reconquer his duchy, which had turned to the French, but he was not listened to. At length, the duke of Lancaster was informed, that if he landed in Brittany with a good army, there were some forts and castles that would surrender to him: in particular, St. Malo, a handsome fortress, and a seaport town. Upon this, the duke of Lancaster, having raised a large army, went to Southampton. He there prepared his vessels and stores, and embarked with many lords, men at arms and archers.

This fleet had favourable winds to St. Malo; and when near the shore, having landed and disembarked their stores, they advanced towards the town, and closely besieged it. The inhabitants were not much alarmed, for they were well pro-

 vided

vided with proviſion, men at arms and croſs-bows, who valiantly defended themſelves, ſo that the duke remained there a conſiderable time.

When the conſtable of France and the lord de Cliſſon heard of this, they ſent ſummonſes every where, and marched to St. Malo to raiſe the ſiege. Many thought that a battle muſt enſue, and the Engliſh drew out their army ſeveral times in battle-array, ready for the combat; but the conſtable and the lord de Cliſſon never came near enough for an engagement.

The Engliſh, therefore, having lain before the town ſome time, and not perceiving any inclination in the inhabitants to ſurrender, the duke of Lancaſter was adviſed to decamp, for he ſaw it was only waſting time: he therefore re-embarked, and returned to England, where he diſmiſſed his army.

The caſtle of Auray was ſtill in the poſſeſſion of the duke of Brittany, who reſided quietly in England: the king of France ſent thither ſeveral lords of France and Britanny, who began a ſiege which laſted a long time. The garriſon of Auray, not ſeeing any hope of ſuccour, entered into a treaty, that if they were not relieved by the duke of Brittany or the king of England, with a ſufficient force to raiſe the ſiege on a certain day, they would ſurrender. This treaty was acceded to; and when the appointed day arrived, the French were there, but no one came from the duke nor the king of England: the caſtle was therefore placed under the obedience of the king of of France, in the ſame manner as the other caſtles and principal towns of Brittany; and thoſe of Auray, who were attached to the duke departed thence.

CHAP. LXII.

THE FRENCH GARRISON OF MONTBOURG IS DEFEATED BY THE ENGLISH AT CHERBOURG.

SOON after Eaſter, in the year of our Lord 1379, king Charles of France, finding the garriſon of Cherbourg was oppreſſing the whole country of Coutantin, appointed ſir William des Bourdes, a valiant knight and good captain, to be chief governor of Coutantin, and of all the fortreſſes round Cherbourg.

Sir William des Bourdes went thither with a handſome body of men at arms and genoeſe croſſbows, and fixed his quarters at Montbourg, which he made a garriſon againſt Cherbourg; whence he formed frequent expeditions, and would willingly have met with the men of Cherbourg; for he wiſhed for nothing better than an engagement with them, as he felt himſelf a good knight, bold and enterpriſing, and had alſo under his command the flower of the men at arms from all the adjacent garriſons.

About the ſame time, ſir John Harleſtone was ſent to Cherbourg, to take command of it. I have

have before mentioned him as having been governor of Guines. He had embarked at Southampton with three hundred men at arms and as many archers, and with them had safely arrived at Cherbourg. There were in this army sir Otho de Grantson*, and among the English sir John Aubourc†, sir John Orcelle‡, with other knights and squires.

On their arrival, they disembarked their horses and armour, with other stores, and remained some days in Cherbourg to recruit themselves, and make preparations for expeditions and for carrying on the war in earnest.

Sir William des Bourdes puzzled himself day and night in endeavouring to find out some means of annoying them. You must know, that these two governors laid several ambuscades for each other, but with little effect; for by chance they never met, except some few companions, who adventured themselves fool-hardily, as well to acquire honour as gain: these parties frequently attacked each other: sometimes the French won, at others they lost.

Such skirmishes continued so often that sir William des Bourdes marched out one morning from Montbourg, with his whole force, towards

* Sir Otho de Grantson—was before mentioned, not as an Englishman, but as one who had an estate on the other side of the sea.

† Sir John Aubourc. May it not be Aubrey.

‡ Sir John Orcelle. Perhaps Worsley, or Horseley.

Cher-

Cherbourg, in hopes of drawing that garriſon out into the plain.

On the other hand, ſir John Harleſtone, who was ignorant of the intentions of the French, had alſo that ſame morning made an excurſion, and had commanded his trumpets to ſound for his men to arm themſelves, as well horſe as foot, and to advance into the plain: he had already ordered who were to remain in the garriſon. He marched forth in handſome diſplay, and ordered ſir John Orcelle, with his foot-ſoldiers, to take the lead as their guide. Having done this, he ſent forward his light troops. Sir William des Bourdes had made a ſimilar arrangement of his army. They both advanced in this array until the light troops of each party met, and came ſo near that they could eaſily diſtinguiſh each other. Upon which, they returned to the main body, and reported all they had obſerved.

The two leaders, on hearing their reports, were quite happy, for they had at laſt found what they had been ſeeking for, and were much rejoiced thus to meet.

When the two knights had heard the news from their light troops, they each drew up their forces with great wiſdom, and ordered their pennons to be diſplayed. The Engliſh foot were intermixed with their men at arms. As ſoon as they were within bow-ſhot, the French diſmounted; ſo did likewiſe the Engliſh: then the archers and croſſbowmen began to ſhoot ſharply, and the men at arms

arms to advance with their lances before them in close order. The armies met, and blows with ſpears and battle-axes began to fly about on all ſides. The battle was hardly fought, and one might there have ſeen men at arms make trial of their prowess.

Sir William des Bourdes was completely armed, and, with his battle-axe in his hand, gave ſuch blows to the right and left that on whomſoever they fell that perſon was ſtruck to the ground. He performed valorous deeds, worthy of being praiſed for ever after; and it was not his fault the Engliſh were not diſcomfited.

In another part of the field, ſir John Harleſtone, governor of Cherbourg, fought well and valiantly with his battle-axe, one foot advanced before the other; and well it needed him, for he had to do with an obſtinate body of hardy men. Several gallant deeds were performed this day; many a man ſlain and wounded. Sir John Harleſtone was ſtruck down, and in great peril of his life; but by force of arms he was reſcued. The battle laſted long, and was excellently kept up, as well on one ſide as on the other. The Engliſh had not any advantage, for they had as many killed and wounded as the French, but at laſt the Engliſh continued the combat ſo manfully, and with ſuch courage, that they gained the field: the French were all either ſlain or made priſoners: few men of honour ſaved themſelves, for they had entered into the engagement with ſo much good heart that they could not prevail on themſelves to fly, but were determined to die or to conquer their enemies.

Sir

Sir William de Bourdes was made priſoner on good terms by a ſquire from Hainault, called William de Beaulieu, an able man at arms, who for a conſiderable time had been attached to the Engliſh in the caſtle of Calais: to him ſir William ſurrendered in great grief, and much enraged that the victory was not his.

The Engliſh that day did much harm to the French. Several were made priſoners towards the end of the engagement; but it was a pity to ſee the numbers killed.

When the Engliſh had ſtripped the dead, ſir John Harleſtone and his men returned to Cherbourg, carrying with them their priſoners and their riches. You may be aſſured that they rejoiced mightily in the ſucceſs of this day, which God had given to them. Sir William des Bourdes was feaſted and entertained with every poſſible attention; for he was perſonally deſerving of whatever could be done for him.

This defeat took place, between Montbourg and Cherbourg, the day of St. Martin *le bouillant* 1379.

When the king of France heard that the garriſon of Montbourg and its governor were either ſlain or made priſoners, and that the country was much alarmed by this defeat, the king, like one well adviſed and attentive to his affairs, immediately provided a remedy, by ſending, without delay, freſh troops to guard the frontiers, the fortreſſes and the country round Cherbourg. Sir Hutin de Bremalles was appointed general of theſe

troops

Whilst the duke of Burgundy was with his army in Picardy, as I have before said, the duke of troops by the king of France, who kept the country against the English.

However, by orders of the king, they afterwards abandoned Montbourg, and all the country of Coutantin, which is one of the richest in the world. They made all the inhabitants give up their handsome houses and other possessions, and retreat out of this peninsula. The French guarded the frontiers at Dune, Carentan, and at St. Lo, and all the borders of the peninsula of Coutantin.

CHAP LXIII.

THE DUKE OF ANJOU UNDERTAKES AN EXPEDITION AGAINST THE ENGLISH IN THE BOURDELOIS.

YOU have before heard related how the duke of Burgundy had made an incursion from the borders of Picardy, which was very honourable to him and profitable to the French; and how he had placed in Ardres, and the other castles of which he had gained possession, governors and men at arms to defend them: especially in the town of Ardres, where he had established for a time sir William des Bourdes, and, in his absence, the viscount de Meaux and the lord de Saimpy. These captains had it repaired and strengthened, notwithstanding it was strongly fortified before.

The king of France had heard the news of this with infinite pleaſure, and conſidered this expedition as having done him great ſervice. He ſent immediate orders to the governor of St. Omer, commanding the town of Ardres to be reinforced and provided with every kind of ſtore and proviſion in the moſt ample manner: which orders were punctually obeyed.

The army was diſbanded, except the troops which were attached to the lord de Cliſſon and the Bretons; but they returned as ſpeedily as they could into Brittany, for news had been brought to the lord de Cliſſon and the other barons before Ardres, that Janequin le Clerc*, an Engliſh ſquire and an expert man at arms, had ſailed from England to Brittany, and had reinforced Breſt with Engliſhmen. Theſe Bretons, therefore, carried with them ſir James de Verchin, ſénéſchal of Hainault. The duke of Burgundy returned to his brother the king of France.

At this period, there was a large body of men at arms aſſembled on the borders of the Bourdelois, in obedience to the ſummons of the duke of Anjou and the conſtable of France, who had appointed a day for attacking the Gaſcons and Engliſh, of which I ſhall ſpeak more fully when better informed than I am at preſent.

---

* Janequin le Clerc,—I imagine to be ſir John Clark, of whom Hollingſhed ſpeaks ſo handſomely in the 3d of Richard II. and who was killed in a battle at a ſea port in Brittany—See Hollingſhed.

Whilſt

Anjou reſided in the good town of Toulouſe with the ducheſs his lady, and was deviſing, night and day, different ſchemes to annoy and harraſs the Engliſh; for he found that various caſtles and towns on the river Dordonne, and on the borders of Rouergue, the Toulouſain and Querci, were ſtill harraſſing the country and thoſe inhabitants who had put themſelves under his obedience. He was anxious to provide a remedy for this, and reſolved to lay ſiege to Bergerac, this place being the key to Gaſcony, and ſtanding on the frontiers of Rouergue, Querci and Limouſin. But as he found there were yet ſeveral great barons of Gaſcony adverſe to him, ſuch as the lords de Duras, de Roſem, de Mucident, de Langurant, de Guernoles, de Carles, and ſir Peter de Landuras, with many more, he determined to raiſe a large force that would not only enable him to oppoſe theſe lords but to keep the field.

He wrote, therefore, to ſir John d'Armagnac, who, in ſuch a buſineſs, would not fail him, and ſent alſo to the lord d'Albret. He had before ſent for the conſtable of France, the lord Louis de Sancerre, the lord de Coucy and many knights and ſquires, in Picardy, Brittany and Normandy, who were all willing to ſerve him and to advance their reputation in arms and renown. The conſtable and marſhal of France were already arrived.

The duke of Anjou knew that there exiſted a coolneſs between the relations and friends of the lord de Pommiers, and ſir Thomas Felton, high ſéneſchal of Bourdeaux, and the Bourdelois. I will

will tell you the reaſon of it, and afterwards clear it up.

Long before this period, in the year 1375, there was a cruel inſtance of juſtice executed at Bourdeaux by the orders of ſir Thomas Felton, lieutenant for the king of England in the Bourdelois, upon ſir William lord de Pommiers, on ſuſpicion of treaſon, which aſtoniſhed every one.

By orders of ſir Thomas Felton, this lord de Pommiers was arreſted in Bourdeaux, together with a lawyer, his ſecretary and counſellor, called John Coulon, a native of Bourdeaux. It was proved on them (as I was at the time informed), that the lord de Pommiers had agreed to ſurrender himſelf and all his caſtles to the French; from which charge they could never clear themſelves, ſo that they were condemned to death.

The lord de Pommiers and his ſecretary were publicly beheaded in the market-place of the city of Bourdeaux, before all the people, who much wondered thereat*. His relations blamed this proceeding exceedingly, and that gallant knight, ſir Aymon de Pommiers, uncle to ſir William, ſet out from Bourdeaux and the Bourdelois very

---

* A. D. 1377, 1378.

Rotuli Vaſconiæ de anno primo Ricardi II—Membrana 16, 17, 18, 19.

1 Proceſſus judicii redditi contra Wilhelmum Sans, dominum de Pomers, pro proditione, in curia Vaſconiæ, et de Caſtris et terris ſuis ſatisfactis ad dominum regem.

indignant at ſuch a diſgrace to his family, and ſwore he would never again bear arms for the king of England. He croſſed the ſeas to the holy ſepulchre, and made ſeveral other voyages. On his return, he changed to the French intereſt, placing himſelf and his territories under the obedience of the king of France. He immediately ſent his challenge to the lord de l'Eſparre, and made war upon him, becauſe he had been one of the judges of his nephew.

Sir John Bleſſac, ſir Peter de Landuras and ſir Bertrand du Franc were alſo implicated in theſe ſuſpicions of treaſon, as well as on account of the ſurrender of the caſtle of Fronſac, which had been delivered up to the French, it being the inheritance of the lord de Pommiers who had been beheaded: they were detained in priſon at Bourdeaux upwards of ſeven months. They were at length ſet at liberty, through the entreaties of their friends, for nothing could be proved againſt them. Sir Gaillard Vighier, however, continued a long time in imminent danger, which ſurpriſed many, as he was not of that country, but had come from Lombardy with the lord de Coucy, and was in the ſervice of pope Gregory, who exerted himſelf in his deliverance as ſoon as he heard of his impriſonment, the knight having inſiſted on his innocence.

By theſe means, much ſecret hatred was cauſed, from which many miſchiefs enſued.

When the duke of Anjou ſaw the time was arrived for his marching from Toulouſe, and that

the

the greater part of his men at arms were in the field; in particular, the conftable of France, in whom he had the greateft confidence; he fet out from Touloufe, and took the direct road to Bergerac. Sir Perducas d'Albret was governor of the place: he refided in a fmall caftle, a fhort league from Languedoc, called Moueux, which is a ftrong fort.

The duke of Anjou and his army marched until they came before Bergerac, when they encamped themfelves all around it, and as near the river as poffible for the greater eafe of themfelves and their horfes. Many great barons were with the duke: in the firft place, fir John d'Armagnac, with a large troop; the conftable of France with another large body; the lord Louis de Sancerre, fir John de Bueil, fir Peter de Bueil, fir Evan of Wales, fir Maurice de Trifiquidi (who had formerly been one of the thirty knights on the French fide at the duel in Brittany), fir Alain de Beaumont, fir Alain de la Houffaye, fir William and fir Peter de Mornay, fir John de Vers, fir Baldwin Cremoux, Thibaut du Pont, Heliot de Calais, and many other able men at arms with large companies. They encamped themfelves to a great extent in thofe fine meadows along the river Dordonne, fo that it was a great pleafure to look at them.

The conftable was lodged very near to the quarters of the duke. Thofe companions who were defirous of advancing themfelves frequently came to the barriers to fkirmifh; many of whom were

 flain

ſlain or wounded by arrows, as in ſuch adventures muſt happen.

At the end of ſix days after the town of Bergerac had been beſieged, the lord d'Albret and ſir Bernard d'Albret, his couſin, arrived in the camp of the duke, well accompanied by men at arms and foot-ſoldiers, where they were received with joy, as the army was by them greatly reinforced.

The duke, with the principal leaders of the army, held a council on the eighth day, to conſider in what manner they could moſt effectually annoy the inhabitants of Bergerac. Many ſpeeches were made, and different propoſals offered. It was long debated to ſtorm the town, but afterwards this meaſure was abandoned, as their men might ſuffer much, and not make any great gain. The council broke up without coming to any determination, except to continue on the ſiege; for they were ſtill expecting large bodies of men at arms from France, and in particular the lord de Coucy.

CHAP. LXIV.

SIR THOMAS FELTON IS DEFEATED AND MADE PRISONER, WITH MANY OF THE PRINCIPAL LORDS OF GASCONY, BY A PARTY OF FRENCH AT THE SIEGE OF BERGERAC.

SIR Thomas Felton, who resided at Bourdeaux, was not at his ease from knowing that his enemies were but twelve leagues distant, and in such numbers that he could not think of opposing them by force, having also learnt the duke of Anjou's summons and intentions: he had, therefore sent information to the king and council in England; but those whom he had dispatched thither had not been able to do any thing, for the kingdom of England was much shaken, and different parties were mutually opposing each other.

The duke of Lancaster, in particular, was unpopular with the common people; from which cause much party animosity and danger happened afterwards in England. No men at arms were sent either to Gascony or to Brittany, on which account, those who were defending the frontiers for the young king were very ill pleased.

It happened that sir Thomas Felton had desired the lord de l'Esparre to go to England, for the better information of the king and his uncles respecting the affairs of Gascony, in order that they might take council to provide for them. The lord de l'Efparre had already left Bourdeaux, and was proceeding on his voyage; but the wind proving unfavourable, he was driven into the Spanifh feas, where he was met by fome fhips from Spain, with whom he engaged unfuccefsfully: he was made prifoner and carried to Spain, where he remained upwards of a year and a half, and fuffered many mortifications from the relations of the lord de Pommiers.

Sir Thomas was a truly valiant man: he had written and fent fpecial meffengers to the lords de Mucident, de Duras, de Rofem and de Langurant, four of the moft noble and powerful barons of Gafcony, and who were attached to England, to requeft, that for the honour of the king their lord, they would not fail, on any account, to defend the principality, and to defire they would come to Bourdeaux with their vaffals; for all knights who were anxious to acquit themfelves towards the king and lord were already arrived there.

When they were all affembled, they amounted to full five hundred lances: they remained at Bourdeaux, and in the Bourdelois, during the time when the duke of Anjou was beginning the fiege of Bergerac. Sir Thomas Felton and thefe four gafcon barons held a council, in which they refolved to march towards the French, and poft themfelves in a fecure fituation, to fee if they could gain any advantage over them. They fet out, therefore, from Bourdeaux with upwards of three hundred lances, taking the road for la Réole, and came to a certain town called Yuret*, in which they quartered themſelves.

The French knew nothing of this ambuſcade, and ſuffered much from it. The ſiege of Bergerac was ſtill going forward: there were many ſkirmiſhes and deeds of arms performed with the garriſon by the beſiegers; but the French were not great gainers, for ſir Perducas d'Albret, the governor, was very active in oppoſing them, that no blame might be imputed to him.

The army called another council, and reſolved to ſend for a large machine, called a ſow, from la Réole, in order the more to haraſs the garriſon. This ſow was a large engine, which caſt weighty ſtones, and one hundred men, completely armed, could be drawn up in it, and attack the walls. Sir Peter de Beuil, ſir John de Vers, ſir Baldwin de Cremoux, ſir Alain de Beaumont, the lord de Montcalay and the lord de Gaures, were ordered to go for this engine: they left the army, in conſequence, with about three hundred men at arms whom they could depend on, and, fording the river Dordonne, rode towards la Réole: they advanced between Bergerac and la Réole, until they came to Yurac, where the Engliſh were in ambuſcade with upwards of four hundred combatants, of which they were ignorant.

---

* Yuret,—probably Yurac,—a village in Guienne, near Bourdeaux.

News was brought to the army and to the constable of France, that the English had taken the field, but it was unknown which way they had marched. The constable, lest his men might be surprised, immediately ordered a large detachment to guard the foragers, who were out between the rivers Garonne and Dordonne, and gave the command of it to sir Peter de Mornay, sir Evan of Wales, Thibaut du Pont and Heliot de Calais: there might be in this detachment two hundred lances of tried men.

Sir Peter de Beuil, and the others who were sent to bring the sow, rode on to la Réole, and, having laden a great many carts with it, set out on their return, but by a different route from that by which they had arrived, for they required a broader road for their convoy, and yet they were to pass by Yurac, or very near to it, where the English were in ambuscade: however, they were so fortunate to meet with a second detachment from their army, when they were within a short league of the town. The whole then amounted to full six hundred lances. They continued their march in greater security, and more at their leisure.

Sir Thomas Felton and the barons of Gascony in Yurac were informed, that the French were escorting that way a very large engine, from la Réole to their siege of Bergerac. They were much rejoiced at this intelligence, and said it was what they wished. They then armed themselves, mounted their horses, and drew up in the best array they were able. When they had advanced into

into the plain, they had not long to wait before they ſaw the French, marching in a large body, and in handſome order. No ſooner was each party aſſured that thoſe whom they ſaw were enemies, who ſeemed mutually eager for the conteſt, than ſticking ſpurs into their horſes, and with ſpears in their reſts, they charged each other, ſhouting their different war cries. I muſt ſay, that in this firſt conflict, many a gallant tilt was performed, and many a knight and ſquire were unhorſed and driven to the ground.

In ſuch deadly warfare, there is no accident but what may happen. Heliot de Calais, a moſt able ſquire and good man at arms was knocked off his horſe, by a violent ſtroke on the throat-piece with a ſpear, whoſe broad point was as ſharp and as fine as a razor. This iron cut through the throat-piece, as well as all the veins: the ſtroke beat him to the ground, when he ſhortly after died: the more the pity. By this accident did he end his days.

Among the French, there was a knight from Berry or Limouſin, named ſir William de Lignac, an excellent man at arms, who this day performed many gallant deeds.

The combat was ſharp, and long continued on each ſide, cloſe to the village of Yurac: when their lances failed, they drew their ſwords, and the attack was more vigorouſly renewed. Many feats of prowеſs were performed, many captures made, and many reſcued. Of the Engliſh ſlain on the ſpot, was a gaſcon knight, called the lord de

Gernos

Gernos and de Calais: of the French, Thibaut du Pont.

This battle was well and long fought: many handſome deeds were done, for they were all men of valour: but in the end the Engliſh could not gain the field: they were fairly conquered by the French. Sir William de Lignac captured with his own hand ſir Thomas Felton, ſénéſchal of Bourdeaux: nearly at the ſame time, the lords de Mucident, de Duras, de Roſem, de Languiant, were alſo made priſoners. Few of the Engliſh or Gaſcons but were made priſoners or ſlain.

Thoſe who could eſcape met, on their return towards Bourdeaux, the ſénéſchal des Landes, ſir William Helman, the mayor of Bourdeaux, and ſir John de Multon; in the whole, about one hundred lances: who were haſtening to Yurac; but, when they heard the news of ſo complete a defeat, they wheeled about, and returned as ſpeedily as poſſible to Bourdeaux.

CHAP. LXV.

BERGERAC SURRENDERS TO THE DUKE OF ANJOU.—THE LORDS DE DURAS AND DE ROSEM, AFTER HAVING PROMISED TO BE OF THE FRENCH INTEREST, RETURN AGAIN TO THE ENGLISH.

WHEN this engagement was over and the field cleared, and all thoſe who had been made priſoners placed under a ſecure guard, they ſet out on their return to the ſiege carrying on at Bergerac.

The duke of Anjou was mightily rejoiced when he heard of the detachments having had ſuch ſucceſs, and that all the flower of Gaſcony, the knights and ſquires his enemies, were either killed or taken, and among them ſir Thomas Felton, who had been very active againſt him, ſo that he would rather have loſt five hundred thouſand francs than that it ſhould have been otherwiſe.

Sir Peter de Beuil, ſir William de Lignac, ſir Evan of Wales and others, continued their march until they came to their army before Bergerac, where they were received with much pleaſure by the duke of Anjou, the conſtable, the barons and knights their friends, who conſidered their ſucceſs as very honourable and profitable to them.

On the morrow, the ſow they had brought was erected near to the walls of Bergerac, which much

alarmed

alarmed the inhabitants, who held a council to consider their situation, and whether they could maintain it. They addressed themselves to their governor, for they found they could not long hold out, as no succour was to be expected since their sénéschal was taken, and with him the chivalry of Gascony, on whose assistance they had depended.

Sir Perducas told them, they were in sufficient strength to hold out for some time, being well provided with provisions and artillery, if they made not any foolish agreement.

Things remained in this situation until the next morning, when the trumpets of the army sounded for an assault, and every one repaired to his banner. The constable of France, who was in the field with a grand array, sent to hold a parley with the inhabitants before the assault began, or any of their men were wounded or slain; in which he remonstrated with them, that having had their leaders made prisoners, from whom alone they could hope for assistance, and who were now in treaty to place themselves and their lands under the obedience of the king of France, they could not look for any relief; and, should the town be taken by storm, it would inevitably be destroyed by fire and flame, and none receive quarter.

These threats frightened the inhabitants, who demanded time to hold a consultation, which was granted to them. The burghers then assembled, without calling in their governor, and agreed to surrender as good Frenchmen, provided they were peaceably and gently dealt with, without

any

any of the army entering their town, which was directly granted.

When ſir Perducas d'Albret, their governor, heard of this, he mounted his horſe, ordered his men to march, and, having paſſed the bridges, made for the fort of Moncin, when Bergerac ſurrendered to the French.

The conſtable of France took poſſeſſion of it, placing therein a governor and men at arms to keep and defend it.

After the ſurrender of Bergerac, the duke of Anjou was adviſed to advance further into the country, and lay ſiege to Caſtillon * on the Dordonne. News of this was ſoon ſpread through the army, when every one began to make his preparations accordingly; that is to ſay, the duke, the conſtable and the other men at arms, except the marſhal of France, who remained behind to wait for the lord de Coucy, as he was expected to arrive that evening (which indeed he did), when the marſhal advanced to meet him with a very large attendance of his men, and received him moſt amicably. They remained all that night in the place which the duke had left.

The duke and his army advanced to a fine mead, on the banks of the Dordonne, in his march to Caſtillon.

Under the command of the lord de Coucy were, ſir Aymon de Pommiers, ſir Triſtan de Roye, the

* Caſtillon,—a town of Guyenne, election of Bourdeaux.

lords

lords de Faignelles, de Jumont, ſir John de Roſay, ſir Robert de Clermont, and ſeveral other knights and ſquires. They marched from their quarters, and continued advancing in company with the marſhal of France and his troops until they arrived at the army of the duke, where they were received with much ſatisfaction.

In the road to Caſtillon, there is a town called St. Foy: before the van-guard arrived at Caſtillon, they marched thither, and, having ſurrounded it, began to attack it briſkly. This town had not any men at arms, and but trifling fortifications, ſo that it did not long defend itſelf. On its ſurrender, it was pillaged.

The ſiege was formed before Caſtillon above the river, and continued for fifteen days: of courſe, there were many ſkirmiſhes at the barriers, for ſome Engliſh and Gaſcons had retreated thither after the battle of Yurac, and defended themſelves valiantly.

The gaſcon barons who had been made priſoners at Yurac, were ſtill in the French camp, and in treaty to turn to the French party. Sir Thomas Felton was not ſolicited ſo to do, as he was an Engliſhman, but had his ranſom fixed by his maſter, ſir William de Lignac, to whom he paid thirty thouſand francs, and obtained his liberty: but this was not immediately ſettled.

After much negociating, the four gaſcon barons turned to the French: they engaged, on their faith and honour, that themſelves and their vaſſals would ever after remain good Frenchmen; for which

which reafon the duke of Anjou gave them their liberties.

The lords de Duras and de Rofem left the duke with a good underftanding, intending to vifit their own eftates: the lords de Mucident and de Langurant remained with the army, and were gracioufly treated by the duke of Anjou, with whom they frequently dined and fupped.

The firft mentioned lords thought the duke very obliging in thus lightly allowing them to depart, which indeed he afterwards repented, as he had good reafon. Thefe two lords, when on their road converfing together, faid; 'How can we ferve the duke of Anjou and the French, when we have hitherto been loyal Englifh? It will be much better for us to deceive the duke of Anjou than the king of England, our natural lord, and who has always been fo kind to us.' This they adopted, and refolved to go to Bourdeaux, to the fénéfchal des Landes, fir William Helman, and affure him that their hearts would never fuffer them to become good Frenchmen.

The two barons continued their journey to Bourdeaux, where they were joyfully received: for they had not then heard any thing of their treaties with the duke of Anjou.

The fénéfchal des Landes and the mayor of Bourdeaux were inquifitive after news, and what fums they had paid for their ranfoms. They faid, that through conftraint and threats of death, the duke of Anjou had forced them to turn to the French; but added, 'Gentlemen, we will truly

tell

tell you, that before we took the oath, we reserved in our hearts our faith to our natural lord the king of England; and, for any thing we have said or done, will we never become Frenchmen.'

The knights from England were much pleased with these words, and declared they had acquitted themselves loyally towards their lord.

Five days afterwards, news was brought to the duke of Anjou and the army before Castillon, that the lords de Duras and de Rosem had turned to the English, which very much astonished the duke, the constable and the other barons. The duke then sent to the lords de Mucident and de Langurant, told them what he had heard, and asked what they thought of it: these barons, who were exceedingly vexed, replied; 'My lord, if they have broken their faith, we will not belie ours; and that which we have said and sworn to you we will loyally keep, nor shall the contrary be ever reproached to us; for by valour and gallant deeds of arms have your party conquered us, and we will therefore remain steady in our obedience to you.'

'I believe you firmly,' said the duke of Anjou; 'and I swear by God first, and then by my lord and brother, that on leaving this place, we will not undertake any one thing before we have besieged the towns of Duras and Rosem.'

Things remained in this state; that is to say, the duke of Anjou much enraged at the conduct of the two gascon barons, and the siege continuing before

before Caſtillon. The town and caſtle of Caſtillon, on the Dordonne, was a town and inheritance of the captal de Buch, whom the king of France had detained in priſon at Paris.

CHAP. LXVI.

CASTILLON, SAUVETERRE AND SEVERAL OTHER PLACES IN GASCONY SURRENDER TO THE DUKE OF ANJOU.

DURING the time Caſtillon was beſieged, there was a great famine, in ſo much that for money there was difficulty in getting proviſions. The French were forced to march twelve or fifteen leagues for forage for the army, and in going and returning they ran great riſks; for there were many caſtles and Engliſh garriſons on the frontiers, from whence they ſallied forth and formed ambuſcades; or they waited in the narrow paſſes and defiles; and whenever they found themſelves the ſtrongeſt, they fell upon the French foragers, killed and wounded them, and carried off their forage. For this reaſon, they never could forage but in large bodies.

The ſiege of Caſtillon was carried on with much vigour, and the garriſon ſo haraſſed by aſſaults and engines that they ſurrendered, on their lives and fortunes being ſpared. The men at arms

 marched

marched out, and as many more as chose to leave it, and went to St. Macaire*, where there is a good castle and strong town.

On the surrender of Castillon, the duke of Anjou received the fealty and homage of the inhabitants, and renewed the officers: he appointed as governor of it a knight from Touraine, called sir James de Montmartin.

When they were about to march from Castillon, they called a council to consider whither they should go next; and it was determined to advance towards St. Marine; but, as several small forts were scattered about the country before they could arrive there, it was not thought proper to leave them in their rear on account of the foragers. They therefore, on quitting Castillon, marched to Sauveterre †, which they besieged.

Other intelligence was brought, respecting the lords de Duras and de Rosem, different from what had been at first reported; that in truth they were at Bourdeaux, but it was not known on what terms.

This news was spread through the army, and was so public as to come to the ears of the lord de Mucident and de Langurant: they mentioned it to the lord de Coucy and sir Peter de Bueil, whom they were desirous to interest in excusing those knights, adding that it was very simple to

* St. Macaire,—a city in Guyenne, on the Garonne, nine leagues from Bourdeaux.

† Sauveterre,—a town in Gascony, diocese of Comminges.

believe

believe ſuch tales ſo lightly told. They replied, they would willingly undertake to ſpeak to the duke, who told them he ſhould be very happy to find the contrary true to what he had heard. The affair remained in this ſtate, and the ſiege of Sauveterre continued:

The town of Sauveterre held out only for three days; for the knight who was governor ſurrendered it to the duke, on condition of himſelf, his troops, with their fortunes, being ſpared. By theſe means they marched and came before St. Bazile, a good town, which immediatel ſurrendered, and put itſelf under the obedience of the king of France.

They then advanced to Montſegur *, which they attacked on their arrival, but did not gain it on this firſt attempt. They encamped and refreſhed themſelves for the night. On the morrow, they prepared for the aſſault, and thoſe within, ſeeing they were in earneſt, began to be greatly alarmed, and called a council, wherein it was at laſt determined that they would offer to ſurrender on having their lives and fortunes ſpared; and upon theſe terms they were received.

The French marched away to another good walled town, ſituated between St. Macaire and la Réole, called Auberoche. They were four days before they could gain it, which was done by capitulation. The French then advanced to St. Macaire.

* A village in Gaſcony, election of Landes.

CHAP. LXVII.

THE DUKE OF ANJOU TAKES THE TOWN AND CASTLE OF ST. MACAIRE BY CAPITULATION,—THE TOWN OF DURAS BY STORM, BUT THE CASTLE RECEIVES QUARTER.

THE army of the duke of Anjou was daily increaſing from all quarters; for ſuch knights and ſquires as were deſirous of renown came to wait on him, and to ſerve him. The ſiege was formed before St. Macaire in a very handſome manner; for thoſe men at arms had retreated thither who had quitted the garriſons which had ſurrendered. The town, therefore, had been greatly reinforced, and better guarded. There were many grand aſſaults and ſkirmiſhes, as well before the town as at the barriers.

Whilſt the ſiege was going forward, the duke of Anjou and the conſtable of France ordered the the leaders of the different corps to make excurſions in various parts. Large detachments, therefore, ſet out, under the orders of the marſhal of France, ſir Perceval de Marneil and ſir William de Moncontour.

Theſe detachments remained for ſix days in the field, took ſeveral towns and ſmall caſtles, and put all the ſurrounding country under the ſubjection of the king of France. None went out to oppoſe them, for the whole country was almoſt empty

empty of men at arms attached to the Engliſh, and the few who were there fled towards Bourdeaux. When they had finiſhed their expeditions, they returned to the army.

The inhabitants of St. Macaire knew well that they could not hold out for a long time, and the beſiegers promiſed them every day, that if they ſuffered themſelves to be taken by ſtorm, they ſhould all without mercy be put to death. They began to be doubtful leſt their career might terminate in this cruel manner, and ſecretly opened a treaty with the French to ſurrender, on their lives and fortunes being ſpared.

The men at arms in St. Macaire had intelligence of this, and, ſuſpecting the inhabitants might perhaps form ſome treaty inimical to them, they retired into the caſtle, which was large and ſtrong, and built to ſtand a good ſiege, taking with them all their own wealth, and a good deal of pillage from the town. Upon this, the inhabitants ſurrendered their town to the king of France.

The duke of Anjou received intelligence during the ſiege of St. Macaire, that his lady the ducheſs had been brought to bed of a ſon at Toulouſe. The duke and the whole army were much rejoiced at this event, and their warlike heroiſm was greatly increaſed.

The men at arms entered the town, for it had large and handſome houſes, in which they refreſhed themſelves, as they had wherewithal, the town being well provided with every ſort of proviſion.

 The

The castle was surrounded on all sides, and engines erected before it, which cast such large stones as greatly astonished the garrison. Whilst this siege was carrying on, true intelligence was brought respecting the lords de Duras and de Rosem, by two heralds who declared they had turned to the English. On hearing this, the duke said, 'Let me but gain St. Macaire, and I will immediately march and lay siege to Duras.' He ordered the attacks on the castle to be renewed with greater vigour, for he was not willing to leave it in his rear.

The garrison seeing themselves thus attacked, without any hopes of succour, and knowing that the duke and constable were determined to have them by fair or foul means, thought they should act wisely if they entered into a treaty, which they accomplished, and delivered up the castle, on their lives and fortunes being spared, and on being conducted to Bourdeaux. Thus did the town and castle of St. Macaire become French.

The duke of Anjou took possession of it, appointed a governor, and then decamped with his whole army, taking the road towards Duras.

The army continued its march until it came before Duras, when an attack was immediately ordered. The men at arms made themselves ready, and the cross-bowmen, well shielded, advanced to the town; some of whom had provided themselves with ladders, in order the more easily to scale the walls.

This

This attack was very ſevere, and thoſe who had mounted the walls ſought hand to hand with their opponents: ſo many gallant deeds were done by each party, that it laſted the greater part of the day.

When they had thus well fought for a length of time, the marſhals ordered the trumpets to ſound a retreat, and every man retired to his quarters for the night. In the mean time, ſir Alain de la Haye, and ſir Alain de St. Pol, arrived at the army with a large troop of Bretons, who had marched towards Libourne*, and had attacked an Engliſh garriſon at Cadillac†, which they had taken by ſtorm, and ſlain all within it.

On the morrow morning, the duke ordered the ſtorming to be renewed, and that each man ſhould exert himſelf to the utmoſt. He had it alſo proclaimed by a herald, that whoever ſhould firſt enter Duras ſhould receive five hundred francs.

The deſire of gaining this reward made many poor companions come forward. Ladders were placed againſt the walls in various places, and the attack began in earneſt; for the young knights and ſquires, who were eager for renown, did not ſpare themſelves, but fought with a thorough good will.

---

* Libourne,—a city of Guyenne on the Dordonne, ten leagues from Bourdeaux.

† Cadillac,—a town in Guyenne, ſeven leagues from Bourdeaux.

The lord de Langurant had afcended a ladder, with his fword in his hand, and fought hard to enter the town the firft, not indeed for the five hundred francs, but to illuftrate his name; for he was exceedingly angry that the lord de Duras had fo lightly turned to the Englifh. The lord de Langurant, as I muft fay, performed fuch deeds that his own people as well as ftrangers were quite aftonifhed therewith, and advanced fo far that his life was in great jeopardy; for thofe within fide the walls tore off the helmet from his head, and with it the hood, fo that he would inevitably have been flain, if his own fquire, who followed him clofe, had not covered him with his target. The knight defcended the ladder by degrees, but he received in his defcent feveral heavy blows on the target. He was much efteemed for this affault, by all thofe who faw him.

In another part, fir Triftan de Roye and fir Perceval d'Ayvenal, mounted on ladders, fought moft valoroufly; and alfo fir John de Jumont and fir John de Rofay, where each for his part did wonders in arms. On the battlements was the lord de Seriel, mounted on a ladder, fighting gallantly hand to hand with thofe on the infide, and all who faw him faid, that if any one was likely to have the advantage of firft entering the town, he was in the road fo to do.

This knight did not thus adventure himfelf for profit, but for glory: however, as fortune is hazardous, he was ftruck down with fuch force by a fword, ſword, that he tumbled into the ditch, and broke his neck. In ſuchwiſe died this knight.

The ſame fate attended a ſquire from Brittany, who bore for his arms two chevrons gules, chequered with or, argent, and azur. This vexed the conſtable ſo much that he ordered the aſſailants to be reinforced, and the fight continued with more vigour than before. The lord de Mucident proved himſelf an able knight, and ſhewed he was indeed a Frenchman from the manner in which he aſſaulted.

The town of Duras was taken by ſtorm, and the firſt perſons who entered it were ſir Triſtan de Roye and ſir John de Roſay. When the men at arms in Duras ſaw that the town muſt be loſt, they retreated into the caſtle, leaving the reſt to its fate. Thus was Duras taken, and all found in it were put to death. The men at arms retired to their quarters, where they diſarmed themſelves, and took their eaſe, having plenty of proviſion with them.

On the morrow morning, the conſtable of France, attended by the marſhal, mounted their horſes, and rode to the caſtle to reconnoitre, and ſee on which ſide they could beſt attack it. Having well examined it, they found it was marvellouſly ſtrong, and ſaid, that without a very long ſiege, it would not be eaſily taken: on their return, they related this to the duke of Anjou. 'That does not ſignify,' replied the duke, 'for I have ſaid and ſworn, that I would not ſtir from hence until I ſhould have this caſtle under my obedience,'

obedience.' 'And you ſhall not forſwear yourſelf,' anſwered the conſtable.

Engines were directly pointed againſt the caſtle, as they were ready on the ſpot. When thoſe within ſaw the great preparations that were making againſt them, as well by thoſe in the town as by the French, and that the attack would be ſevere, and probably fatal to them, they thought it adviſable to enter into a negociation. They opened a treaty with the conſtable, who agreed to ſpare their lives and fortunes on their ſurrendering the caſtle. The duke of Anjou was therefore adviſed by the conſtable not to fatigue or hurt his men, but to grant them quarter, which he did. On the third day they marched out of the caſtle, and were conducted whither they wiſhed to go, and the conſtable took poſſeſſion of it; but I believe the duke of Anjou ordered it to be razed to the ground.

CHAP. LXVIII.

THE DUKE OF ANJOU RETURNS TO THE DUCHESS AT TOULOUSE, AND THE CONSTABLE TO THE KING OF FRANCE.—EVAN OF WALES LAYS SIEGE TO MORTAIN SUR MER.

AFTER the conqueſt of the town and caſtle of Duras, the duke of Anjou ordered ſir John de Jumont, ſir Triſtan de Roye, and ſir John

John de Rosay, to remain in the town of Landurant* (for the lord of it had turned to the French since he had been made prisoner at the battle of Yurac), with one hundred good spears to guard the frontiers against the Bourdelois: he himself wished to return to Toulouse to see his duchess, who had been delivered of a handsome boy, for he was desirous of holding a grand feast at Toulouse to celebrate this event.

He therefore ordered men at arms to the different towns and castles which he had conquered. On dismissing Evan of Wales, he said to him; 'You will take under your command the Bretons, Poitevins, and Angevins, with whom you will march into Poitou, and lay siege to Mortain sur mer, which the lord de l'Estrade† holds; and do not quit the place for any orders which you may receive in the king's name until you have had possession of it; for it is a garrison that has done us much mischief.'

'My lord,' replied Evan, 'as far as shall be in my power I will loyally obey you.' The duke, the constable, and the lord de Coucy, then ordered all those who were to accompany Evan into Poitou. Upon this, full five hundred good men at arms left the duke, and took the road to Saintonge, in order to advance towards St. Jean d'Angeli.

---

* Landurant,—should be Landiras,—a town in Guyenne, near Bourdeaux. William Shalton was lord of Landirans.—See Rolles Gasconnes.

† The souldich de l'Estrade.—See Anstis.

The duke of Anjou, the conſtable of France, the lord de Coucy, the marſhal of France, ſir John and ſir Peter de Bueil, returned to Toulouſe, where they found the ducheſs newly recovered from her lying-in. On this event, there were very great rejoicings and feaſtings at Toulouſe.

The conſtable and the lord de Coucy then returned to Paris; the marſhal de Sancerre into Auvergne, to aſſiſt the dauphin of Auvergne and the barons of that country, who were carrying on the war againſt the Engliſh that had remained in Limouſin, Rouergue, and on the borders of Auvergne.

Let us now ſay ſomething of Evan of Wales, how he laid ſiege at this ſeaſon to Mortain, and how he haraſſed its garriſon. Evan of Wales, being deſirous of obeying the orders of the duke of Anjou, (for he knew well that whatever the duke did was by the directions of the king of France his brother, as he had paid all the expenſes of the different expeditions he had made) had advanced as far as Saintes. He had halted to refreſh himſelf and his companions in that rich country between Saintes and Poitou, and in the beautiful meads which are on the banks of the rivers in thoſe parts. Many knights and ſquires of Poitou were with him, ſuch as the lords de Pons, de Touars, de Vivarois, the lord James de Surgeres, and ſeveral more. On the other hand, from Brittany and Normandy, were ſir Maurice de Triſiquedi, ſir Alain de la Houſſaye, ſir Alain de St. Pol, ſir Perceval d'Ayneval, ſir William de Montcontour,

Montcontour, the lord de Mommor, and Morelet his brother.

Theſe troops, when ordered, marched away, and laid ſiege to Mortain. The caſtle is ſituated on the Garonne, near to and below its embouchure with the ſea: it is the handſomeſt and ſtrongeſt fort in all the borders of the countries of Poitou, la Rochelle, and Saintonge.

When Evan of Wales, the barons and knights were arrived there, they formed the ſiege very prudently, and provided themſelves by little and little with every thing they wanted; for they were well aware that they could never conquer the caſtle by ſtorm, but that it muſt be won by diſtreſſing the garriſon with famine and a long blockade.

Evan, therefore, ordered four block-houſes to be erected, ſo that no proviſion could enter the place by ſea or by land.

At times, the young knights and ſquires who wiſhed to diſplay their courage, advanced to the barriers of the caſtle, and ſkirmiſhed with the garriſon. Many gallant deeds were there performed.

There was a knight in Mortain called the Souldich, who was from Gaſcony, a valiant knight and able man at arms, whoſe orders they obeyed as if he had been their governor. The caſtle was plenfully ſupplied with wines and proviſion, but they were in great want of ſeveral ſmaller neceſſaries.

CHAP. LXIX.

KING CHARLES OF FRANCE INSTIGATES THE SCOTS TO MAKE WAR ON ENGLAND.—THE SCOTS TAKE THE CASTLE OF BERWICK.

KING Charles of France, notwithſtanding he always reſided at Paris, or at various other places in France which pleaſed him more, and that he never bore arms himſelf, kept up a very ſharp war againſt his enemies the Engliſh. He had formed alliances, as well in the empire as with the adjoining kingdoms, in a greater degree than the four or five preceding kings of France had ever done. He paid great attentions to all from whom he thought he ſhould derive any aſſiſtance; and becauſe king Richard of England was young, and his kingdom unſettled, he had ſent to renew his alliance with the Scots, and with their king, Robert Stuart, who had ſucceeded his uncle king David Bruce, and to excite them to make war upon the Engliſh, ſo that they ſhould be diſabled from croſſing the ſeas.

Upon this, king Robert, after the death of Edward and the coronation of Richard, aſſembled his council at Edinburgh, where he had ſummoned the greater part of thoſe barons and knights from whom he looked for aſſiſtance. He remonſtrated with them againſt the Engliſh for having in former times done them much miſchief by burn-

ing

ing their country, razing their caſtles, killing and ranſoming the inhabitants: that the time was now arrived when they might revenge themſelves for all theſe diſgraces; as king Edward was deceaſed, who had been ſo ſucceſsful againſt them, and a young king was now on the throne.

The barons of Scotland and the young knights preſent, being deſirous of advancing themſelves and revenging the injuries which the Engliſh had formerly done to their country, replied unanimouſly, that they were willing and prepared to invade England, either to-day or to-morrow, or whenever he pleaſed.

This anſwer was very ageeeable to the king of Scotland, who returned them his thanks for it.

Four earls were appointed captains of men at arms; namely, the earl of Douglas, the earl of Moray, the earl of Mar and the earl of Sutherland; ſir Archibald Douglas conſtable of Scotland, and ſir Robert de Verſi * marſhal of the whole army.

Summons were immediately iſſued for the aſſembling of the forces by a certain day in the Merſe, which is the country bordering on England. Whilſt this ſummons was obeying, a valiant ſquire of Scotland, named Alexander Ramſay, ſet off with forty men from his company, determined to perform a gallant enterprize. They were all well mounted, and, having rode the whole night through bye roads, came to Berwick nearly at day-break.

---

* Sir Robert de Verſi. Q.

A ſquire attached to the earl of Northumberland, called William Biſſet, was governor of the town of Berwick; and a very able knight, called ſir Robert Abeton *, was conſtable of the caſtle.

When the Scots were arrived near Berwick, they concealed themſelves, and ſent a ſpy to obſerve the ſtate of the caſtle. The ſpy entered it as far as the ditches, wherein there was not any water, nor indeed could any be retained in them, for they were of moving ſands: he looked about him on all ſides, but did not ſee a ſoul: upon which, he returned back to his maſters.

Alexander Ramſay directly advanced with his companions, without ſpeaking a word, and paſſed the ditches: they had brought good ladders with them, which they placed againſt the walls. Alexander was the firſt who mounted them ſword in

* Sir Robert Abeton—ſir Robert Boynton. Dr. Fuller, in his hiſtory of Berwick, 1799, ſays, 'that ſeven intrepid Scotſmen in 1377 took poſſeſſion of Berwick caſtle by ſtorm in the night, and continued maſters of it for eight days, though it was beſieged by ſeven thouſand Engliſh archers and three thouſand cavalry, and only loſt two of their number, which had increaſed to forty-eight when they were ſubdued. Notwithſtanding this heroic achievement, they were all put to the ſword.

'Upon entering the caſtle, they killed the governor, ſir Robert Boynton, but liberated his lady for two thouſand marks.

'When the earl of Northumberland ſummoned theſe heroes to ſurrender, they boldly replied;

'That they would not yield it either to the kings of England or Scotland, but would retain and defend it for the king of France.'

No authority is mentioned.

hand,

hand, and entered the caſtle followed by his men without any oppoſition.

When they had all entered, they haſtened to the great tower where ſir Robert Boynton ſlept, and began to cut down the door of it with the axes they had brought. The governor was ſuddenly awakened. he had ſlept all the night, and kept but a poor watch, for which he paid dear. He heard the door of his chamber broken, and thought it might be done by ſome of his own men who wanted to murder him, becauſe he had quarrelled with them the preceding week. With this idea, he opened a window which looked on the ditches, leaped out of it without further conſideration, and thus broke his neck and died on the ſpot.

The guards of the caſtle, who towards day-break had been aſleep, awakened by his groans, found the caſtle had been ſcaled and taken: they began to ſound their trumpets, and to cry out, 'Treaſon! treaſon!'

John Biſſet, the governor of Berwick, on hearing their cries, armed himſelf, as well as all the able men of the town, and advanced toward the caſtle, when they plainly heard the noiſe of the Scots; but they could not gain entrance, for the gates were ſhut, and the draw-bridge raiſed. Upon this, John Biſſet, having conſidered a ſhort time, ſaid to thoſe with him; 'Come quickly: let us break down the ſupports of the bridge, ſo that none can ſally out, nor get away without danger from us.'

They ſoon got hatchets and wedges, and the ſupports of the gate next the town were deſtroyed. John Biſſet ſent off a meſſenger to the lord Percy at Alnwick, which is but twelve ſhort leagues off, to requeſt he would come immediately to his aſſiſtance with all his forces, for that Berwick caſtle had been taken by the Scots. He alſo ſaid to Thomelin Friant *, who was the perſon he ſent, 'Tell my lord of Percy the ſtate you have left me in, and how the Scots are ſhut up in the caſtle, and cannot get away, unleſs they leap the walls; ſo let him haſten here as faſt as he poſſibly can.'

Alexander Ramſay and his men, having ſcaled the caſtle of Berwick, thought they had done wonders, as in truth they had: they would have been maſters of the town, if John Biſſet had not acted ſo prudently, and ſlain whomever they pleaſed, or ſhut them up in the tower, for ſuch was their intention: they ſaid, 'Let us now go into the town; it is ours, and ſeize all the riches, which we will make the good men of the town carry away for us, and then we will ſet fire to it, for it cannot now make any reſiſtance: in three or four days time, ſuccours will come from Scotland, ſo that we ſhall ſave all our pillage: and on our departure we will ſet the caſtle on fire, and by theſe means repay our hoſts.' All his companions aſſented, for they were eager for gain. They tightened on their

* Thomelin Friant. Q.

arms,

arms, and each grafped a fpear, for they had found plenty in the caftle, and, opening the gate, let down the draw-bridge. When the bridge was let down, the chains which fupported it broke, for the pillars on which it fhould have refted were deftroyed, and the planks carried into the town.

When John Biffet, and the inhabitants who were there affembled, faw them, they began fhouting out, 'Oh what, are you there? keep where you are, for you fhall not go away for a certainty without our permiffion.'

Alexander Ramfay, feeing their appearance, foon found they intended to keep them confined in the caftle, and that they muft get away as well as they could: he therefore fhut the gates, to avoid their arrows, and ordered his people to inclofe themfelves within, intending to defend the caftle. They flung all the dead into the the ditches, and fhut up the prifoners in a tower. They thought the place was full ftrong enough to hold out until fuccours fhould come from Scotland, for the barons and knights were affembling in the Merfe and in that neighbourhood: the earl of Douglas had even left Dalkeith, and arrived at Dunbar.

We will now return to the fquire whom John Biffet fent to Alnwick, and fpeak of his arrival, and of the information he gave to the earl of Northumberland.

CHAP. LXX.

THE EARL OF NORTHUMBERLAND RETAKES THE CASTLE OF BERWICK.

THOMELIN Friant made haste until he arrived at Alnwick, and entered the castle from the knowledge he had of it; for it was so early that the earl of Northumberland was not out of bed. Having arrived at his bedside to speak to him, for the business was very pressing, he said; 'My lord, the Scots have this morning taken Berwick castle by surprise; and the governor of the town sends me to inform you of it, as you are the lieutenant of all these countries.'

When the earl heard this news, he made every possible haste to order succour to Berwick: he sent off letters and messengers to all knights and squires of Northumberland, and to those from whom he expected any assistance, desiring them to repair to Berwick without delay, and informing them that he was marching thither to besiege the Scots, who had conquered the castle.

This summons was soon spread over the country, and every man at arms, knight, squire and cross-bowman left their houses. The lord Neville, the lord Lucy, the lord Gastop *, the lord Stafford, the lord de Blelles †, the governor of

* Gastop. Q. † Blelles. Q. Bellasis.

New-

Newcaſtle, and a right valiant and expert man at arms, called ſir Thomas Muſgrave, were there; but the earl of Northumberland firſt arrived at Berwick with his people; and forces daily came thither from all parts.

They were in the whole about ten thouſand men, who ſurrounded the caſtle ſo cloſely on all ſides that a bird could not have eſcaped from it without being ſeen. The Engliſh began to form mines, the ſooner to accompliſh their purpoſe againſt the Scots and regain the caſtle.

Intelligence was brought to the barons and knights of Scotland, that the earl of Northumberland, with the chivalry of that country, were beſieging their countrymen in Berwick caſtle: they therefore determined to march thither, raiſe the ſiege and reinforce the caſtle, for they conſidered what Alexander Ramſay had performed as a moſt gallant achievement. Sir Archibald Douglas, the conſtable, ſaid; 'Alexander is my couſin, and it is his high birth that has cauſed him to undertake and execute ſo bold a feat as the taking of Berwick caſtle: it behoves us to do all in our power to aſſiſt him in this buſineſs, and if we can raiſe the ſiege it will be to us of great value: I am of opinion, therefore, that we march thither.' He immediately ordered part of the army to remain behind, and the reſt to advance toward Berwick.

He choſe five hundred lances from the flower of the Scots army, and ſet off well mounted and in good order, taking the road to Berwick.

The

The English who were before Berwick with ten thousand men, including archers, soon heard how the Scots intended to raise the siege and reinforce the garrison: they called a council, and resolved to extend their ground, to wait for them and offer battle, as they were anxious to meet them.

The earl of Northumberland ordered all to prepare themselves, and march into the plain to be mustered, when they were found to amount to full three thousand men at arms and seven thousand archers.

When the earl saw his army so numerous, he said; 'Let us keep to this ground, for we are able to combat all the force Scotland can send against us.' They encamped on an extensive heath, without the walls of Berwick, in two ba talions and in good array.

This had been scarcely done an hour before they perceived some of the scouts of the Scots army advancing, but too well mounted to be attacked by the English: however, some English knights and squires would have been glad to have quitted their line to have checked their career, but the earl said, 'Let them alone, and allow their main body to come up: if they have any inclination for the combat, they will themselves advance nearer to us.'

The English remained very quiet, so that the Scots scouts came so close they were able to reconnoitre their two battalions and judge of how many men they were composed. When they had sufficiently observed them, they returned to their lords, and related what they had seen, saying; 'My lords,

lords, we have advanced ſo near to the Engliſh that we have fully reconnoitred them: we can tell you, they are waiting for you, drawn up in two handſome battalions, on the plain before the town: each battalion may conſiſt of five thouſand men: you will therefore conſider this well. We approached them ſo cloſe that they knew us for Scots ſcouts; but they made not the ſmalleſt attempt to break their line to purſue us.'

When ſir Archibald Douglas and the Scots knights heard this account, they were quite melancholy, and ſaid, 'We cannot think it will be any way profitable for us to advance further to meet the Engliſh; for they are ten to one, and all tried men: we may loſe more than we can gain: and a fooliſh enterprize is never good, and ſuch is what Alexander Ramſay has performed.'

Sir William Lindſay, a valiant knight and uncle to Alexander Ramſay, took great pains to perſuade them to ſuccour his nephew, ſaying; 'Gentlemen, my nephew, in confidence of your aſſiſtance, has performed this gallant deed, and taken Berwick caſtle. It will turn to your great ſhame, if he ſhould be loſt, and none of our family in future will thus boldly adventure themſelves.'

Thoſe preſent anſwered, 'That they could not amend it, and that the many gallant men who were there could not be expected to riſk their own deſtruction in the attempt to prevent a ſingle ſquire from being made priſoner.' It was therefore determined to retreat further up in their own country among the mountains near the river Tweed, whither they marched in good order and at their leiſure.

When the earls of Northumberland and Nottingham, and the other barons of England, found the Scots were not advancing, they ſent off ſcouts to enquire what was become of them, who brought back intelligence that they had retreated towards the Merſe beyond the caſtle of Roxburgh *.

On hearing this, each man retired quietly to his quarters, where they kept a ſtrict guard until the morrow morning about ſix o'clock, when they all made themſelves ready for the attack of the caſtle. The aſſault immediately began: it was very ſevere, and continued until the afternoon. Never did ſo few men as the Scots defend themſelves ſo well, nor was ever caſtle more briſkly attacked; for there were ladders raiſed againſt different parts of the walls, in which men at arms aſcended with targets over their heads, and fought hand to hand with the Scots. In conſequence, many were ſtruck down and hurled into the ditches. What moſt annoyed the Scots were the Engliſh archers, who ſhot ſo briſkly that ſcarcely any one dared to appear on the bulwarks. This aſſault was continued until the Engliſh entered the caſtle, when they began to ſlay all they could lay hands on. none eſcaped death except Alexander Ramſay, who was made priſoner by the earl of Northumberland.

* There ſeems ſome miſtake of geography here.

In

In this manner was Berwick caſtle regained. The earl of Northumberland appointed John Biſſet conſtable thereof, a very valiant ſquire, through whoſe means, as you have already heard, it had been reconquered. He had every part of it repaired, and the bridge which he had broken down reſtored.

CHAP. LXXI.

THE EARLS OF NORTHUMBERLAND AND NOTTINGHAM ENTER SCOTLAND WITH A LARGE ARMY.

AFTER the re-capture of Berwick caſtle, the earls of Northumberland and Nottingham, the two moſt powerful barons of the army, determined to make an excurſion after their enemies, and if they could find them to offer them battle. As they had reſolved, ſo did they execute: early on a morning they marched away taking the road to Roxburgh up Tweedſide. When they had marched about three leaguss, they called a council, and the two earls thought it adviſable to ſend a detachment to Melroſe, a large monaſtery of black monks, ſituated on the Tweed, which is the boundary of the two kingdoms, to know if any Scots were lying thereabouts in ambuſcade; whilſt they with the main body would march into the Merſe; by which means they would not fail of hearing ſome news of the Scots.

That

That valiant knight ſir Thomas Muſgrave was appointed commander of this detachment: it conſiſted of three hundred men at arms and as many archers. They left the army, which, on the ſeparation, took a different route, one marching to the right and the other to the left. Sir Thomas and his ſon rode on to Melroſe, where they arrived at an early hour, and took up their quarters, to refreſh themſelves and their horſes, as well as to make enquiries after the Scottiſh army.

They ordered two of their ſquires, well mounted, to ride over the country, to endeavour to find out the ſituation of the Scots, and in what order they were. Theſe two ſquires, on leaving their commanders, continued their route until they fell into an ambuſcade of the Scots, commanded by ſir William Lindſay, who had poſted himſelf in hopes of meeting with ſome adventure, and to hear news of Berwick, and alſo what had been the fate of his nephew, Alexander Ramſay, and into whoſe hands he had fallen: this he was very anxious to learn: he had with him about forty lances.

The Engliſh were ſeized immediately on their entering this ambuſh, which gave the knight very great pleaſure. He demanded from them whence they came: but they were afraid of ſpeaking leſt they ſhould betray their maſters: however, they were forced to be explicit, for the knight aſſured them that he would have them beheaded, if they did not truly anſwer all the queſtions he ſhould put to them.

When things became ſo ſerious, and they ſaw no

no means of eſcaping, they related how the caſtle of Berwick had been regained, and all found within put to death except Alexander Ramſay: they afterwards told how the earls of Northumberland and Nottingham were marching along Tweedſide in ſearch of the Scots, and how ſir Thomas Muſgrave, his ſon, ſir John Seton and ſir Richard Breton, with three hundred ſpears and as many archers, were lodged in the abbey of Melroſe, and that theſe knights had ſent them out to diſcover where the Scots were.

'By my troth,' replied ſir William Lindſay, 'you have found us, and you will now remain with us.' They were then taken aſide, and given up to ſome of their companions, with orders to guard them well under penalty of their lives.

Sir William Lindſay inſtantly ſent off one of his men at arms, ſaying; 'Ride to our main army, and tell them all you have heard, and the ſituation of the Engliſh: I will remain here uutil morning, to ſee if any thing elſe may happen.'

This man at arms rode on until he came to a large village beyond Morlane *, which is called Hondebray †, ſituated on the Tweed, among the mountains, where there were large meads and a plentiful country; for which reaſons the Scots had quartered themſelves there. Towards evening,

* Morlane. 'Lambirlaw.'—*M'Pherſon's Geographical Illuſtrations of Scottiſh Hiſtory.*

† Hondebray. 'It ſeems Hadingtoun; and, if ſo, the river ought to be Tine.'

M'Pherſon's Geog. Illuſt.

the

the ſquire arrived; and, as they knew he had brought ſome intelligence, he was conducted to the earls of Douglas, Murray, Sutherland, and to ſir Archibald Douglas, to whom he related all you have juſt read.

The Scots were much vexed on hearing the recapture of Berwick caſtle; but they were reconciled by the news of ſir Thomas Muſgrave and the other Engliſh knights being quartered at Melroſe. They determined to march inſtantly, to diſlodge their enemies, and make up from them for the loſs of Berwick.

They armed themſelves, ſaddled their horſes, and left Hadingtoun, advancing to the right of Melroſe, for they were well acquainted with the country, and arrived a little before midnight. But it then began to rain very heavily, and with ſuch a violent wind in their faces that there was none ſo ſtout but was overpowered by the ſtorm, ſo that they could ſcarcely guide their horſes: the pages ſuffered ſo much from the cold, and their comfortleſs ſituation, that they could not carry the ſpears, but let them fall to the ground: they alſo ſeparated from their companions, and loſt their way.

The advanced guard had halted, by orders of the conſtable, at the entrance of a large wood, through which it was neceſſary for them to paſs; for ſome knights and ſquires who had been long uſed to arms ſaid, they were advancing fooliſhly, and that it was not proper to continue their courſe in ſuch weather, and at ſo late an hour, as they ran a riſk of loſing more than they could gain.

They

They therefore concealed themſelves and their horſes under oaks and other large trees until it was day. It was a long time before they could make any fire from their flints and wet wood: however, they did ſucceed, and ſeveral large fires were made; for the cold and rain laſted until ſun-riſe, but it continued to drizzle until the hour of ſix. Between ſix and nine o'clock, the day began to get ſomewhat warmer, the ſun to ſhine, and the larks to ſing. The leaders then aſſembled to conſider what was beſt to be done, for they had failed in their intentions of arriving at Melroſe during the night.

They reſolved to breakfaſt in the open fields on what they had, to refreſh themſelves and horſes, and ſend out parties to forage. This was executed, and the greater part of their foragers ſpread themſelves over the country and adjacent villages. They brought hay and corn for the horſes, and proviſion for their maſters.

It happened that the Engliſh quartered in the abbey of Melroſe had that morning ſent out their foragers, ſo that the two parties met, and the Engliſh had not the advantage: ſeveral of their party were ſlain and wounded, and their forage ſeized. When ſir Thomas Muſgrave and the Engliſh knights in Melroſe heard of it, they knew the Scots were not far diſtant: they ordered their trumpets to ſound, and their horſes to be ſaddled, whilſt they armed themſelves, for they were determined to take the field. They left the abbey in good order, and in handſome array.

The

The Scots knights had received information from their foragers of their enemies being near: they therefore made all haſte to refreſh their horſes, to arm and draw themſelves up in order of battle, alongſide and under cover of the wood. They were full ſeven hundred lances, and two thouſand others, whom I call luſty varlets, armed with hunting ſpears, durks and pointed ſtaves.

The lord Archibald Douglas and his couſin the earl of Douglas ſaid; 'We cannot fail to have ſome buſineſs ſince the Engliſh are abroad. let us therefore be on our guard, for we will fight with them if the parties be nearly equal.' They ſent two of their men at arms to obſerve the order of the Engliſh, whilſt they remained ſnug in their ambuſh.

CHAP. LXXII.

SIR THOMAS MUSGRAVE AND THE ENGLISH UNDER HIS COMMAND ARE DEFEATED BY THE SCOTS.

SIR Thomas Muſgrave and the knights of Northumberland, being deſirous of meeting the Scots on equal terms, ſet out from Melroſe, and took the road to Morlane: they left the Tweed on on their left hand, and, by an ascending road, made for a mountain called St. Giles *.

Two Scots scouts were posted there, who, having well considered the English, immediately set off to their own troops, and related their observations on the English; in what order they were marching, and that they had only seen three banners and ten pennons.

The Scots were highly pleased with this intelligence, and said with a hearty good will, 'In the name of God and St. Giles, let us march towards them, for they must be our prisoners.' They then shouted their war-cry, which I think was, 'Douglas, St. Giles!'

They had not advanced half a league before both armies came in sight, and each knew a combat was unavoidable. Upon this the earl of Douglas knighted his son, and sir James Douglas displayed his banner. He also knighted the lord Robert and lord David, sons of the king of Scotland, who in like manner displayed their banners. There were made on the spot about thirty knights in the Scottish army, and one from Sweden, called sir George de Besmede, who bore on a shield argent a mill-iron gules with an indented bordure gules.

On the other hand, sir Thomas Musgrave made his son Thomas a knight with others of his household. The lord Stafford and lord Gascoyn made some likewise. They drew out their archers,

* St Giles Q this mountain

posting

poſting them on their wings; and, this day, the Engliſh cry was, 'Our Lady of Arleſtone!'

The engagement then commenced with vigour, and the archers by their ſhooting confounded the men at arms; but the Scots were in ſuch numbers, the archers could not be every where. There were between the knights and ſquires many a tilt and gallant deed performed, by which ſeveral were unhorſed.

Sir Archibald Douglas was a good knight, and much feared by his enemies: when near to the Engliſh, he diſmounted, and wielded before him an immenſe ſword, whoſe blade was two ells long, which ſcarcely another could have lifted from the ground, but he found no difficulty in handling it, and gave ſuch terrible ſtrokes, that all on whom they fell, were ſtruck to the ground; and there were none ſo hardy among the Engliſh able to withſtand his blows.

The battle was ſharp and well fought as long as it laſted; but that was not any length of time, for the Scots were three to one, and men of tried valour. I do not ſay but the Engliſh defended themſelves valiantly: in the end, however, they were defeated, and ſir Thomas Muſgrave, his ſon, with ſeveral other knights and ſquires, made priſoners. The Scots took ſeven ſcore good priſoners; and the purſuit laſted as far as the river Tweed, where numbers were ſlain.

The Scots, after this victory, reſolved to march ſtraight for Edinburgh, as they learnt from their priſoners that the earls of Northumberland and

Nottingham were in the neighbourhood on the other ſide of the Tweed, on their road to Roxburgh, and that they were in ſufficient numbers to engage with all the force the Scots could bring againſt them: on which account, they thought they might as well abandon their expedition, in order to ſave themſelves and guard their priſoners.

They had wiſely determined to retreat without making any halt; for, had they returned that evening to their former quarters, they would have run a riſk of being conquered, as I ſhall now relate.

When the earls of Northumberland and Nottingham, and the other barons of England had ſeparated from ſir Thomas Muſgrave, they advanced directly towards Roxburgh. They learnt from their ſpies, that the Scots, whom they were ſeeking to fight with, were quartered at Hondebray, which pleaſed them much, and they reſolved to have a ſkirmiſh with them: they were marching thither that ſame night the enemy had left it: but in rained ſo hard that they could not accompliſh their purpoſe: they therefore took up their quarters in the woods until the morrow, when they again ſent out their ſcouts to find where the Scots were, who returned, ſaying that they could not ſee any thing of them.

They then determined to advance towards Melroſe, in order to gain intelligence of ſir Thomas Muſgrave and his companions. When they had dined, they marched along Tweedſide, on their way thither, and ſent ſcouts over the river to learn ſome news of them.

After the defeat on the plains of St. Giles, which I have juſt related, the ſcouts met ſeveral of their fellow-ſoldiers flying like men diſcomfited, who told them as much as they knew of the battle. Upon this, they returned, and with them the run-aways, who related truly what had paſſed between the Engliſh and Scots: they well knew they had been defeated, but were ignorant who had been killed or who made priſoner.

The lords of Northumberland, on hearing this unfortunate intelligence, were very melancholy, and with reaſon. They had two cauſes for vexation; for having loſt the battle, and for having miſſed finding the Scots, whom they had been in ſearch of.

A numerous council was aſſembled in the field, whether or not to purſue the Scots; but as they did not know which way they had marched, and night approaching, they reſolved to make for Melroſe, and fix their quarters there.

Before they could accompliſh their march to Melroſe, they heard the truth of the event of the battle; that ſir Thomas Muſgrave, his ſon, with ſeven ſcore men at arms, had been made priſoners by the Scots, who were carrying them off, and had taken the road to Edinburgh.

Theſe barons then found that they muſt ſubmit to their loſs, for help it they could not. They paſſed the night as well as they were able, and on the morrow they decamped, when the earl of Northumberland gave permiſſion for every one to return to his home: he himſelf retired into his own country. Thus was this expedition put an end to.

The

The Scots returned to Edinburgh, but not all, for the earl of Douglas and his son took the road to Dalkeith. This great success which they had obtained was a great novelty for Scotland. The knights and squires treated their prisoners handsomely, ransomed them courteously, and did with them the best they could. We will now leave off speaking of the Scots, and relate other events which happened in France.

CHAP. LXXIII.

THE DEATHS OF THE QUEENS OF FRANCE AND OF NAVARRE, AND THE RENEWAL OF THE FEUDS BETWEEN THEIR TWO HUSBANDS.

THIS year, in the month of February, the queen of France died, and, as the physicians said, by her own fault. She was with child of the lady Catherine, who was afterwards duchess of Berry. The queen, as I have before said, was not very far advanced in her pregnancy; but the doctors had forbidden her bathing, as being full of danger: however, she would persist; and continued using baths, which brought on a mortal disorder. King Charles of France never married again.

Soon after the death of the queen of France, the queen of Navarre died also. She was sister-german to the king of France. Upon her death diſputes aroſe among the lawyers of the county of Evreux in Normandy: they ſaid, that that county was, by rightful ſucceſſion from the mother, devolved to the children of the king of Navarre, who were ſeparated from him, under age, and in the guardianſhip of king Charles their uncle.

King Charles of Navarre was ſo much ſuſpected of having cauſed, in former times, many ills to France, that he was not thought worthy of poſſeſſing any inheritance in that kingdom under the name of his children. The conſtable of France, therefore, returned from Aquitaine, where he had been a conſiderable time with the duke of Anjou, and brought with him the lord of Mucident, that he might ſee the king and become acquainted with him.

The conſtable was received by the king with great joy, as was the lord de Mucident on his account.

There were many ſecret councils and converſations between the king and conſtable, which were not immediately made public, reſpecting the ſituation of France and Navarre. We will ſhortly return to this buſineſs; but, in order to chronicle juſtly all the events which at this period happened in the world, I will relate to you the beginning of that grand ſchiſm which deſolated the church, by which all Chriſtendom was ſhaken, and from which many evils were engendered and ſpread abroad.

CHAP.

CHAP. LXXIV.

THE DEATH OF POPE GREGORY XI.—AFTER THE SUDDEN DEATH OF HIS IMMEDIATE SUCCESSOR, THE CARDINALS ARE CONSTRAINED TO ELECT URBAN VI. WHICH CAUSES A SCHISM IN THE CHURCH OF ROME.

YOU have before heard how pope Gregory XI. filled the papal chair at Avignon. When he found there was not any likelihood of his bringing about a peace between the kings of France and England, he was much displeased, for he had laboured hard at it, as well as the cardinals by his orders. He resolved, as a matter of devotion, to revisit Rome and the holy see, which St. Peter and St. Paul had edified and augmented; for he had made a vow to God, that if he should ever be raised to so eminent an honour as the papacy, he would never hold his seat but where St. Peter had placed it.

This pope was of a delicate constitution and sickly habit, so that he suffered more than another; and during his residence at Avignon he was much engaged with the affairs of France, and so much pressed by the king and his brothers, that he had not time to attend to his own concerns: he therefore said, he would place himself at a distance, that he might enjoy more repose,

He made preparations in the moſt ample manner becoming ſuch a great perſonage, on the riviera of Genoa and on all the roads. He told his brethren the cardinals to provide for themſelves; for, being reſolved to go to Rome, he ſhould certainly ſet out. On hearing this, the cardinals were much ſurpriſed and vexed, for they remembered the Romans, and would willingly have turned him from taking this journey, but they could not ſucceed.

When the king of France was informed of it, he was in a violent paſſion; for when at Avignon he had him more under his power than any where elſe. He wrote, therefore, directly to his brother the duke of Anjou, at Toulouſe, ſignifying, that on the receipt of the letter, he ſhould ſet out for Avignon, and endeavour, by talking to the pope, to make him give up his intended journey.

The duke of Anjou did what the king had ordered, and went to Avignon, where he was received with great reſpect by the cardinals. He took up his lodgings in the palace of the pope, that he might have more frequent opportunities of converſing with him.

You may eaſily imagine that he acquitted himſelf ably in the different converſations he had with the pope, to diſſuade him from his intentions of going to Rome; but he would not liſten to him on this ſubject, nor give up any thing that related to the affairs beyond the Alps: he ordered, however, four cardinals to remain at Avignon, to whom he gave full powers for them to act in all

reſpects

respects, excepting some papal cases, which he had not the power to delegate out of his own hands.

When the duke found that neither reason nor entreaties could prevail with his holiness to remain where he was, he took leave of him, and said at his departure; 'Holy father, you are going into a country, and among people by whom you are but little loved. You leave the fountain of faith, and a kingdom wherein the church has more piety and excellence than in all the rest of the world. By this action of yours, the church may fall into great tribulation; for should you die in that country (which is but too probable, as your physicians declare) these Romans, who are a strange people and traitors, will be lords and masters of all the cardinals, whom they will force to elect a pope according to their wishes.'

Notwithstanding these speeches and reasons, he would not put off his journey, but set out and arrived at Marseilles, where the galleys of Genoa had been ordered to wait for him. The duke of Anjou returned to Toulouse*.

Pope Gregory embarked at Marseilles with a numerous attendance, and a favourable wind landed him at Genoa. After having re-victualled his galleys, he again embarked, and, making sail for Rome, disembarked not far from it.

---

* Denys Sauvage says in a note, that it was after this return to Toulouse, he undertook the expedition mentioned in the lxiiid chapter of this volume.

You muſt know, that the Romans were exceedingly rejoiced at his arrival: the conſuls and all the principal nobility of Rome went out to meet him on horſeback with great pomp, and conducted him with triumph into that city. He took up his reſidence in the vatican, and often viſited a church within Rome which he was much attached to, and to which he had made many conſiderable additions: it was called Santa Maria Maggiore. He died ſoon after his arrival in this ſame church, in which he was buried, and there lies. His obſequies were performed in a magnificent manner, as was becoming ſo eminent a perſonage.

The cardinals, ſhortly after the death of pope Gregory, aſſembled in conclave at the vatican. As ſoon as they had met to elect a pope, according to the uſual modes, who might be worthy and of ſervice to the church, the Romans collected in great numbers, in the ſuburbs of St. Peter: they were, including all ſorts, upwards of thirty thouſand, encouraging each other to do miſchief, if things did not go according to their wiſhes. They came frequently before the conclave, and ſaid; 'Liſten to us, my lords cardinals: allow us to elect a pope: you are too long about it. Chuſe a Roman, for we will not have one of any other country: if you ſhall elect another, neither the Roman people nor the conſuls will conſider him as pope, and you will run a riſk of being all put to death.'

The cardinals heard theſe words, and being in the power of the Romans, were not at their eaſe,

nor

nor aſſured of their lives: they therefore appeaſed their anger as well as they could. The wickedneſs of the Romans aroſe to ſuch a height that thoſe who were neareſt the conclave broke in, to frighten the cardinals, in order that they might the ſooner decide in favour of him whom they wiſhed. The cardinals were much alarmed, fearing they would all be put to death, and fled, ſome one way, ſome another.

The Romans, however, would not ſuffer them to depart, but collected them again together whether they would or not. The cardinals, finding themſelves in their power and in great danger, made quickly an end of the buſineſs, to appeaſe the people; and, though it was not done through devotion, yet they made a good election of a very devout man, a Roman, whom pope Urban V. had raiſed to the purple: he was called the Cardinal of St. Peter.

This election pleaſed the Romans exceedingly, and the good man had all the rights attached to the papacy; but he only lived three days, and I will tell you the reaſon. The Romans, being deſirous of having a pope from their own nation, were ſo much rejoiced at the election falling as it had done on the cardinal of St. Peter, that they took the good man, who was at leaſt one hundred years of age, and placing him on a white mule, carried him in triumph for ſuch a length of time, through Rome, out of wickedneſs and in exultation of their victory over the cardinals by having gained a Roman pope, that the fatigue was too

much

much for him. On the third day, he took to his bed, and died, and was buried in the church of St. Peter.

The cardinals were much vexed at the death of the pope; for, as they saw things were taking a wrong turn, they had determined, during the life of this pope, to have dissembled with the Romans, for two or three years, and to fix the seat of the church elsewhere than at Rome, at Naples or Genoa, out of the power of the Romans. This would have been carried into execution, but the pontiff's death deranged every thing. The cardinals assembled in conclave in greater danger than before; for the populace collected in large bodies before St. Peter's, shewing plainly that they would not scruple to destroy them unless they elected a pope according to their pleasure. They kept crying out before the conclave, 'Consider, my lords cardinals; consider well what you are about, and give us a Roman pope, who will reside among us; otherwise we will make your heads much redder than your hats.'

Such speeches and menaces frightened the cardinals, for they wished rather to die confessors than martyrs: to free themselves from all danger, they began to deliberate on the choice of a pope, but it fell not on one of their brother-cardinals. They elected the archbishop of Bari, a very learned man, who had laboured much for the church. With this promotion to the papacy the Romans were satisfied.

The cardinal of Geneva put his head out of one

of

of the windows of the conclave, and, calling out aloud to the Roman populace, ſaid, 'Be appeaſed, for you have a Roman pontiff, Bartholomew Prignano archbiſhop of Bari.'

The people unanimouſly anſwered, 'We are ſatisfied.'

The archbiſhop was not at this moment at Rome, but, as I believe, at Naples. He was immediately ſent for, and, being much pleaſed at the event, came directly to Rome to ſhew himſelf to the cardinals.

On his arrival, great feaſts were made: he was elevated, and had all the powers of the papacy. He took the name of Urban VI. This name was very gratifying to the Romans, on account of Urban V. who had much loved them.

His elevation was publiſhed in all the churches in Chriſtendom, and made known to the different potentates, emperors, kings, dukes and earls. The cardinals wrote alſo to their friends, to inform them that they had choſen a pope by a good and fair election, of which ſeveral repented afterwards.

This pope renewed all the graces and pardons which his predeceſſor had given, ſo that divers left their own countries and repaired to Rome to receive them.

We will now for a while leave this matter, and return to the principal object of our hiſtory, the affairs of France.

CHAP.

CHAP. LXXV.

THE KING OF NAVARRE SENDS AMBASSADORS TO FRANCE, IN HOPES OF REGAINING POSSESSION OF HIS CHILDREN.—TWO OF HIS PEOPLE ARE CONVICTED OF HAVING ATTEMPTED TO POISON THE KING OF FRANCE.

YOU have before heard, that after the death of the queen of Navarre, ſiſter to the king of France, there were many perſons who, from love to one and hatred to the other, had declared that the inheritance of the children of the king of Navarre, which had fallen to them on their mother's deceaſe, was legally their due; and that the king of France, their uncle by the mother's ſide, had a right to the guardianſhip of them, and the management, in their name, of all the lands which the king of Navarre held in Normandy, until his nephews ſhould be of age*.

The king of Navarre was ſuſpicious of ſomething being propoſed like to the above, for he was well acquainted with the laws and cuſtoms of France. He therefore determined to ſend the biſhop of Pampeluna and ſir Martin de la

* Denys Sauvage ſays, in a marginal note, that he does not underſtand this; for the kings of Navarre, from father to ſon, were the legal inheritors of the county of Evreux; nor how the children could claim any right from their mother.

Carra

Carra into France, to entreat the king in the moſt amicable manner, that out of love to him, he would ſend him his two ſons, Charles and Peter; and that, if it were not agreeable to the king to allow of both coming to him, heat leaſt would let him have Charles, for a treaty of marriage was in contemplation between him and the daughter of king Henry of Caſtille. He reſolved, notwithſtanding this embaſſy to France, to order his caſtles in Normandy to be ſecretly inſpected and reinforced, that the French might not ſeize them; for, if they were not ſtrengthened in every reſpect, they might do ſo; and, ſhould they once get poſſeſſion, he could not regain them when he pleaſed.

He made choice, for this buſineſs, of two valiant men at arms of Navarre, in whom he had great confidence, whoſe names were Peter de Baſille and Ferrando.

The biſhop of Pampeluna and ſir Martin de la Carra arrived in France, and had long conferences with the king, to whom, with much reverence, they recommended the king of Navarre, and entreated of him that he would ſuffer his two ſons to depart. The king replied, that he would conſider of it.

They afterwards received an anſwer in the king's name, his majeſty being preſent, that 'the king wiſhed to have his nephews, the children of Navarre, near him: that they could not be any where better placed: and that the king of Navarre ought to prefer their being with their uncle, the

king

king of France, to any other perſon: that he would not allow either of them to leave him, but would keep them near his perſon, and form them a magnificent eſtabliſhment, ſuitable to their rank as ſons of a king, and his own nephews.' This was all they could obtain.

During the time theſe ambaſſadors were in France, Peter de Baſille and Ferrando arrived at Cherbourg with many ſtores. Theſe two viſited, by orders of the king of Navarre, the whole county of Evreux, renewed the officers, and placed others in the different forts, according to their pleaſure.

The biſhop of Pampeluna and ſir Martin de la Carra returned to Navarre, and related to the king, whom they met at Tudelle*, all that had paſſed in France. The king was not well pleaſed that he could not have his children, and conceived a violent hatred againſt the king of France, which he would have ſhewn if he had had the power; but he was incapable of hurting that kingdom, and beſides he had not formed any alliances. He thought it, therefore, better to diſſemble, until he ſhould have greater cauſe of complaint, and more real evils be done unto him.

The king of France and his council received information that the king of Navarre was reinforcing all the caſtles and towns in Normandy, which he called his own; and they knew not what to think of his conduct.

At this time there was a ſecret armament formed

* Tudelle,—a village in Armagnac, dioceſe of Auch.

in England, of two thousand men at arms, who were embarked, but without any horses, of which the duke of Lancaster and earl of Cambridge were the commanders.

The Normans, hearing of it, had informed the king of France that this expedition was certainly intended for the coasts of Normandy, but they could not say whither it had sailed. Others supposed it to have been undertaken by the advice of the king of Navarre, who meant to deliver up to the English his strong places in Normandy.

The king of France was also told, that he must hasten his preparations, if he wished to be master of these castles, and that it had been too long delayed; for, if the English should once gain them, they would be enabled to harass France very much, and they could not obtain a more convenient entrance into the kingdom than by being possessors of the towns and castles of the king of Navarre.

Two secretaries of the king of Navarre were arrested in France, a lawyer and a squire: the name of the first was Peter du Teitre, and the other James de Rue: they were conducted to Paris for examination, and were found so intimately connected with the king of Navarre's intentions of poisoning the king of France that they were condemned to death, and were executed and quartered at Paris accordingly.

CHAP. LXXVI.

THE KING OF FRANCE ORDERS THE POSSESSIONS OF THE KING OF NAVARRE TO BE SEIZED, AS WELL IN NORMANDY AS IN LANGUEDOC.—THE KING OF NAVARRE FORMS AN ALLIANCE WITH THE ENGLISH.—THE TERMS OF THAT ALLIANCE.

THESE machinations and wicked attempts of the king of Navarre were ſo numerous that the king of France ſwore he would not undertake any thing before he had driven him out of Normandy, and had gained poſſeſſion, for his nephews, of every town and caſtle which the king of Navarre held there.

Every day brought freſh information, and worſe news reſpecting the king of Navarre, to the palace of king Charles. It was currently reported that the duke of Lancaſter was to give his daughter Catharine to the king of Navarre, who, in return, was to deliver up to him the whole county of Evreux.

Theſe reports were readily believed in France, for the king of Navarre had but few friends there. The king of France, at this period, went to reſide at Rouen, where he had ſummoned a large body of men at arms, and had given the command of it to the lords de Coucy and de la Riviere, who advanced to Bayeux, a city in Normandy attached to Navarre.

Navarre. These barons had with them the lord Charles and lord Peter, the two sons of the king of Navarre, to shew to the whole country and to the county of Evreux, that the war they were carrying on was in behalf of these children, and for the inheritance which belonged to them in right of their mother, and which the king of Navarre wrongfully withheld.

However, the greater part of the men at arms were so much attached to the king of Navarre, that they would not quit his service: the Navarrois who were collected in Bayeux, as well as those whom he had sent thither, maintained the war for him handsomely.

The king of France ordered commissioners to Montpellier, to seize all the lands and lordships which were in the possession of the king of Navarre.

When these commissioners, sir William des Dormans and sir John le Mercier, were arrived at Montpellier, they sent for the principal inhabitants, to whom they shewed their instructions.

Those of Montpellier obeyed. Indeed it was necessary for them to do so; for had they acted otherwise they would have suffered for it, as the duke of Anjou and the constable of France had entered their territories with a considerable force, who wished for nothing better than to carry the war thither.

Two knights of Normandy, governors of Montpellier for the king of Navarre, were made prisoners by orders of the king of France, as were alſo ſir Guy de Graville and ſir Liger d'Argeſi, who remained a long time in confinement. Thus was the town of Montpellier and all the barony ſeized by the French.

We will now return to the army of Normandy, and relate how the lords de Coucy and de la Riviere went on. They advanced to Baveux, and laid ſiege to it. The garriſon-towns of Navarre had cloſed their gates againſt the French, and ſhewed no intentions of ſpeedily ſurrendering them.

When the king of Navarre heard that the French had ſeized the town and territory of Montpellier, and that a large army was in the county of Evreux, where they were pillaging and deſtroying his towns and caſtles, he held many conferences on theſe ſubjects with thoſe in whom he placed the greateſt truſt. It was determined in theſe councils, that as he could not receive any aſſiſtance but from England, he ſhould ſend thither a perſon in whom he confided, with credential letters, to know if the young king Richard and his council were willing to form an alliance with him, and to aſſure them, that from henceforward he would ſwear to be true and loyal to the Engliſh, and would place in their hands all the caſtles which he poſſeſſed in Normandy.

To execute this embaſſy to England, he called to him a lawyer in whom he greatly truſted, and ſaid to him, 'Maſter Paſchal, you will ſet out for England, and manage ſo as to return to me with good news, for from this day forward I will be ſteady in my alliance with the Engliſh.'

Maſter

Master Paschal prepared to do what he had been ordered; and, having made himself ready, he embarked, made sail, and landed in Cornwall, and from thence journeyed on until he arrived at Sheen, near London, where the king resided. He approached his person, and recommended to his majesty his lord the king of Navarre.

The king entertained him handsomely. There were present the earl of Salisbury and sir Simon Burley, who entered into the conversation and answered for the king, saying his majesty would shortly come to London, and summon his council on a day fixed on between them.

Master Paschal, at this council, informed the king of all that he had been charged to say: he harangued so ably and eloquently that he was listened to with pleasure. The council for the king replied, that the offers which the king of Navarre had made were worth attending to; but that, in order to form so extensive an alliance as the king of Navarre was desirous of making, it would be necessary for him to come over himself, that he might more fully explain every thing, for the affair seemed well deserving of it.

On this, the council broke up, and master Paschal returned to Navarre, when he related to the king that the young king of England and his council were desirous of seeing him. The king replied, he would go thither, and ordered a vessel, called a lin*, to be prepared, which sails with all

* Lin,—a felucca, or small frigate.—Du Cange.

winds, and without danger. He embarked on board this vessel, with a small attendance: he, however, took with him sir Martin de la Carra and master Paschal.

The king of France, some little time before he set out for Rouen, had conceived a great hatred against the king of Navarre: he was informed secretly, by some of his household, of all his negotiations with England: in consequence, he had managed so well with king Henry of Castille, that he had sent the king of Navarre his defiance, and had commenced a severe war against him.

The king of Navarre had therefore, before his embarkation, left the viscount de Castillon, the lord de Lestrac, sir Peter de Vienne and Bascle, with a large body of men at arms, as well from his own country as from the county of Foix, with orders to defend his kingdom and his forts against the Spaniards.

He embarked with a very favourable wind, which landed him in Cornwall; from whence he journeyed until he came to Windsor, where king Richard and his council were. He was received there with great joy; for they thought they might gain much from him in Normandy, more especially the castle of Cherbourg, which the English were very desirous of possessing.

The king of Navarre explained to the king of England and his council, in a clear manner, with eloquent language, his wants, and his reasons for coming, so that he was willingly attended to, and received such promises of succour that he was well satisfied.

satisfied. I will inform you what treaties were entered into between the two kings.

The king of Navarre engaged to remain for ever true and loyal to the English, and never to make any peace with the kings of France or Castille without the consent of the king of England. He engaged to put the castle of Cherbourg into the hands of the king of England, who was to guard it for three years at his own costs and charges, but the lordship and sovereignty of it were to remain in the king of Navarre. If the English should be able, by force of arms, to gain any of the towns or castles which the king of Navarre then had in Normandy, from the French, they were to remain with the English, the lordship, however, resting in the king of Navarre*.

The English were much pleased with these terms, because they gained a good entrance to France through Normandy, which was very convenient for them.

The king of England promised to send, at this season, a thousand spears and two thousand archers, by the river Gironde from Bourdeaux to Bayonne; and these men at arms were to enter Navarre, and make war on the king of Castille. They were not to quit the king nor the kingdom

* See Rymer—for the passport to the king of Navarre, and the treaty at length, an. reg. Ric. II.

The passport for Charles of Navarre is dated a year later than Froissart mentions. It is in Rymer dated the 12th August, from the manor of Clarendon, 1370, to continue to the feast of St. John Baptist following, for five hundred persons.

 of

of Navarre ſo long as there ſhould be war between the kings of Navarre and Caſtille. But theſe men at arms and archers, on entering the territories of Navarre, were to be paid and clothed by the king of Navarre as was becoming them, and on the ſame footing as the king of England was accuſtomed to pay his ſoldiers.

Different treaties, alliances and regulations were drawn up, ſigned, ſealed and ſworn to, between the kings of England and Navarre, which were tolerably well obſerved. In this council, the king named ſuch members as were ordered to Normandy, and thoſe who were to go to Navarre: becauſe neither the duke of Lancaſter, the earl of Cambridge, nor the duke of Brittany, were preſent at theſe treaties, it was reſolved to ſend copies ſealed to them, in order that they might haſten to invade Normandy.

CHAP. LXXVII.

THE LORDS DE COUCY AND DE LA RIVIERE TAKE SEVERAL PLACES IN THE COUNTY OF EVREUX, FROM THE KING OF NAVARRE.

KING Charles of France, being wiſe and ſubtle (as his whole life plainly ſhewed), had received information of the armament in England, but was ignorant, whither it was to ſail, to Normandy

mandy or Brittany. On account of these doubts, he had kept in the latter country a large body of men at arms, under the command of the lords de Clisson, de Laval, the viscount de Rohan, the lords de Beaumanoir and de Rochefort. They had besieged Brest by block-houses only, to prevent any provision from entering.

The governor of Brest was a valiant English squire called James Clerk.

Now, because the king of France knew of the king of Navarre's voyage to England, in the hopes of forming an alliance with his adversary the king of England, he suspected that this naval armament would land in Normandy, and seize by force those castles which belonged to the king of Navarre: he therefore in haste sent orders to the lords de Coucy and de la Riviere, stating to them his suspicions, with orders to conquer, by the speediest modes possible, all castles, more particularly such as were near to the sea-coasts, by force or by negotiation. He knew that Cherbourg was not easy to be taken, and also that it could not be reinforced on the land side.

The king of France had likewise ordered large bodies of men at arms to Valognes* from the lower parts of Brittany. Sir Oliver du Guesclin commanded the Bretons, and the lord d'Ivoy and sir Perceval were the leaders of the Normans.

---

* Valognes,—a town in Normandy; it lies between Cherbourg and Carentan.

The lords de Coucy and de la Riviere had besieged the city of Bayeux with a great force, which was daily increasing from the additions the king of France was sending to them from all quarters. Bayeux is a handsome and strong city near the sea, which at that time belonged to the king of Navarre. The citizens (finding themselves thus besieged by their neighbours, who told them, that if the town were taken by storm, they would all inevitably be destroyed, both men and women, and the town re-peopled with another set of inhabitants,) began to be seriously alarmed. They saw no appearance of assistance coming to them, but, on the contrary, found themselves in opposition to the lord Charles de Navarre, to whom the county of Evreux belonged, in right of succession to his late mother. The inhabitants also listened to the harangues of the lords de Coucy and de la Riviere, who, with impressive language, shewed them the dangers into which they were running: knowing likewise that their bishop was well inclined towards the French, they thought, considering all things, it would be much better for them to surrender their city from affection, as they were required to do by the above mentioned lords, than to remain in such peril.

The inhabitants of Bayeux demanded a truce for three days; during which time, a treaty was so far concluded that the lords de Coucy and de la Riviere entered the city, and took possession of it for the king of France, as his acknowledged commissaries.

The

The attorney-general was ſent thither on the part of the children of Navarre, who were preſent during all the negotiations.

The two lords renewed all the officers of the city, and, for fear of a rebellion, left a body of good men at arms: they then marched off to lay ſiege to Carentan, a handſome and ſtrong town ſituated on the ſea-ſhore, and in the diſtrict of Caen.

The inhabitants of Carentan were without any governor of note: indeed, they had not had one ſince ſir Euſtace d'Ambreticourt, who had been their governor for four years, and had died there; ſo that they had not any to look to for advice but themſelves: they knew alſo that the admiral of France, ſir John de Vienne, in conjunction with the Spaniſh admiral and a large force, were before Cherbourg, but were ignorant of the treaties of the king of Navarre, as well as unacquainted with the reſult of his journey to England.

They were attacked every day in two different manners; by words and arms; for the lords de Coucy and de la Riviere were very anxious to gain this town, and ſucceeded in winning it by capitulation: they put it under the obedience of the king of France, reſerving the rights of the two ſons of the king of Navarre.

Theſe lords of France readily granted very favourable terms, in order to get poſſeſſion of ſuch towns and caſtles as they wanted by the moſt expeditious means. They took poſſeſſion of Carentan, reinforcing it with men at arms: they then departed,

departed, and came before the castle of Molineaux*, which in three days capitulated. They advanced to Conches†, and encamped on the banks of the beautiful river Orne, which runs by Caen, and there refreshed themselves, until they knew the inclinations of the inhabitants, who shortly surrendered on terms; for the lords de Coucy and de la Riviere having the heir of Navarre with them gave a good colour to their proceedings.

However, when any town or castle surrendered itself to the king of France, or to his commissaries, there was a condition in the treaty, that all those who chose to depart might go wherever they pleased: those who did depart only went to Evreux, of which Ferrando, a Navarrois, was governor.

After the conquest of Conches, which was gained, as you have heard, by treaty, they advanced before Passy‡, where there was an assault: many were killed and wounded on both sides. That same day the castle surrendered to the king of France: they then marched away. In short, all that the king of Navarre possessed in Normandy surrendered, excepting Evreux and Cherbourg. When they had won different small forts, and placed the whole country under the obedience of the king

* Molineaux,—a village in Normandy, election of Caen.

† Conches,—a market town in Normandy, near Evreux.

‡ Passy,—a town in Normandy, four leagues from Evreux.

of

of France, they laid siege to Evreux, which was cut off from any communication with Cherbourg.

In Evreux, there was, according to custom, the strongest garrison of Navarrois in Normandy; and the inhabitants never perfectly loved any other lord but the king of Navarre. The place was closely besieged. It held out for a long time; for Ferrando the governor, performed in person several gallant deeds of arms.

About this time the king of Navarre, being returned to his own country, expected to have had some assistance from the English; but it does not appear that he had any succours from them, for the duke of Lancaster and the earl of Cambridge, before these treaties had been entered on, had experienced very contrary winds for their voyage to Normandy, and so numerous a levy as had been ordered of four thousand men at arms and eight thousand archers could not immediately be assembled at Southampton, where they were to embark. It was St. John Baptist's day before they were all collected and had sailed from England. The earl of Salisbury and sir John Arundel were still at Plymouth, who ought to have reinforced Brest and Hennebon*; but they had wanted wind, so that they joined the duke of Lancaster and e rl of Cambridge's army.

They landed on the Isle of Wight, where they remained some time waiting for intelligence, and to know whether they should il for Normandy or

* Hennebon. Denys Sauvage thinks it should be Aub-ay, or Derval, instead of Hennebon.

Brittany:

Brittany: they there learnt that the French fleet was at sea, on which sir John Arundel was ordered back to Southampton, with two hundred men at arms and four hundred archers, to defend that place.

CHAP. LXXVIII.

THE DUKE OF ANJOU RETAINS LARGE BODIES OF MEN AT ARMS AGAINST THE ENGLISH.—THE SPANIARDS LAY SIEGE TO BAYONNE.

ON account of the information the king of France had received from the Normans, that the English were in great force at sea, but doubtful whither it was directed: he had issued a special summons throughout his realm for every knight and squire, according to his degree, to keep himself fully prepared to march to whatever part he should be ordered.

The duke of Anjou had also, at this period, retained large bodies of men at arms from all quarters, with the intention of laying siege to Bourdeaux. He had with him his brother the duke of Berry, the constable of France, and all the flower of knighthood from Gascony, Auvergne, Poitou and Limousin. In order to carry their enterprize, he had raised an immense army, and had also, with the consent of the king of France, collected

two

two hundred thoufand francs in Languedoc; but he could not at prefent undertake this fiege, for the king of France had recalled the duke of Berry, the conftable and other barons, on whofe affiftance he had depended, as it was well known the Englifh were at fea, but uncertain in what part of the kingdom they would attempt to land.

Notwithftanding this expedition from Languedoc had failed, the poor people who had been fo hard preffed to pay fuch large fums were never repaid any part.

The king of Caftille, about this time, laid fiege to Bayonne with full twenty thoufand Spaniards and Caftillians: he began the fiege in the winter, and continued it through that whole feafon. Many gallant deeds were performed there by fea and land, for Roderigo le Roux, don Fernando de Caftille, Ambrofe de Boccanegra and Peter Bafcle, lay at anchor before Bayonne with two hundred veffels, and gave fufficiency of employment to its inhabitants. The governor of the town at the time was a right valiant knight from England called fir Matthew Gournay.

His good fenfe and prowefs were, as I have been informed, of great affiftance to the townfmen. I have heard from fome of thofe who were befieged, that the Spaniards would have fucceeded in their attempt on Bayonne, had not a great mortality afflicted their army, fo that out of five who were taken ill three died.

King Henry had with him a necromancer from Toledo, who declared that the whole air was poi-

foned

ſoned and corrupted, and that no remedy could be had for it without riſking the death of all. In conſequence of this deciſion, the king broke up the ſiege; but the Spaniards and Bretons had conquered a number of ſmall forts and caſtles in the adjacent country, into which they entered; and the king went to refreſh himſelf at la Coulongne*. He ſent his conſtable, with ten thouſand men, to lay ſiege to Pampeluna.

In that city were the viſcount de Caſtillon, the lord de Leſcut and le Baſcle, with two hundred lances in the whole, who carefully guarded the place. The king of Navarre, who had but lately returned from England, reſided at Tudelle, impatiently expecting the ſuccours which were to come to him from England, and which indeed had been ordered; for, by directions from the king and council, the lord Neville and ſir Thomas de Termes † were at Plymouth, or in that neighbourhood, with about one thouſand men at arms and two thouſand archers, and were laying in their ſtores for the voyage to Bourdeaux; but they had not met with a paſſage according their wiſhes.

With regard to the great army under the command of the duke of Lancaſter, at laſt it landed near to St. Malo: news of which was ſoon carried to the Breton lords of the French party, and immediately the viſcount de Belliere, ſir Henry de Malatrait and the lord de Combor left their habi-

* La Coulongne. Sala calls it Calongne Q. if not Orogne.

† De Termes. Q. Sir Thomas Trivet.

tations,

tations, and flung themſelves into St. Malo with two hundred men at arms, to the great joy of Morfonace the governor, who otherwiſe would have been hardly puſhed.

END OF VOL. IV.

CPSIA information can be obtained at www.ICGtesting.com
Printed in the USA
BVOW06s1235190215

388467BV00016B/131/P